TALES OF
PUGILISM

By Jamie Boyle

www.warcrypress.co.uk
Jamie Boyle (c)

ISBN: 978-1-912543-03-8

TALES OF PUGILISM: Produced by www.wacrypress.co.uk (part of Roobix Ltd: 7491233) on behalf of Jamie Boyle, Northallerton. Copyright © Jamie Boyle 2018. Jamie Boyle has asserted his right as the author of this work in accordance with the Copyright, Designs and Patents Act 1988.

Printed and bound in Great Britain by Clays, St. Ives

Find out more at: facebook.com/TalesOfPugilism/

Please return this book on or before the due date below

t,

HA

Chapters

Introduction 1

Kevin Mitchell 7

Davey Robinson (Repton ABC) 21

Matthew Burke 33

Andrew Buchanan 48

Richy Horsley 68

Alex Morrison 79

Colin Hart 87

Joe Maphosa 92

John Spensley 101

Francis Jones 114

Matt Hamilton 139

Alan Temple 153

Dominic Negus 172

Peter Richardson 190

Josh Warrington 201

Jon Lewis Dickinson 214

Bradley Welsh   223

Nick Manners   234

Gary Sykes   252

John Pearce   267

Afterword   297

"They were so sanctimonious, so pompous, so horrible and so fucking stupid I could have easily battered them all, everyone".

Paul Sykes on the BBBoC before his licence was granted.

Introduction

It was the 18th of November 1990 and I was sat watching the old football show on ITV Saint & Greavsie. I was watching it with my Dad waiting for my beloved Glasgow Celtic to come on. I was a massive football fan growing up and had been brainwashed as a child, really since I could walk, to follow Celtic. With Scottish parentage and living in Glasgow at times in my life it was never going to be any other way really!

Not only did I follow football, but I played it and was a half decent player when I was very young. I don't think it registered that I wasn't actually going to play for Celtic until the age of around 12. I was the kid off the estate who would carry a football with me and wear a Celtic shirt every day, some would say I'm still like that now! Going back to Saint & Greavsie though, I'll never forgot that day instead of my fix of football coming on, it was a good 15 minutes of the grudge fight Britain stood still to see, and that was the WBO middleweight champion Nigel Benn defending his title against the undefeated pantomime villain Chris Eubank. I remember being seriously in a strop as a 10-year-old boy that so much of my favourite weekly program was being taken up by stupid boxing which I had no interest in whatsoever! I vaguely remember the Frank Bruno/Mike Tyson fight the year before, but this is really my first boxing memory.

To be honest as annoyed as I was this was taking up my beloved footy programme I couldn't take my eyes off these two fella's who were telling the whole world what they were going to do to each other later that day. I didn't have a scooby doo about boxing then but there was something about Chris Eubank I found absolutely fascinating. I knew Chris Eubank was going to win, and the reason why is that no human being could possibly be that confident of something if he wasn't going to win, it was a no brainer to my young undeveloped mind. I can remember him clearly saying in the interview about Nigel Benn, "He doesn't realise the ability I have" whereas all Nigel kept saying was "I'm gonna give this boy a hiding". All day I waited with great anticipation for the fight which was shown around 10pm that night and went live to over 13 million viewers around Great Britain.

To this day that fight is the best fight I've ever seen, it had everything. On the way to the ring Nigel Benn had Chris Eubank's "Simply the Best" song by Tina Turner totally sabotaged and cut off within 12 seconds of it playing. It was sheer violence at its most brutal for the 9 rounds it lasted. Chris Eubank stood at the end looking up to the sky letting out a medieval roar and leaving Nigel Benn crying on the referee Richard Steele's shoulder very much a broken man.

Ever since then really, I would say I've had the boxing bug. Of course, I grew up in a time when your Chris Eubank's, Michael Watson's, Nigel Benn's, Frank Bruno's and Prince Naseem Hamed's were regularly shown on terrestrial television and like your top footballers of the time and throughout the early 90s they were household names. Sky Sports didn't really take over all the big fights until 1995 so it was normal for the average family to sit around the front room glued to the telly for The Big Fight Live which was normally presented by that man who looked like the Devil to me as a child, the popular Jim Rosenthal.

It wasn't only watching boxing that I would become obsessed with, the moment I went in my best friend at the times bedroom and I saw all his boxing trophies I wanted to be like him. I didn't give a shit if I lost every week I just wanted to be like him and have these big marvellous fuck off trophies.

As a kid I'd turn up at these boxing shows and the first thing I would do is go see how big the trophies were, it become an obsession as a schoolboy to have trophies in my bedroom window, didn't matter how badly I got my brains rattled as long as I got a trophy to put in my bedroom window.

Boxing can influence so many people's lives and change it for the better. It doesn't matter if you're an elite champion or just a keep fitter, if you're dedicated at whatever level you're at, it becomes a way of life. When I was growing up 15-16 years old, at a time when all my friends were hanging on street corners drinking bottles of White Lightening and smoking, I was too busy keeping fit and having somewhere to go 3-4 times a week because I belonged to an amateur boxing club. I had somewhere to go to keep me away from trouble.

In my opinion boxing will always save more lives than it takes. Of course, fatal injuries are going to happen every couple of years because it's in the small print and it will continue whilst the object of the game is to clobber your opponent very hard to the head. Boxing's really a skill though, it's such a beautiful art! When you watch two top fighters trying to outmanoeuvre, out think and outsmart it's such a wonderful thing to watch. You don't have to be a good fighter on the streets to be a good boxer.

People who don't really understand boxing would like to portrait as a thuggish sport but it's far from it.

Over the years I've met real hardened guys on the streets but put them in a boxing ring or even when I've sparred with them and they haven't got a clue as to how to even stand properly let alone throw a punch.

I really despise violence, if I was in a pub and I've seen people fighting I've turned away and winced because violence is ugly, whereas if you stuck the same two pissheads in boxing gloves and told them to continue under the Queensbury rules I could watch them all day. If you imagine building a house, then the first thing you do is build it on strong foundations before you even start. Well it's the same with boxing. If you can't put your feet in a correct manner, then you can't throw a proper punch and you can't receive a punch also. Balance/foundations is everything before a bell has even rang.

Many years ago, when I was helping out at an amateur club in Middlesbrough there was a ridiculously talented young fighter by the name Shafiq Chubzy Asif. Even Anthony Joshua has said he used to sit back in awe watching him train in GB training camps. I'd like to say it was an absolute privilege and a pleasure just to take that guy on the pads he was magical to watch up at close quarters, he was frightening. He only ever went in four national competitions as an amateur, two junior ABA'S and two Boys Clubs and the guy won all four. He did things in the gym most fighters could only dream about. He also went pro and was 6-0 before he walked away from boxing for good aged just 20 years old. The reason I'm using him as an example is because although he was a superstar amateur boxer on Team GB, the guy literally has never had a fight in his life outside boxing. If somebody was to go up to him and say "Let's have a fight" he'd walk away, but if anybody did have a fist fight with him he'd hit them six times before they'd even got their hands out of their pockets. Shafiq now has a life away from boxing and he's happy so good luck to the guy although it's a crying shame in my eyes as he would have been phenomenal.

Although boxing's a rough and ready sport I have no problems taking my 10-year-old son into boxing this year. My hope is that my boy Jameson Lennon sticks to boxing and that he can be moulded properly into a disciplined young man. Regardless of if he wants to compete or not, the training and discipline of boxing will give him the perfect start to becoming a gentleman and that it will stay with him for life.

Boxing humbles people and my good friend John Pearce is no finer example of that as I dare say he's the most liked person in the town of Middlesbrough and I'm not talking about his boxing ability there also. I've certainly never heard anybody say a bad word about him anyway in over the last 25 years or so.

Boxing to this day means a great deal to me. I'd say along with football it's the biggest passion in my life. Just because we're not all champions in boxing doesn't mean we can't be extremely passionate about the game and know what's what and who's who in it. This book I bring you is twenty different people's outlooks on boxing and what it means to them. Some face's you'll already have heard of, some you won't but all have a tale to tell regarding the most noble art of all.

Have you ever wondered how people ever become an astronaut and go into space! I have. Well it's the same with how people decide to become involved in a life where you get punched in the face for a living!

I always remember East Ender Dominic Negus telling me in a previous book of mine, he said "Us boxers aren't the most academic of people and fighting's the only thing some of us know". Of course, you get the occasion Shafiq Chubzy Asif in boxing where real fighting isn't a natural thing, but you'll get far more guys from the street who've had nothing so fighting becomes a way of life to them as natural as breathing. This is the real reason there's been so many great fighters out of the East End of London because it was the most deprived area in the country. Growing up for many of them whoever punched the hardest in a street fight could steal some food for the day and other kids would back off and leave them alone.

I started this book in early September 2017 when I was going through one of the worst times in my life. Last year was definitely my Britney Spears 2007 year. Everything was going Pete Tong and I just needed a change of scenery for a week. I ended up heading for London, the home of boxing, armed with just my debit card, Dictaphone and sleeping bag, that's why the first few chapters of this book are all "Cock-er-neys".

Many of the people I've had the pleasure of interviewing have been personal friends but as much as I love the fight game I could never really come close to finding out what these guys have experienced in boxing or the raw emotions of being shit on from a great height by the boxing baddies. Why is it us folk, who are civil citizens, enjoy watching two men pulverise each other on a weekend? Why is it the nation stands still for these big PPV fights? If you talk to the average guy on the street he'd say its brutally Neanderthal like, then you could walk into the next street and ask another Joe public and he'll say it's the greatest sport in the world.

I hope you enjoy reading this book as much as I've have done spending the hours writing it. Thank you to the twenty "proper boxing folk" who've agreed to be in it. You are all and none before the other, my absolute hero's and I salute each and every one of you.

Happy reading, many thanks always a pleasure. Jamie x

Kevin Mitchell

In September 2012 I was living in Saltburn, East Cleveland. I travelled the 200 miles up to Glasgow just to watch the Ricky Burns Vs Kevin Mitchell weigh-in the, day before the fight at the SECC, Glasgow (there's something about men in undies acting hard). That fight was the first and probably the last time I will ever support an English man over a Scotch man in my life.

As much as I love Ricky Burns, and have signed photos up of him in my house, I'd always admired Mighty Mitchell and followed his career since he won the ABA'S as an 18 year old in 2003. I tend to stick to watching our British fighters over say the Cotto's, Mayweather's and Paquiao's of this world. I'd rather watch say the British Super Bantamweight title fight than Mayweather Vs Paquiao, but that's how I've always been regarding boxing!

I would personally describe Dagenham's Kevin Mitchell as being the complete box fighter, he could do it all i.e. move, box, punch as well as fight on the back foot.

Not many know this but even though Kevin Mitchell fights out of an orthodox stance (right handed) he's actually left-handed, hence the reason his left hook was so good. Oscar De La Hoya and Miguel Cotto were the same, as well as Marvellous Marvin Hagler but he was the other way around. If any young fighter today is thinking of starting up boxing, then go and take a look at Kevin Mitchell Vs K.O. Machine and recent Amir Khan conqueror Breidis Presscott on Youtube! This fight took place in December 2009 and this fight to me, better than any other, is what pugilism is all about. Hit and not be hit, being smart and using your brain as well as your feet. Hands high and not taking any risks! Many people always look for the spectacular knockouts, but what boxing is really about is hit and not being hit.

Kevin didn't do anything foolish that night and boxed to a strict game plan to win a wide unanimous points decision. I will never tire of watching that fight and I'll be showing my young boy Jameson Lennon this fight when the times right for him to study the sport of boxing. If you've never watched the fight YouTube it now and after one round, you'll get the drift of what I'm saying.

I managed to get hold of Kevin through his close friend, the likable Brendan O'Connor. Brendan's been a close friend of the Mitchell family for years and he arranged for me to meet Super Kev outside Liverpool Street station in East London. I walked across the beautiful city of London the 5 miles from my hotel in Victoria, South London to meet with Kevin and when I was 15 minutes away from Kevin he texts me saying, "I'm in the Hamilton Hill pub I'm waiting for you". I managed to get there and saw what was a very smartly dressed Kevin Mitchell sipping a large glass of red wine. Although Kevin hadn't fought for 20 months and had now retired, I couldn't help but notice how fit he looked. Kevin was no longer the lightweight, but now he was a solid super middleweight easy. He had a wide back the type that powerful punchers normally have. He was much bigger than I'd expected him to be being around 5ft 8 in height.

Kevin and I sat talking for a good hour over bits and bobs. I didn't really want to tell him he was my favourite British fighter 'ever' in case I looked like a right stalker, Ha! I found Kevin to be very funny and switched on with his boxing history on past fighters. What first struck me about Kevin Mitchell is, how can I say this, very cock-er-ney ha... He was real apples 'n' pears, jellied eels, pie 'n' mash and Chas 'n' Dave indeed. I'd seen him many many times over the years but his level of 'cock-er-ney blew me away. That's not a bad thing, truth be told I'd always been ridiculously intrigued with the real EastEnders since I first discovered the Michael Caine 'Jack the Ripper' film when I was about 11years old. Then my interest in the Kray twins around 13 years old, not the normal reading for your average teenager I grant you.

Before I recorded Kevin and asked him about his glamorous career I had to call my good friend Alex Morrison in Glasgow. I let Kevin talk to Alex for a bit and went to the bar to get myself a drink. It's a little habit I've developed over the years, what I mean is one day in 2013 Alex rang me and said, "Jamie I have someone here who wants to talk to you"! Then Alex passed the phone to a guy and then I heard the unique unmistakable soft voice saying, "HEY JAMIE ITS RAY LEONARD". It's funny because all the people I've ever told that tale to they've always replied the same "DID YA FUCK SPEAK WITH SUGAR RAY LEONARD"! So, over the years when I've been to boxing do's I've always returned the favour, none as big as Sugar Ray Leonard mind! I knew of course that Kevin fought Alex's close friend and boxer Ricky Burns so I knew that they'd have things to chat about. The pub was getting a little bit "rowdy" and I knew I'd need to take him somewhere quieter to chat with him, so my Dictaphone would pick him up properly, so we left the Hamilton Hall and went to the English restaurant just around the corner. Kevin sat down and told me how he got involved with pugilism over a bite to eat.

Kevin says:

I started boxing really because I was an aggressive young kid and my mum thought it would channel my aggression into something positive. I started boxing at 10 years of age. I was never a bully, but I used to beat up bullies growing up in the East End. I would just love any kind of fighting, I liked to fight, and I was a natural at it. My first ever amateur gym was the Hornchurch & Elm Park ABC.

My full amateur record was 50 fights and with that I won 45 with 29 KO'S. That many KO'S was highly unusual in the amateur ranks so I'm told. I had 5 losses and a couple of those were to friends of mine Nick MacDonald and Matthew Edmonds. The other losses came in a fight which was England Vs France which I took with only a week's notice, the Multi Nations tournament versus an Italian, but I felt I was robbed and the junior Olympics in America and that was also an incredibly close decision, so I only lost to top guys in my amateur days.

Titles wise I'm on the list of only about 10 people ever to win 4 schoolboys titles. You can only go in it 4 times, so I won it every time I entered along with Mark Tibbs and Naseem Hamed etc. I also won the junior ABA'S, NABC'S as well as the full Senior ABA title in 2003 when I was just a boy at 18 really. I beat a kid in the final called Gareth Couch from Thame ABC. I also beat Liverpool's Stephen Smith from the Rotunda. Stephen and his brothers have gone on to become great pro's, all four of them have held major belts.

Some TV stations and many promoters approached me after I won the ABA'S. With me knocking everyone out in the amateurs I was getting a lot of attention to sign up with this one, that one etc.

At the end of my amateur days I had 5 fights in 3 weeks and won all 5 by KO so looking back I was red hot, just a young kid coming up the ranks.

One of my best amateur wins was over Liverpool's David Mullholland from the Gemini ABC. I beat David then he went on to win the ABA'S twice so that was a great win for me on paper. When I decided I was going to go, pro as just an 18 year old boy, I had a lot of sharks trying to sign me up. Physically I was mature for an 18 year old as even at 15 I was beating grown men up.

I eventually signed up with Frank Warren and I had my first pro fight against the Northern Irish boy Stevie Quinn in the Goresbrook Leisure Centre, Dagenham and won by KO in the first round. I would go on to fight in London, particularly The York Hall, Bethnal Green. That place became like my second home, I was a big ticket seller.

The way the promoters work is they build you up in your hometown, then they branch you out in Liverpool, Manchester and Glasgow because that's how it works.

The first professional title I fought for was the IBF intercontinental belt. I beat the French national champion Mohammed Medjadja in just 6 rounds. It was on the undercard of the big grudge match between Danny Williams Vs Audley Harrison in their first fight.

When I won that title I was just a kid 19 or 20 years of age with no sense and still learning. I would go on to win the vacant Commonwealth title and vacant WBO intercontinental at Super Featherweight, which really brought me to Carl Johanneson for the British title. Out of all my 43 fights, Carl Johanneson was the hardest by far believe me! The fight was on the undercard of David Haye Vs Enzo Maccarinelli at the 02 Millennium Dome in March 2008. I sold the arena out that being that I was the main ticket seller on the card, David Haye didn't sell tickets. Against the hard-punching Carl Johanneson, I was certainly slung in at the deep end, if I was a fake then this was the fight I was going to get found out in and it would be painful. I was around 21-22 when I fought Carl. Bloody hell he's one hard man let me tell you. In the fight with Carl I had my jaw busted and both my hands broke by the 6th round. Just look at my hands, I've always been able to punch even though I've got such small hands but at least they make my cock look big eh(laughs). Carl Johanneson was a proper warrior though and a nice man, he's a real gentleman and I respect him greatly. After I fought Carl I was seriously busted up and in a lot of pain for a good few weeks after it. I think the relief was there to see when I stopped him in the 9th round and I jumped on the ropes to a standing ovation, the place was packed with people who had all come to see me and there were cheering my name. That was a great night for me for sure. There was a show on at the 02 about 6 months after which I wasn't on, and it was buy a ticket get one free so that just shows you something doesn't it.

After I beat Carl Johanneson I won the British title at Super Featherweight, but I never defended my belt and had to give it up. I never made the 9st 4lbs limit again from that night because it was killing me. I was even due to face the unbeaten Puerto Rican thunderous puncher Roman "Rocky" Martinez but I just couldn't get anywhere near the weight again, so I had to pull out. It turns out my close friend Nicky Cook took my place in facing Martinez but was beaten in 4 rounds. I knew I had to continue at the 9st 9lbs limit at lightweight and I felt much healthier and stronger. I'll never forget when Frank Warren rang me and he put forward the Breidis Presscott fight. I know Frank was thinking I was gonna turn it down but I bit his hand off and said yes damn right I'll take it! Breidis Prescott had completely pole-axed the unbeaten Amir Khan only the year before but I knew I had the beating of him if I was on my game. I'll say one thing for Breidis Prescott, when he came over to face me he spent the full build up trying to intimidate me, he was constantly angry and one aggressive fella. I don't think I heard him speak only kinda growl towards me and staring like a dog. He looked like he'd try to eat your kids, he was one bad looking geezer. The fight itself panned out like I knew it would. Prescott was loading up and trying to take my head off with every punch but I was too cute and switched on for him. When I saw him load up I would just brace myself for the onslaught and get out of range. I was just a little bit smarter in my ring craft than him and I shocked a few people that night by beating him so convincingly.

The fight which came after the Prescott victory was against Ignacio Mendoza and I knocked him out in two rounds, which led me to the reason I'd become professional in the first place, a world title fight finally! I was to face dangerous Australian Michael Katsidis at my beloved West Hams Upton Park in the May of 2010. Katsidis was a real warrior, a real-life gladiator if you like and I should never have even been in the ring with him that night. Mentally and physically I was a complete and utter mess. My whole build up for that fight was wrong! That camp was everything that your modern day athlete shouldn't do. I was a barely functioning alcoholic and drank during the whole build up to that fight. At times I wouldn't train so I could go out on the drink, then I'd stay out sofa surfing at friends houses or at times I slept in my car. I'm ashamed to say it but the truth of the matter is, I was training for the biggest fight of my life, but I was more bothered about being in my mates' pubs and getting the place rocking. I was my own worst enemy because I was suffering from alcoholism, but I wouldn't admit it. I looked like a fighter in the ring, but I was completely reckless outside it. Myself, looking back, especially as a trainer, would never let one of my fighters have a camp like that I'd fucking kill him before he got in the ring. I knew in the Katsidis fight I was fucking done for when I was doing the ring walk! I made the mistake of taking that fight and it's something I've got learn to live with for the rest of my days.

After the Katsidis fight Michael came in my dressing room and cried. He told me that he actually didn't think he was gonna win the fight. Fair play to him he was on his game and I wasn't! My loss to Michael was the catalyst of an extremely dark time for me. I fell out with my partner, the mother of my two boys. My mum would often catch me asleep in my car, quite often I'd sleep in the car because I was in such a state and didn't want her to see me. She would come and get me out of the car and quite often put me to bed I was in that much of a state. When I look back at the Michael Katsidis fight I find it a fucking miracle I even made the weight. That loss broke my heart, I'd never lost before so I hadn't any experience in how to handle it, I thought the pub would make it all better. I took that defeat so badly for around nine months. In that short space of time I spent £180 grand on partying. I'd think nothing of going out with six grand from my safe and staying out for days and nights on end. Eventually my going out led to days, weeks and to months where I never even went near a boxing gym, unless there was one above one of the many pubs I would frequent. It was nine months of my life where to be quite truthful, I never even knew what day of the week it was. Many days I would go find a pub in London where I wouldn't be recognised so I could just booze in peace without people telling me I was throwing my career away. There's no doubt in my mind I was an alcoholic with a serious problem. These days though I can have a drink and I've sorted the problem out with me and the booze. Back then though I would find the shitiest little pubs in the whole of London and I'd be buying every tramp in the area drink after drink. I'd then go partying with complete strangers and end up in all kinds of shitholes. My last bender before I sorted myself out was a costly one. I would often take bundles of money out rolled up in thousand pound bundles. So, this time I went out with my last six grand for a few days. I was out for as long as it took me to spend it I guess. The last night I was in

Romford and I had around £300 in one pocket, and my last £1000 in the other rolled up. I tried to enter the club and a few of the door staff wouldn't let me in the club because I was in a bit of a state. After a few minutes arguing and telling the bouncers I was gonna kick off if they refused me entry they let me in. I went in and spent the £300 in a couple of hours buying bottles of champagne like a dick. As I'd entered the club I'd noticed some poor homeless fella sat by the door, this had obviously stuck in my mind, he was fucking freezing and I just felt so sorry for him so I walked up to him and said, "ERE YA GO GEEZER, GO AND HAVE A GOOD TIME ON THAT" and give him the last £1000 I had to my name. Nine months earlier I'd had £180K in a safe. I now had no money left in the world and I must have quickly realised that about 30 seconds after walking off, because I had to go back over to him and ask to lend £20 so I could get a taxi to my Mums. I woke up rough as fuck without £1 to my name, that's a true story!

From that moment on in my life the only way to go in life was up! I started going to AA meetings and spending time with other wrecks like me. At AA meetings I met guys that had come back from Afghan and Iraq and you think, fuck me, is this what the worlds coming to? They come back from war and yet they've got no help. They've got nothing to help with their stress. So, they hit the bottle. That's the way the world works. People finish work on a Friday, they're stressed out, so what do they do? They go for a beer. The world doesn't realise, booze is a depressant. There's no doubt 'id have ended up in prison if I'd carried on boozing. Depression was a massive problem for me also at this time, there were ups and downs and people don't understand the stresses of boxing. I used to crave and want to go on the booze after a fight. I'd be depressed for months. I was moody and stressed I didn't want to go out, I didn't want to do anything. I wouldn't clean, I'd be murder. It all stems from drinking. My kids would go from seeing me four days a week, every Monday, Tuesday and every weekend to hardly seeing me after a fight because I'd make excuses for nothing, then go back on the booze again. When you're that low it tends to only be one way and I started slowly but surely sorting my shit out.

I was then offered the John Murray fight, so I knew I'd have to be in top shape to keep that strong fucker off for 12 rounds. Getting that fight at the time I did gave me a structure in my life once again. I would train like a demon for what I knew was gonna be a brutal war and I was right. When I fought John Murray he had the longest unbeaten run in British boxing of 31-0. I get on fabulously with John Murray now but back then in the build up we had our moments with great tension between two fighters. John was the red hot favourite to smash me up because a lot of people in the boxing world had heard how I'd been living the past year. I was a 9/2 underdog at the bookies. I was being seriously written off with most of the top pundits saying I'd fall to bits just like I had with the Katsidis fight. I went into that fight as good as I could have gone into it and in the shape of my life with supreme confidence. The rest is history as me and John had an absolute barnstormer! I'd just like to say credit to John Murray for being a tough, tough man. I have great love for John Murray now and I was actually invited up to his retirement party with all the boxing world Anthony Crolla, Sky Sports' Ed Robinson, Jonny Nelson and Anthony Farnell etc. I myself got up and delivered a speech for John and the fight we had, he's an absolute warrior of the highest order let me tell you. He walked through many of my hardest punches when many a fella never. Funnily enough after I beat John Murray in 2011 I was the one promised the world title against Brandon "BAM BAM" Rios but I never got it. It ended up with John Murray getting the fight for the WBA title, I still to this day don't know how that happened I tell you! My next move was to take a fight and a homecoming one in the East End at The York Hall, Bethnal Green against Felix Lora and I outpointed him over 10 rounds. That put me in line to face a very good friend of mine, Ricky Burns in Glasgow.

In the past I'd sparred many rounds with Ricky Burns, even though he edged it in sparring I was flying in the gym and I really thought I was gonna get the win over him. It turns out the better man won on the night and I made a friend for life in Ricky Burns, he's a terrific fella and so are his team, the Morrisons and his family, I love Ricky. When Ricky beat me in September 2012 I took it quite well, how could you not losing to a lovely fella like him. I had a busy season in 2013 with 3 wins from my 3 fights. I had another 2 wins in 2014, both by KO and I was really back in love with my boxing now. This is how I really should have been in the Katsidis fight.

In 2015 Eddie Hearn had got me to face the tough Mexican (aren't they all) Danie Estrada, that was a great win for me and I really punched Estrada's head in to win the WBC silver title. Estrada would never fight again after I stopped him in 8 rounds at Wembley Arena on the Froch / Groves 2 undercard. That marvellous performance set me up for a world title shot and this time I wasn't gonna fuck it up I was well ready. I was to take on Venezuela's Jorge Linares who was the main guy in the lightweight division. Even Oscar De La Hoya went public to say how much he was looking forward to watching me against Linares.

Although I was to fight once more against Ismael Barroso in my final fight which I lost, it was really the Jorge Linares fight which finished me because I should have won his world title. I had him down, but I never finished him, part of me never got over that because everyone who's watched that fight knows I should have been world champion.

When I watched Jorge Linares fight Manchester's Anthony Crolla twice after our fight Linares had it all his own way both fights. When Linares fought me he was scared to come forward at times because he was terrified of my power, he knew I could dig as he'd already picked himself off the deck once. Like I said that was the night my passion for the games light went well and truly out. I never got over it. I was in such a state from the Linares fight and a complete mess. I had a golf ball for a left eye and a cut to my nose. I just thought fuck this from then on. I hung up my gloves aged 31 which is still relatively young really. I was training for a European title bout and I was in the gym training, but I wasn't enjoying it, I wasn't enjoying my bag and pad work, so I told my then trainer Tony Sims I was calling it a day. I'd been boxing 22 years and I just felt it was time to do something different, start a new chapter of my life.

As a young man, I lived the party lifestyle, partying and training don't go together. I'd say the last two or three years, I worked on my career but if I could go back, that's something I would have done differently. I had 43 fights, 39 wins and I won 29 by way of KO. I know I'm still young enough to come back but I wouldn't ever do it. It's gone from what I had as a young lad, the fire, the drive the buzz for the game has well and truly gone so I got out at the right time. The fight game is a young man's game! When I was 18 you could have put me in with King Kong I wouldn't have given a fuck. Me, myself these days, I'm in a good place in my life. I've got my two boys and a new baby daughter so I'm very happy. I'm happy to stick to boxing outside the ropes being a trainer now.

If someone asked me how I'd like to be remembered I'd say, as a fighter who left everything in the ring. I was a kid from the East End with nothing, so I suppose I didn't do too badly out of boxing. I've always had time for the fans and young fighters and I always bloody will. I think that's important to be like that as they paid their hard earned money to come and watch me, so it's the least I can do to pose for a few pictures or sign autographs. I was just like that myself, so I know what it's like. Even when I'm out in pubs and I've had guys full of drink wanting to pick a fight with me I've never walloped them. Worst case scenario is I've open handed slapped them because it would be a fucking liberty me banging someone's lights out. If I had to do something like that, then that person would have had to have done something really bad let me tell you. I'm a nice guy (Kevin smiles) a lot of people say to me Kevin, "You're equal in Britain to Herol "Bomber" Graham as the best fighter to never win a world title". Well I'm happy with that. I was an exciting fighter who left it all in the ring no matter what and my 4 losses coming by KO probably prove that. I had a bloody good career and a good time in boxing most of the time. Now it's time to get my hands dirty with Tony Sims as a trainer. He is an amazing man to be around and a bit like me, he's been through his ups and downs and made a great life. I love boxing and I owe it everything.

For anyone wanting to contact Kevin you can do so by following him on Twitter @KevinMitchell6

"Never fight ugly people, they have nothing to lose".

Wayne Kelly

Davey Robinson (Repton A.B.C.)

In the heart of London's East End, Bethnal Green to be precise, within the sound of the Bow Bells, in what was just an old bath house sits the world famous Repton Boys Club. This truly wonderful setup is literally a stone's throw away from where the Kray twins Ronnie & Reggie grew up on Vallance Road. It's also only a 10 minute walk from the mecca of world boxing The York Hall.

Over the years, on my journeys to the capital I have popped down to the Repton several times and I've always been given a warm welcome. It has a real aura in that place and in my experience of studying boxing I can confidently say the boxing club is the most successful and well known in Great Britain by some distance. You only have to look at some of the calibre of fighters that have come from the Repton conveyer belt to wear them famous green vests such as John H Stracey, Maurice Hope, Audley Harrison, Darren Barker, Andy Lee and of course film tough guy actor/EastEnd boy done good Ray Winstone. Winstone would go on to have 88 amateur contests winning 80 times in the Repton ABC colours, now that's some going, and he obviously could fight a bit!

Of course, the most notorious of all to ever come out of the club were the Kray twins Ronald and Reginald Kray. Whatever they went on to become in life, they first started out as young boxers and learned their craft in the Repton. Reggie had 55 amateur contests winning 50, Ronnie was beaten far more than his twin because he never had the temperament. Ronnie Kray was all about brute force and would try to walk through his opponents with sheer aggression. When he came up against a classy stylish boxer he would run out of ideas and often got disqualified several times. Reggie could really have had a future in boxing and become a champion in the game. Of course, his brother wouldn't allow that, and Reggie chose another path in life. The rest is history! The Krays always had a great affinity with the club even when they were locked away for 30 years. Tony Burns the head coach for the Repton went on to become Reggie Krays best man when he married Roberta Jones at Maidstone prison in 1997.

Speaking from a personal point of view and having half an idea on boxing, it really was quite something when in 2013 I went down to London with a pro named Josh Leather to Frank Warrens office for him to sign papers, well that day we popped in the Repton to watch the juniors train, that really was quite something to watch believe me! In all my years of being around boxing gyms as a kid or helping out coaching I'd never seen kids say 10-11 sparring and throwing combinations like right uppercut-left hooks with perfect balance. What I was watching was sublime and not like watching children of that age train. These kids were properly well schooled in the art of pugilism and I've often talked about it over the years to people who also follow the most noble art of them all.

In amateur boxing around the country there are far too many cowboys/coaches and I've seen my fair few. Putting their kids in when they can't keep their feet apart or their hands up correctly. The Repton gym from what I watched that day is how every gym should be in Britain. It's a gym like that that I'd want to take my son to in a year or so because boxing's a hurtful business, particularly when your 6 stone and don't know any better and it's up to the coaches to look after their kids as the Repton do.

Now boxings boxing and the object of the game is to knock the other opponent out so of course it does come with a little bit of pain or the odd bloodied nose. If you go out in the rain you want to have the best waterproof Mac money can buy, it's the same with boxing. You go into a game as brutal as boxing and you want to be sure you've been taught and trained well enough to protect yourself in the storm. To know you have the ability to get on your bike around the ring and away from the big typhoons that will blow you over. You don't play at getting punched in the face or your ribs broken so it's not a sport you want your child in if the coach hasn't got a Scooby-Doo and isn't good enough to train your pet hamster. That's the very least a father can do for any son when getting him involved in boxing and taking him to a place like the Repton I can only applaud. If only I lived closer to the place for my son!

I'd already had the pleasure of spending a bit of time with Davey "diamond" Robinson in 2012, I'd came down to watch the ABA finals at the York Hall, Bethnal Green. Davey gave me a guided tour of the grand place. It was a real honour that Davey granted me a little time out of his hectic schedule for this book as on the day I saw him he was extremely busy moving things around in his gym in and out of his work van. I sat in his office and in his own words he told me what the Repton ABC meant to him and how he even came about to get involved in boxing. He was another fella who was also very cock-er-ney... Diamond Dave told me:

I'm 71 now and I was born in London's West End in Soho where I lived along with my 4 brothers. I didn't even come to the East End of London until I was 16 years of age. How it came about is that I met an East End girl and I just kind of stayed in the East End ever since. When I was a lad I myself went to various boxing clubs in London, believe me there was plenty of them about in them days. Everybody loved to box it was just the normal thing to do, just like playing football for a kid now. If I'm being honest about it, I only had a few bouts and I very quickly realised I wasn't the greatest, so I packed it up.

In my days, as a boy I didn't have no father to guide me or keep me off the streets, after the war, where I grew up in the West End it was a bloody rough and ready place so as a young boy I would find it hard not to get myself in spots of bother. I never had the guidance from anyone, so boxing wasn't really a big part in my life when I was very young, not like it is now.

I didn't really become involved in boxing until I took my second oldest son Jamie to the Repton when he was about 8 years of age in 1975. I've been here ever since, that's 42 years now!

The actual building our gyms in was originally a bath house. We've been in here since 1975, before that we were at Victoria Park. It used to be called the Robert Browning club and it was more of a youth club truth be told.

Our main man/coach Tony Burns has been with us since before the start of time. His father Harry Burns started it before him. Harry came up with the name The Repton and we've been The Repton ever since. I've been involved 42 years but of them 42 years I've been the chairmen 28 of them. This makes me the longest serving chairman of a boxing club in the country.

I was first handed the keys to where we are now in 1975, if you look over there (Davey points to a picture on the wall) there's the picture of me with Albert Jacobs the mayor of Tower Hamlets. That man guided me at the start I must say, his plan was to make this club go on for 100 years at least. Our club owe Albert Jacobs a huge amount of gratitude for where it is today. That man had a wonderful vision and dream for the Repton boys club and it needs to be remembered.

When I first came to the club in 1975 we had John H Stracey here, Billy Taylor the Olympian, Paul Lawson and Harry Lawson. It was quite peculiar because Paul boxed for England and Harry boxed for Scotland.

In more recent years we've had Mark Tibbs, Gary Barker and Darren Barker. Darren's a lovely lad and he often still sticks his head around the door. The Rowlands were here too along with Audley Harrison who went on to win the 2000 Olympic Games in Sydney. We don't see much of Audley now as he lives in America.

I've seen some fantastic skills in our gym by some magical boxers. My son Jamie won the schoolboys three years in a row. He's the last Repton boy to win the Schoolboys, Boys Clubs and Jnr ABA'S in one season, a clean sweep!

We're now on the up after a big turnaround in our club. Our long term junior trainer Bobby Becks has just left us, but we'll recover. We're Repton and we'll always be Repton it's what we do.

The Repton is a massive part of my life. I can't ever see my leaving, they'll have to carry me out of the place. Every year I say to my wife, "oh I'll just do another year" and she just looks at me and laughs. She says, "You'll stay in there and stay in there" and in reality, she's right. I think I kid myself at times because I can't ever imagine a time when I'm not there. I can't see me going by my own free will that's for sure! I know all our sponsors, local councillors, trainers and fighters and they all accept me at the Repton. At our club we really are one big happy family. I've been here 42 years and, in all honesty, I can see me being here another 15, that's if him upstairs allows me.

As I've gotten older I've had to hand over the reins on certain things in the gym, for instance I have a good boy called Lionel Omar, he boxed for us as a lad for many years and he's doing things with the Seniors. Young Kelvin Wings has also joined to steady the ship. I counted last night funnily enough, and we have 46 carded senior boxers here so we're gonna have a ridiculously huge team this season. Our juniors need to be rebuilt at the moment. We've lost a lot of the lads and with old Bobby Becks retiring we need totally rebuilding. I have to come in here myself and help out with training with the boys at times. We must get back up and running to get back to how things were. My little grandson Monty is just about old enough to join the junior squad, so I need to take stock there. I'm not that worried though, they'll be a bright future there and besides Repton's Repton. Us Repton lot won't have just anyone in our gym training the boys you know! They must be good calibre and know what they're doing, got to be trustworthy and honest. A few years back we did have one guy some absolute scruffy little chancer by the name of Ben Doughty. He was only here a short while maybe six months that's all, before he was found out for what he was. When Ben was here he was kicked out of his hostel and he moved his stuff under the ring in the gym and thought he was gonna live in here. In the end Tony Burns was getting seriously irritated by him and what he was up to and he came to see me and said, "Dave this geezers got to go you don't know where you are with him he's full of himself". He just wasn't a Repton type of person. When you look at coaches like Georgie Bowers, George Oddwells, Darkie Smiths and the crème de le crème of amateur boxing Tony Burns. That's the kind of standard we have here! Tony Burns' nickname in boxing is "The special one". Wherever we go whether it be New York or France, he gets people coming up to him saying "Mr Burns MBE" and they'll wanna chat with him and a photo. Tony's a great character and what he's done for this club will never be forgotten as well as his old man Harry Burns.

At one point many moons ago, this club was really struggling financially, that was until Harry introduced me to some East End business men. It's because of this that we've made strong progress with regular sponsorship. Unfortunately, this year we've lost a lovely man called Brendan Reilly, Bren was an old Irish fella and he was an extremely generous man to our club. He thought the world of our club and what he did for us was fantastic. He's greatly missed.

Our colours green and gold are known throughout the world. Nobody boxes for us until they're right and they can really box! If that means they stay in the gym for 2 years, then so be it. If they have a problem with that then they'll have to go find another club. We look after our boys and we don't embarrass ourselves by putting these kids in who clearly aren't ready for it. I often say to these kids if you're only here because your dad wants you to be here then that's no good to me! They must really want it and be fully focused, because even in an amateur boxing match you can get badly hurt don't worry about that. Like I've already said I've seen some wonderful boys come through our club but the ones who really stand out off the top of my head are Gary Barker(God rest him) and Colin Derrick. Particularly Colin Derrick because that boy could do everything. His concentration was just perfect for a fighter and he could hit very hard. One Sunday morning in our gym Lloyd Honeyghan came over to spar with Colin and Colin picked him to pieces. To me he should have become a world champion easy. Darren Barker was another brilliant kid, but his younger brother Gary would have gone on to be even better than Darren was he and went on to become a world champion. Gary tragically died aged only 19 due to falling asleep at the wheel of his car. Their father Terry Barker also won an ABA title for our club in 1981 so the Barker family really have our club all through their veins. You can't fault the Barker's for their dedication to our club, the whole family were blessed with the highest of boxing skills and I can only speak highly of them.

We've now got young Georgie Barker with us, so the Barker family are still very much with us today fighting in our colours. These days Darren Barker has his own gym called 12 x 3 in Aldgate with another of the old Repton boys Ryan Pickard. They've made their gym a mini Repton, I wish them both huge success and I love them both.

Another ex Repton boy I'd like to mention is Tony Cesay our old club captain for many years. Tony won the ABA'S in 1999 and in them days it meant more than it does today. Today you can win the ABA'S and you'll only be the 4th best in the country because all the best isn't allowed due to being part of the GB squad based in Sheffield. It doesn't even allow them to enter the ABA'S which I think is a disgrace. Back in the day whoever won the ABA'S went to the Olympics but it's sadly not this way no more. This makes a mockery of the ABA'S it really does but what can you do.

Ray Winstone has never forgotten his Repton roots and he comes to see us now and again. He's about to move to Sicily but he'll always be an East End boy at heart.

The Repton without a shadow of a doubt is like my home from home, I feel very comfortable here. I still remember the first day I came in here, it was a Saturday morning and I looked about in the gym and at the pictures on the walls and I knew this gym was magical. It has a real aura about it. When you walk in our club you realise the potential here and you can feel the history of the place, the fighters of the past. I just can't help but get a certain buzz when I watch our boys of today training, I still get that buzz now 42 years on and I bloody live in here. I often sit in here on my own and I find it so relaxing so tranquil. I've been around all the gyms London, America, Italy and dozens in Europe but you won't see a better set up than this place. If you look up on that wall son (Davey points to the wall) you can see our motto "NO GUTS NO GLORY" that's what we're about here in this club. Now and again we get the odd gangster come for a look in our gym but there always very sociable to us. The ones who've been in are very respectful because they know the good we do by keeping the kids of the East End off the streets, away from crime. Many times, we've had donations from this one or that one and they applaud us for what we do, they never do us any harm. They'll always be villains coming out of the East End and there always has been it doesn't mean their bad people, just means they do a slightly different job to the average 9-5 man in the street. Where your job is working for the council, their job is robbing banks.

The area around here's changed so much to when I first came in 1962. Back in them days it was all proper East End cockneys as well as a lot of Jewish families around, particularly in Whitechapel. These days the old true East Enders have all moved on and they've been replaced by the Asian communities.

Everyone in our club has a part to play, even the cleaners. Money is secondary to us, what matters is we look after our kids. Sometimes on a Saturday morning there's 30-40 kids in here and we only charge £1 a head. That's two and a half hours training for that, we couldn't do it no cheaper than we do it now. None of the other clubs in London are as cheap as us I tell you! We're a very giving club we're not here to take it off the lads, in fact we even pay for the medicals and they get the vest with that.

The gym hasn't always been used for boxing, the film Lock, Stock and Two Smoking Barrels was filmed in here. The bit where Lenny McLean cheats and the boy loses the card game was filmed in our ring. Take That the band from the 90s shot their first video also in our ring. Robbie Williams was dancing around in our club for the shoot of the video. Robbie Williams popped in the gym to see us last year. He walked up to me and said, "I remember you, you're the guvnor aren't ya when we did that video 24 years ago". I said, "Yes that's right Robbie I remember you". He said, "I'll see you in another 24 years" and walked out. Olly Murs has also shot stuff in our place. The reason I think these famous folks choose our gym is we've always kept it looking traditional. Like a proper East End boxing club should look like. I remember back in 1975 Bill Cox who was the chairman back then said to me, "right Dave we need you to do this and I want you to put a tin of paint over that" etc... I told him nah you don't Bill, this place is perfect how it is. My business for a living is in the stone industry so I'd like to think I knew what I was talking about. I told him we needed to keep it grimy and smelly like a proper old school boxing club which is really what we are in fact. Keep the toilets clean and the changing rooms immaculate but our gyms unique. The old fight posters up on the walls keep it natural. Big Audley Harrison says this in his book on our place "Clean magnolia walls don't belong in a boxing gym. The only smell in here is blood and sweat".

When boys walk through this door and talk to me, the first thing I tell them is you're in the Repton now. I don't wanna know your background, I don't wanna know what you're like with your parents, but you will give us respect! No back chat! If you stay here we'll do our very best for you. I'm not bothered if I'm talking to a 10 year old kid or a 25 year old that's just got out of Pentonville prison. If you don't want to give us respect, then don't turn up here it's as simple as that. Our trainers give up hours and hours of their time for nothing so at the very least your gonna behave in here! I don't care if they're black, white or Irish travellers as long as you're prepared to wear the green and gold in that ring you're ok with me.

We always have a good laugh in this club about everything. If you look up there (Dave points above his head) where it says pay your sub money somebody's crossed it out and wrote "Davey's holiday fund". That's just one of the boys thinking he's clever (Dave laughs). Me and Tony have great craic among ourselves and the rest of the lads. Nobody is ever safe there's always some poor bleeder getting the micky taken out of them. Tony's from just near the York Hall so he's as cockney as they come like most of our boys. We're all extremely proud of our East End roots.

If you want to learn more about the Repton ABC you can do so by following them on Twitter @ReptonBC or on Facebook under Repton Boxing Club.

"The only places a boxer is allowed to hit are the places worth hitting, and like chess, one makes a move, the other makes a move, but instead of winning or losing bishops and rooks, its teeth and senses that are lost".

Paul Sykes.

Matthew Burke

Matthew Burke is a name I remember from my time in amateur boxing as a schoolboy. Largely down to his two national finals with one of my childhood friends Stephen Truscott. Matthew beat Stephen in 1994 in the schoolboy final, then they met again in 1996 in the NABC finals with Stephen getting revenge that time.

I'd often see his name in the magazine 'Amateur Boxing Scene' which was out in the 90s, his name would appear with news of Matthew winning this, that or the other.

I'd spoken to Matthew for many years via social media and even by phone, so I knew what Matthew was about before I went down to his fabulous setup 'The Left Hook gym' on Martha Street, Shadwell East London. I spent a couple of hours with Matthew, who made me very welcome in his gym which is listed in 'Time Out London' as being on the best 50 gyms list in the whole of the capital.

Matthew was another seriously Cock-er-ney person just like Kevin Mitchell who I'd met the day before! That joke Micky Flanagan tells about being so cockney it hurts was for people like those two. I sat on the corner of the ring in his gym and pressed record on my Dictaphone and listened to our Matt tell me how he became involved in the sport of boxing.

Matthew said: -

I grew up in Stratford in East London and I'm almost 37 years of age now. What got me into boxing really, well my first memory is that one day I went into school and a good friend of mine called Tony Chapman brought one of his trophies in to show off. Well I was bloody mesmerised by this thing he'd won at the weekend, I was well jealous of him and the attention he got, and I wanted to be just like him. Tony was a top amateur and his old man Joey Chapman ran the Newham ABC boxing club which was in my area. Funnily enough when I see Tony these days I still talk to him and it often gets brought up about that trophy he won, how every kid in the school wanted to be him for that day. I would eventually follow suit and go along to his dad's gym the Newham ABC to see if I could score any of these big glamorous trophies for myself, that's all I was thinking about as an 8-year-old boy.

The gym at the time was very strong with a great set of boys such as Dougie Wood, Teddy Day, Paul Souter, Terry Driscoll and of course Joey's son Tony. I started competing initially in gym shows, these days they're skills bouts and I had around 10 of these. You couldn't win in these bouts, but you couldn't lose either. The main thing was that you got a trophy/medal which was really what I was in the game for, so I bloody loved it. As a kid this was the best thing in the world, as much as I wanted to be like Tony and show off all my trophies and medals I never really did, as I was a very shy kid, whereas Tony always was a cheeky chappie, even to this day he is!

I would go on to have my first real competitive bout aged 11 and I won that on points. I would get hugely frustrated as a boy, because when I won one I would think I would be the best and keep winning, only to then lose which always brought me back down to earth and I'd be on the brink of depression - for a whole day. In my first season I couldn't get two back to back wins for the life of me. I think I lost about 8 fights in my first season, it was a case of win, lose, win, lose, win, lose... It was only really after my first year that I started getting back to back wins and I progressed greatly in the following seasons, even going unbeaten for two years solid.

Tony Chapman was my main sparring partner in our gym for many years. We would go for sparring at other gyms in London such as Mickey May's West Ham Boys, which wasn't far from us. I sparred many top boxers as an amateur including Marc Callaghan from Barking who would go on to become British super bantamweight as a pro. Also, Nicky Cook, who won title after title as an amateur and pro. I often sparred with Patrick John boy Humphries who could really bang. He had the sort of power that when he hit you, your fingers and toes would buzz! He went on to become a half decent pro himself fighting for the British title. I boxed Patrick three times as an amateur winning one and losing two. In our third and final fight he stopped me, he caught me with a great shot, I was straight up on my feet and wanted to continue but the ref called it a day. That's when he had really developed his punch power, I was just the first unfortunate one to find out! Patrick John boy Humphries would go on to stop his next 9 opponents after me, boy he could hit!

The best I ever sparred with on the London scene throughout my years boxing was a young Kevin Mitchell. I sparred him when we were both pro, Kevin had the fastest hands I'd ever seen in boxing and he could bang with both hands.

Looking back on my amateur career I had around 65 bouts winning approx. 50 of them, I got to 3 national finals winning 2 of them. I beat your friend Stephen Truscott from Middlesbrough and a Welsh kid called M White from Porthcawl ABC. The final I lost was the Boys Clubs and it was my old nemesis Truscott. I had the fucker down in the first round with a monster right hand. I don't know how the hell he got up from that but unfortunately for me he did and battled back to get the decision. I went in to that fight with a bad back injury (I'd damaged a disc training for these championships), we went to the semi-finals of the championships to weigh in knowing I couldn't fight, but luckily for me my opponent withdrew, I had a reputation as a big puncher by then. I was then rested for the finals with Stephen. In hindsight I should have gone for the finish when I dropped him in the 1st, as I had no fitness due to the injury. That fight is on YouTube if anyone wants to have a look and you'll see my bemusement at how the fuck he got up. Speaking to one of Stephen's family years later they told me Stephen said it was the hardest he'd ever been hit. Prince Naseem Hamed was there for that fight at ringside watching it.

Another lad I boxed from up north was Darlington's Stuart Hall. Stuart Hall went on to win a world title at bantamweight in 2014. I fought Stuart twice, the first bout in Darlington which he won (It was a poor judging decision and was met with disbelief), then he came down to London and I beat him convincingly.

Another fella who I boxed as an amateur who wasn't a bad pro was Martin Welsh from Swanley, Kent. Martin Welsh was the first one to ever really hurt me in boxing when I boxed him at just 13 years old. I was coming down ill on the day of that fight and it really affected me. After facing him I thought "FUCK THIS GAME" as every time he hit me it was like being hit with a hammer. That was my most unpleasant experience in boxing and because I was ill, the beating he gave me was magnified. It was my home show for Newham ABC and I only never pulled out because I didn't want to let anyone down. Now as a Coach I would never let one of my youngsters' box whilst ill. You can play football, basketball and volleyball but you don't play boxing let alone go to war less than 100%. He beat me and to be honest I wanted to pack in. I managed to come back from that defeat and beat him twice so that was a great personal achievement for me. When I met Martin a good 15yrs later he told me he always looked up to me as an amateur boxer and always followed my progress. I was quite touched by that to be honest. He's a good guy.

I remember one day when I got home from school (my GCSE year) I'd had a call from Joey, he asked if I could fight that night, one of our guys was meant to be fighting but had pulled out, their opponent had come over all the way from Ireland and were desperate to fight. Joey said, "They will give you £30 if you fight!" - "I'm in", I said. So, we rushed to this show and weighed in, that's when Joey looked at this kid's card from Ireland and said to their coach "I don't think we should take this one, my boy will be a bit too good for you." Their coach took one look at me and said, "We will take it, our boy will be strong enough" (I was always very skinny and didn't look like a boxer at all, especially one that had knock out power). I always joked, it was my disguise.

I was due to box for England a week later and remember Joey saying, "This kids strong, don't get stopped or you'll not box next week." I love those words of wisdom! That's Joey, straight to the point, no bullshit.

The 1st bell went, and this kid came straight at me, throwing bombs. I remember vividly to this day how I felt in there, I was taking a few on the arms and thinking, yeah...he is strong! I better keep it tidy and not get caught.

Then 30 seconds later he was down and staying down. I'd landed one of my trademark right hands and he was out. They even needed the doctor in to help him up as he couldn't get himself up.

Those coaches learnt the valuable lesson that day of "don't judge a book by its cover" and I'd earned the easiest £30 of my life.

As an amateur I was always being linked to fight Irelands Bernard Dunn because he was my weight and the best in his country the same as me. It never materialised but I'd have loved to have tested myself against Dunn and of course he went on to become a world champion himself as a pro.

A future world champion I did fight was the Repton's Darren Barker. He was incredibly slick, and he may well be the best amateur I ever fought. Darren beat me in the London ABA'S in 2001 on points, it was a good close fight, but he was just too slick on the day.

West Ham's Benny Tokely was another top amateur I boxed, he beat me twice in my first year of boxing, I would have loved to get a rematch later on, but we just never ended up crossing paths again.

I myself boxed for England 6 times and the most memorable moment was going to Russia with Ricky Hatton, Nicky Cook, Tony Dodson and David Barnes, all of whom went on to win titles as amateurs and pros. When I was in Russia Ricky Hatton flattened the first Russian he fought. Then the Russian amateur boxing coaches found the biggest and best guy at the weight to put in with Ricky, then Hatton did the same thing and flattened him in the same fashion. The Russians nicknamed Hatton "little Tyson".

I first knocked an opponent out when I was 14 years of age, and I do mean out, I rapidly gained a reputation as a big puncher around the London amateur boxing scene. On my route to winning my second national title I stopped 2 kids on their feet, KO'D 2 and the one guy who went the distance I dropped, I really had finally gained my punch power. I remember one National semi-final I had, I was walking through the hall before my fight and a man grabbed me and said, "alright Burke, so what round you gonna win this one in?" I just laughed, and he then said, "I'm serious, what round?" so, I just said "2nd" (I thought that gives me time to work him out). I stopped the guy in the 1st and after the fight the same guy came up and said, "You told me the 2nd, you lost me money there".

Of course, being so heavy handed always leads to a fighter with hand problems. Once when I boxed for England V Ireland I broke both hands in the first round. I carried on through the pain barrier and managed to gain a victory via points. That Irish guy had the hardest head I've ever punched! I remember my dad having an argument with one of my coaches at the time. The coach was saying I had nearly thrown the fight away by not working hard enough in the fight. My old man heard this and come barging in saying, "OI, JUST LOOK AT HIS FUCKING HANDS, they're ruined but he still won the fight, what more do you want"?!

I decided I'd had enough of the unpaid ranks and that I wanted to give the pro ranks a go. I was signed by Matchroom's Barry Hearn as I had a successful amateur career. I was 21 when I turned pro and I would often spar many rounds with talented fighters, some of those boxers I got rounds with included Kevin Mitchell, Colin Dunne, Graham Earl and Kevin Lear. I was involved in sparring preparation for Kevin Lear leading up to his fight with Manchester's Michael Gomez for a world title. He hit me with a left hook and dislocated my jaw, so I couldn't eat for a week! I had 4 professional contests and my coach was the much-respected Johnny Eames. In my first bout I beat Joel Viney and followed it with another victory over Andrew Robinson, both points victories over 4 rounds. My third bout and first loss was against Greenock's teak tough John Simpson. John Simpson went on to become British & Commonwealth featherweight champion as well as fighting

39

for a version of a world title, so I suppose it was no shame. John beat me on points 39-37 and he just came forward all night. It wasn't until the last round that I discovered he didn't like body shots, with me being so tall I used to neglect the body and mostly go head hunting, I caught him with a beauty, but by then it was too late, and I let him off and lost the fight. It's ironic that John Simpson's 3 losses as a pro by KO by Lee Selby, Tommy Coyle and John Murray have all come from body shots. My fourth and final fight was against a guy who really went on to do well and fight for a genuine world title, a fella I've just mentioned… Manchester's John Murray. I faced Murray in his backyard of Manchester in only his second bout. The fight ended after the first round. We just went at it from the opening bell and we were both landing good shots, then all I can remember is being hit by what felt like a concrete slab, turns out it was his hard head. My nose was completely fucked (broke), and that was the end of the fight. I was walking to the ring that night though wishing I wasn't there, I didn't want to be boxing, I guess it's because I knew I hadn't been training properly.

Looking back on going pro I turned over when I didn't even really wanna be boxing. I wasn't mature enough to say I needed a break from boxing. I really should have maybe had a year or two off from the sport like many do nowadays and it's not frowned upon. It had been part of my life for so long and I was feeling utterly burnt out. I didn't want it enough at the time. I was majorly cutting corners in my training. I wasn't doing my roadwork, I wasn't going to bed at the right time and I was messing around with girls. Mentally I just wasn't there, looking back yes, I regret turning pro when I did. I didn't even wanna be boxing truth be told! I wish I'd have waited till around 25/26 when I'd filled out and gained my man strength.

Nowadays I'm still very much involved in boxing on a day to day basis. I Coach regular boxing classes for anyone wanting to learn the art of boxing or just get fit. I'm the Head Coach at Left Hook gym as well as for my amateur club Left Hook ABC. My amateur club is going from strength to strength and we are in to our 3rd season. We've already got 6 titles between 2 of our boxers, including National and International Champions, which is not bad going for a club only in their 3rd season. My amateur team is constantly growing with some real talented fighters. I have big plans for my female boxer Marie Connan. Marie spars with the men in my gym and they don't have to hold back, that's how good she is. She's a real role model, her commitment and dedication are second to none, and she trusts me. That's very important to me as a Coach, to have my Boxers trust. I'm loving building up my amateur stable Left Hook ABC. When I see my guys winning it means more to me than when I was boxing and winning fights. Honestly, helping my guys win championships means more to me than when I got my England Vests! These are my kids and I love them like they're my own flesh and blood. I see it as my duty to look after them and guide them using my experiences in boxing, because it's not all fucking rosy in boxing there's bad people out there that will take the piss. It's my job to save the young Matthew Burkes and prevent them from making the same pigs ears I did because boxing's an unforgiving sport. It can be a bad mistress and brutal.

The people who shout for boxing to be banned are ridiculous! It will straighten more fella's life out then it will ever take. We know what we're doing going into the ring and we know the risks, but there's risks with everything in life, even crossing roads. I think head guards should be removed because they only block your vision and you can't judge slipping the shots properly because your bloody heads bigger. They don't help with concussion either in my opinion, as I knocked out more people that were wearing head guards than those that were not. Go figure!

I'm not really one for getting in trouble or into street fights, and the main reason for that is I don't want to get into trouble with the law. If I wasn't such a goody two shoes when it came to it, I'd probably be fighting weekly. As there is always some bugger giving it the big one. There was this one time I was out with a couple of my mates, and I ended up having to put a bully in his place, and this guy was one BIG bully. I'm not kidding, he made Anthony Joshua look average size. It started out a great night, just having a laugh and a good drink. We had booked a VIP table and a few bottles of champagne so we just chilling out. I'd gone with one of my mates to the dance floor, to have a little butcher's at what was going on, enjoying the sights. Then this guy towering over me grabbed my drink in my hand, so I pulled away. At first, I thought he had mistaken me for someone else and had thought I was holding his drink for him. Then he grabbed at it again. I said, "What you doing mate"? He just said, "I want some of your drink". I just laughed and politely said no, then again and again and again he tried. I was looking up at him and I knew it was going to go off, I just remembered thinking, fuck I don't need this as he was soooo big! After what must have been a minute of me being polite I just said, "Look mate, there's no way you're having my drink". It was at this point he grabbed my wrist and said, "One way or another I'm having your fucking drink". With that a friend I was with tried to be the peacemaker and got between us. I just whispered to my mate "take my glass and get out of the way", he knew what was coming and he stepped away from the big lump. The big lump then grabbed my neck so within a second of him doing that to me it was BANG BANG BANG!!!! Tables went crashing. I hit him with three good shots and he stopped dead for a second, it felt like I was hitting those Easter Island heads. Then he stumbles forward on to me, he was so tall and heavy he actually slumped over my shoulders, all I had in front of me was this muscular torso in a tight top, so instinctively I hit him with three body shots. That took all the fight out of him. It's funny because rather bizarrely I remained so calm, when I hit him with the body shots I saw my watch spinning around my wrist, the impact had unclipped it, so I took my watch off and put it in my pocket safe. Within seconds after that the bouncers came rushing over, I was calm and just explained what had taken place. The big lump had now regained his senses and started to come at me again, only for 3 of the door staff to escort him out of the building. The head doorman asked me to leave but I told him "look mate, I'm calm, he attacked me. I'm from here, I might go out to face ten of his mates". He said, "Don't worry there's ten of us". That really reassured me I wasn't in the bad books and I gathered they knew I hadn't instigated it. As I was being led out one of the bouncers asked me to wait in the lobby, as I waited there another doorman came up to tell me I couldn't wait there, "Your colleague told me to wait here" I said. With that the doorman looked me up and down and said, "YOU did that to him?" The bully was now outside not far from us but with blood streaming down his swollen face holding his ribs. Ironically this big bully was by now moaning to the police outside. Just what I needed I thought! At that point the general manager of the club came over and asked for my I.D. I showed him, and he said "right, I need to go chat to the old bill". So, then I grabbed my I.D and said, "don't worry I'll leave"! With that the manager of the club told me he was going to sort it for me with the old bill but either way you need to speak to the old bill. I just stood back for a while trusting the club manager whilst I was sent to the VIP area once again. Then 20 minutes later he came back in with my I.D and held out his hand saying, "Good job Mr Burke" while shaking my hand. What did make me laugh is one of the doormen said, "He won't show his face in here now for a while". They told me Mr Bully was a regular troublemaker in their place. I was on the edge all night after that though, really did ruin my night. I was also pissed off that I didn't knock the man mountain out. Funny thing is I'm such a friendly guy, had he just come and said hello to me and had a chat I'd have probably offered him a drink as we had shit loads we were never gonna drink.

What really makes me happy now is keeping my kids off the streets. Helping them change their lives for the better, away from gangs, smoking, drink and drugs, many a time I'm a father figure/social worker, trainer all rolled into one.

Our gym is a friendly place, it's like one big happy family. If someone comes into my gym with a chip on their shoulder they don't last long. I won't stand for any crap! If people want to come to use the gym to be a keep fitter, to lose weight then I tell them to enjoy the training and I'll make sure in my gym they're treated with respect and looked after. If you come to my gym and want to compete for me as an amateur boxer then there's no messing and you do as I say. You can't fuck about in boxing!

The East End of London will always be the home of boxing. The York Hall is where it was born, and it has a special aura about it. I boxed there many times as an amateur and it doesn't matter where you sit, there's not a bad seat in that place. I'm so proud of my East End roots. I love boxing, but I remain bitter because I blew my chance as a fighter. I can't turn back the time and be 21 again. That bitterness I carry around with me drives me on to take someone else to a championship, I didn't reach my potential for the ability I had I know that, I'm not being big headed there either! One thing I can say is, I'm very proud of what I'm part of now, Left Hook gym is a very welcoming, multicultural gym and we offer boxing training for everyone, no matter what your ability or background.

I could never see a time in my life when I'm not involved in boxing, if I was a millionaire tomorrow I would still train the amateurs. When they've won a title or even just a club bout and they message me saying, "oh thanks Matt for what you've done for me", that to me is what it's all about and it makes me happy in life. I'd like to give a huge thanks to my great friends (more like family now), Enzo Giordano and Oner Avara (they are best friends and co-owners of Left Hook) who've trusted me to run Left Hook ABC from day one and it's their trust in me that also drives me on to make Champions.

I'd also like to say thanks to Brad Nathan of Lynx Equity Limited. Brad is a solid guy who I first met through coaching (he's not a bad boxer himself). When I told him we don't get any funding for our amateur team he offered to buy us some kits and he always supports us and offers his help when we need to raise funds for taking our team abroad for championships. I learned a great saying from him and I truly believe it, "the harder you work, the luckier you get." He's a Mensch.

If anyone is wanting to find out more about Matthew's gym they can do so by following @LeftHookBoxing on Facebook, Instagram and twitter. Better still call in to see him at his gym at 1, Martha Street, Shadwell, London E1 2PX. He's got time for everyone and is a lovely fella, just make sure you can speak fluent Cock-er-ney…

Matthew's friend and owner of Left Hook Gym, Oner Avara, has also come up with a brilliant platform that will benefit all involved in boxing. Nurturing the grassroots of boxing is incredibly important and that's why recourses like MyNextMatch, a sports software management tool, are very useful. Boxing would really benefit by bringing all athlete data under one central hub. Not only would it make the sport much fairer on the matchmaking side, but the use of the digital medical passport would also help prevent the occurrence of serious injury, if an athlete tries to avoid suspension by jumping to a different sport.

You can see more about this exciting new platform at www.mynextmatch.com

"I like boxing, there's nothing like a punch in the face to remind you you want to live".

Atticus

Andrew Buchanan

I first heard of the name Andrew Buchanan in January 1993 in Brandon WMC at the Schoolboy Championships. Growing up around the northeast boxing scene his name was a name you couldn't avoid, he was that good! Andrew literally won everything around. Being the same age, I often watched him beat the other lads around who I knew or lads that went to my gym such as John Cronin and Gareth Maloney from the Old Vic ABC in Middlesbrough. I would like to add on a personal note, for as good as Andrew was as a kid, he was always humble and never looked down on kids like me who were nowhere near his level like some kids at the age of 14-15 are capable of.

I would often see "El cannon" around the northeast amateur boxing shows and often speak to him and his younger brother Paul, who was also a champion boxer. When I would watch Andrew boxing, in most of his contests he was often too good for his own good. His style was extremely cautious, and he boxed intelligently in every move he'd make.

I always thought he came across as if he couldn't be bothered at times, as if he was that good he knew he was going to win without going into the trenches. He just did enough to win and stayed in second gear.

Andrew would often box kids with maybe 30 contests less than he had and didn't really have to push himself. It was only when he got to fight the national elite that he would really have a fight on his hands and he could not just go through the motions.

Andrew fought a ridiculous number of bouts and had vast experience at such a young age that he would always seem like a veteran to kids his own age. On more than one occasion I would see Andrew get byes to the next round. This was often because kids would pull out rather than face him. This may sound stupid, but I know Andrew almost had this Tyson image that you were "beaten before you boxed him" as I had watched my friends pull out against him.

When I was a kid of around 15 years of age I remember I used to think, if any of the kids I know now go on to be a good pro, it will be Andrew Buchanan! He was just that cut above everyone else at the time. A handful of times I myself went to northeast training at Terry Dagnam's gym in Washington. It was held once a month on a Sunday for the kids of the northeast to get together and train. I don't mind admitting that I used to watch Andrew training and be in awe of his natural skills and overall ability moving and gliding around the punch bags. The only time I can remember an opponent even catching Andrew Buchanan cleanly was at St Paul's gym in December 1995. Andrew faced the Scottish champion Tony McPake from Forgewood. It was the third and final round and McPake hit Buchanan that hard with a right hand he was out on his feet. It came at the end of the round and I remember Andrew needing a helping hand back to his corner after the fight. I wanted McPake to win as he had the same tartan shorts as me, and he told me he was a Celtic supporter before the fight. He'd seen the Celtic shirt I had on and I got talking to him and his club mate John Dunbar, who was there boxing my gym mate John Cronin in the light flyweight division. Never mind Andrew, even Floyd Mayweather got tagged now and again. I think Andrew went on to bribe the judges as he went on to get the decision that day and I thought McPake was a clear winner. I've often joked to Andrew over the years that he definitely rigged the fight to get that decision or even the ref not to stop it in the third.

I'd like to say now Andrews a friend of mine and he often pops to my house with his lovely family, Wife Jen and kids Abby and Cole, and I go to his house with my Wife and son Jameson Lennon. I went through early one Saturday afternoon to get this interview done. On that night I went to the annual Buchanan Halloween bash. I went as everyone's favourite serial killer the bay harbour butcher AKA Dexter Morgan, Andrew went as Ash from The Evil Dead. Before we got dressed up and I fought off Finn (Andrew's dog) from trying to shag my arm, I sat in Andrews front room and he told me about what got him into boxing in the first place, and how he went on to become one of the north east's top names in amateur boxing.

Andrew said:

I'm 37 years old now and I've been retired a couple of years from boxing. I started boxing because when I was aged 5-6 years old, I went to Karate and the karate match I had I got disqualified in because I punched the kid in the face. Karate was non-contact, so I was kicked out of the match and the other boys hand was raised, I was well gutted to have lost. From that day forward my father Gordon told me to forget about karate and he promised to take me to a boxing club close by. My old man took me and my younger brother Paul to boxing. My dad would give up all his time, effort and money to get us into the boxing game, so we were properly ready for the years to come.

The first club our dad took us was West Denton ABC. It was just an old library, it had John Davison the former British and WBC international featherweight champion training there at the same time as us. To us as kids it was like Muhammad Ali sharing a gym with us and we looked up and idolised John at the time. When John boxed abroad for one of his title fights, he returned to our gym with a big box of white T-shirts with his picture on and gave everyone in the gym one. Me and my brother used to wear it every day when it wasn't in the wash. Its little things like that, that mean the world to you as a child and it still stays with me today.   Dominic McGuigan the lightweight who was also a decent pro also trained with us at West Denton ABC, he's on the boxing board of control now in the north east. Jimmy Johnson was one of the coaches and it was a real old school gym. Paint peeling off the walls, mouldy smelly leather punch bags and when you walked into the place it had that distinctive smell only an old boxing gym has. Only ex boxers could really understand that awful unique smell. The gym was just a made-up ring in the corner of the room with saggy ropes. It really was just a tiny scruffy little place but to me it was like the Kronk and it was my life at the time, I just loved them foisty smelly gloves.

That gym was just around the corner from my mam and dad's house and it was mine and my brothers everything growing up as young lads getting into the sport of boxing. If me or my brother ever misbehaved at school, we were never allowed to go to the gym and we would be heartbroken. My dad Gordon used to go with us and watch over. In the end he became part of the team i.e. sweeping up or clock watching. It was a place me, Paul and dad would go to three times a week and how we loved it. That's how we first started with the boxing, from there me and Paul never stopped till we became adults. Me and my brother Paul used to spar when we were little but as we got older and more powerful my dad made us stop. Saying it was too much for him to watch so out of respect to our dad we never did it again.

We stayed at West Denton ABC for around a year, but we became devastated when the gym closed. We then had to move to Benwell ABC. The gym was in the Green Tree pub, just out the back in fact. Quite often when we were training there, the door would open, and we'd get a lungful of smoke from the bar. How times have changed eh. Again, we only stayed at Benwell ABC a year because that place closed too. We had to up sticks again and this time we joined Teams Valley ABC when I was around 9-10. I would go on to have my first bout for Teams and stay there for many years. Joining the Teams gym, I would say was a make or break situation for me looking back. At the time I often wondered if it was my dad's idea of child torture because many times when I was learning my trade there, I would get some right hidings in the gym. Boxing can be a pretty harsh environment to be in when you're just a boy 11years old and 5 stone something.

I used to spar with John and Tony Marsden and these two would beat the crap out of me. Sometimes at school I used to think 'SHIT' I've got to go to that place tonight and get my brains rattled. I often got 'chinned' but as I got older and stronger I started to hold my head above water and I could hold my own with them.

When I first started competing in boxing I wasn't great. I would win one, lose one then win three lose two it wasn't until I was around 14 years of age that I started to become successful. I had to have a year out due to me suffering from Osgood Schlatter's disease in my knee. Looking back the rest had done me good the world of good because since I was around 7 to around 13, I'd had very intense training in the gyms day in day out which obviously isn't great for a growing lad as well as making weights etc. ... The time I had off for around 15 months was a Godsend, even though I was inconsolable at the time seeing my brother win this trophy and that trophy etc.... When I went back to training at around 15 years old I won my first national title. The reason I would wait so long to win a national title was down to a fine young gentleman called Dave Carter from Hartlepool. Dave was the No.1 in the country and the reason I would go out in the schoolboys in the first round was usually him. I boxed him 5 times losing 4 of them. I managed to beat him on my return from coming back from my knee operation, so I suppose I salvaged some pride and got a win over the legendary Dave Carter. Dave won a couple of national titles before he walked away from the sport aged 14. Dave Carter had something like 38 bouts winning 33 of them he was so good. He went on to beat Nigel Wright a good few times. I also had the pleasure of sharing a ring with Shildon's Mr. Wright, 5 times and losing 5 times. Fucking southpaws should be banned!!! Nigel Wright went on to become a good pro and boxed for the Commonwealth title a couple of times.

Just before my 16th birthday in 1996 I would move gym again, me, Paul and dad went along to the north east's most successful gym Birtley ABC in Gateshead as Teams closed down. Things started happening for me at Birtley and it was around this time that I really started to believe in myself. I went over to Ireland with Birtley and I beat a really half decent kid which gave me so much needed confidence which I was lacking in at the time. From then on, I kept winning and winning and it was around then that I thought maybe I could make a living in boxing more rather than it just a hobby. At the time I was really in love with the game, mainly down to Naseem Hamed who was at his peak of his powers. I would watch Naz and try to copy how he moved. I was forever asking my dad and the other coaches at Birtley when can I start boxing southpaw to be like Naz! I would just get a clip round the ear and told, "DON'T BE SO FUCKING STUPID MAN" (laughs)

Head of Birtley was the legendary Ronnie Rowe, he's a fabulous coach and he's still the main man there today holding the gym together. Ronnie took both Jon-Lewis Dickinson and Travis Dickinson to Prizefighter titles among other titles. Both lads are a product from the Birtley ABC. The Birtley gym has gone from strength to strength in the last 20 odd years since it started up. When I arrived it already had Mark and Andy McClean who were elite boxers. As well as Paul Gardner and Danny Temperley, who'd all won national titles. Then there were also some terrific little juniors coming through like Tommy Ward who is British Champion now. Me and my brother Paul bedded in well and we both won national titles for Birtley ABC. I stayed at Birtley ABC for the next 3 years, only to leave with going pro in the back of my mind. I joined Glenn McCrory's gym up on North road. I'd just lost to the best light middleweight in the country at the time Chris Bessey in the semifinals of the ABA'S in 1999. It was no disgrace really as Chris Bessey was a 6-time ABA champion. I'd always been training with England at Crystal Palace training camps since I was 16. In 1999 I was getting more and more invites, but I very foolishly turned them down, thinking I'm going pro anyway so what's the point! So, it was to be that I turned pro and was trained by Glenn McCrory's brother Gary. I was to get the usual promises you get in boxing that you're going to be given this, that and the other and at the time I was very happy. It was all so exciting to me at that time, I was still a teenager. My first promoter who I signed with was Frank Warren. I signed with Frank, but I never actually had a fight with him. There was always talk of Frank putting a big show on up in the North East and putting me, my brother Paul, Sunderland's David Dolan, cruiserweight Shaun Bowes and Ross Murray from Newbiggin but nothing ever became of it. We were all training hard in the gym for months, but no big show was even slightly in the making and it was all a waste of our time.

We'd often go to other gyms sparring and one of them was the Collyhurst & Moston gym in Manchester. That gym had fighters in it like Michael Jennings, Anthony Farnell, Robin Reid and Thomas McDonagh. To be fair it was only due to Glenn McCrory's contacts that we would go to places like this. That time in question was because Glenn had to go interview Robin Reid who one of the top middleweights in the world, for Sky Sports so he took us lot along. I sparred many rounds with Robin Reid that day and Anthony Farnell. I remember Anthony in the amateurs as he is around my age, he would wear gowns with 'Body snatcher' on it and I used to laugh thinking who the fuck does this guy think he is. To be fair Anthony Farnell, he was knocking kids out with body shots and looking back he was more suited to the pros then. It doesn't surprise me that Anthony Farnell is doing well as a pro trainer now. It was little trips like this that really tilted my head into the pros in the first place. Who Glenn McCrory doesn't know in the boxing world is really not worth knowing. Another invaluable experience I gained through Glenn was the time we went to spar Mads Larsen and Mikkel Kessler in Denmark. To even be offered to go was amazing never mind getting paid for the privilege!

In my time around amateur boxing I must have had 120 bouts winning around the 90 mark. Most of my losses were when I was just starting off in the sport as a child. As a senior I only ever lost to England's No.1 Chris Bessey, in which he beat me twice. As a junior the ones that stick out were Birmingham's Leigh Hallet who is the only person amateur or pro, boxing or sparring to make me hit the deck. That day I fought Leigh I was getting carried away and I entered the ring with tassels on my boots thinking I was Sugar Ray Leonard, so I probably deserved dropping for being a knob. Another fighter I lost to was Larry Mosely (Shane's cousin) and that was in the European juniors, I faced some big horrible Azerbaijan who just stuck his fucking stupid big arm in my face all day. That was the most frustrating fight I've ever had, and I felt like taking my gloves off and telling him to fuck off. I even rocked him in the final round but by then I'd lost heart. I just wanted the fight to finish so I could go get myself a pasty! I managed to get a fabulous victory over Leo O'Reilly the Londoner who was highly rated and big things were planned for him as a pro. Also, I beat Birmingham's Nathan Smith in the schoolboys. Nathen was 42-1 going into the fight with me and was a big favourite in the Amateur Boxing Scene magazine.

There were some terrific fighters in that European Juniors in 1997. I think I was the youngest in the tournament as I was still only 17. Scotland's Craig Docherty who would go on to win the Commonwealth title as a pro was there, as was Felix Sturm who went on to get robbed by Oscar De La Hoya so blatantly. Sturm was outstanding in that competition. Another fighter in my weight in that tournament was Lucian Bute from Romania. I watched a lot of the fights from that tournament, it was the Russians who stood out for me. Every one of them was freakishly strong.

I boxed at every level for England i.e. Schoolboy, England Youth, Young England, England under 19s and Full England Seniors. I won the Liverpool multi-nations in 1999 and the year after it was an Olympic qualifying event, so it obviously meant something. I just wish I'd have stayed amateur for another five years and waited till I was 24 with my man strength. I completely regret turning pro when I was just a boy. I should have hung around the amateurs because the No.1 at my weight Chris Bessey was coming to an end and I was No.2 in the division of 71KGS. Hindsight's a wonderful thing isn't it?! Looking back, I wasn't doing the weight well at 71KGS which is light middle. My diet was utter shite, I didn't train properly as an amateur. I would leave everything until the last minute and I would leave dropping the weight to the very last hour.

You learn lessons only when you become older in boxing. Then you know you must put in the graft or it's rather painful. As a lad growing up I would go to the gym and I would only want to spar, spar, spar... If my training regime could be sparring every single night, then I'd be happy. Of course, boxing's not like that and you've got to do your long boring runs, you've got to do your strenuous groundwork which really tones your body for the professional game. You couldn't shy away from these gruelling sessions at Crystal Palace England camps as much as I'd have liked to. In all my time boxing, child, man, amateur or pro, the only time I've ever really been fazed was when I went down to the Wellington ABC to spar with John Pearce. John Pearce was a bit of a legend in amateur boxing. He was a 2-x time ABA champion and Commonwealth gold medallist. In fact, he should have been 3 x time ABA champ because I was there in the quarter finals of the ABA'S when he fought Carl Froch and I thought John beat him. Froch went on to get the decision by a majority decision but many ringside had a Pearce win. Not to mention John Pearce boxed him with one hand as he broke a hand in the first round. Even though Froch beat Pearce, it was Pearce who'd get the pick over Froch for the England teams so work that one out, who was best? When I sparred the many rounds I did with John Pearce I had to be as sharp as I'd ever been, or I'd have ended up with broken ribs. Pearce was a devastating body puncher and I'd seen him first hand cut opponents in half from his left hook to the body. John Pearce was your Golovkin type who knew how to cut the ring off and to stalk his opponents down. Not only this but he was an extremely intelligent fighter, I took a lot away from sparring with such a legend coming up into the seniors.

Another huge reason I should have stayed pro was because at the time I left, all the funding had come into amateur boxing. I would have been eligible at the time because I was at the top of my rankings, but of course like every young lad does, I knew best, and I wasn't going to listen to anyone.

I eventually turned over and fought in the paid ranks aged 20 in the year 2000. As a pro I had 11 bouts winning 8 drew 2 and lost 1.

One thing I'll say for the record from my own personal experiences is amateur and professional boxing are completely different. Think football and rugby, in both sports you're playing with a ball right, well in boxing your aim is to punch each other's brains out. Doesn't sound that different but it so is I can assure you. In my first 3 fights I boxed decent kids who'd come to win, they weren't coming to just be paid like a journeyman would. I would have a record of 3-0 but then I had a big break due to contract disputes. It's all water under the bridge now but at the time it didn't end well with my team Glenn and Gary McCrory. At the time it was difficult, I was inexperienced and very naïve about which way to go. I made the move away from the McCrory's and we didn't part on the best of terms. It was a real shame because Gary McCrory was a friend and a good man so that was hard for me to deal with. I ended up in the boxing wilderness for a good few years, drinking and eating whatever I wanted. It was one of them things where I thought I'll get signed with someone else and stay in the gym, but I never did. Truth be told I put boxing to bed and to the back of my mind and then I met Jen (my Wife).

I was working on the doors in Whitely Bay most weekends poor as owt, trying to scrape up enough just to live and get by. I did manage to come back and have one final fight against Jason Collins from the West Midlands. I signed up with North East promoter Tommy Conroy. Tommy was a canny fella and a bit of a name around the North East among boxing circles. After the fight with Collins which proved disastrous, I had words with Tommy Conroy and we had a fall out. To cut a long story short I had a very bad virus, but I never pulled out, I felt I was forced to go through with it. I should have been pulled out. 99 times out of 100 I'd have beat Jason Collins. After the first round against Collins I struggled to keep my hands up, I thought I was dying in there. It was ridiculous because Collins really gave me a hiding and although I could see them coming, I couldn't do anything about it but stay there and cop it sweet. I just tried my best to hear the final bell which I did miraculously. After the 4th and final round I collapsed in my corner and was rushed to hospital. The medics told me I was severely dehydrated. I was knackered from the weight issues as well as pissing blood. It was a real fatal lesson and one that cost me my unbeaten record. I was so fucked off with boxing truth be told, I wouldn't box again for over 3 years.

It wasn't until my brother Paul invited me to his gym in Hartlepool that I would have anything to do with boxing again. I'd never so much as put a glove on in 3 years. It was 2005 and I followed my brother Paul to Peter Copes gym. I was living in Whitely Bay so Hartlepool for me was a 70-mile round trip just to even get to the gym, still I was doing it and I was only 25 so I was still young enough to fight. Financially I was still as broke as owt and me and Jen had just had our first bairn Abby. I tried to make boxing work and I took a fight against Howard Clarke under Hartlepool promoter Gus Robinson I won the fight on points, I had him down in the 3rd and my team were happy with us. The fight was on sky and I was on my old amateur rival Nigel Wrights undercard along with my brother Paul. I thought this was the start of a new beginning and I liked working with Gus Robinson, but it was not to be. I faded away from boxing yet again, I had no money and needed to get a real job. Plus, it was costing to even get to the gym, so I forgot about boxing and me and Jen got married. I got myself a fulltime job and put boxing to bed yet again, this time I thought it was definitely for good. I never thought I would make another comeback until, it must have been around 2012. Me and Jen were at a boxing show in Newcastle. Truth be told I only went because I'd won a pair of tickets on Facebook so me and Jen went along. I was probably the size of a house back then, but I was sat watching the boxing, sipping away at my pints and snacking at the buffet, when Jen told me I looked a picture of sadness. I think it suddenly dawned on me that I'd missed my prime years because I couldn't afford to fight anymore. I never fought from 2005 to 2013 for financial reasons alone and that made Jen sad. "You need to go back don't you?" were Jen's words… She was right! I needed to go back at 33, even just to check if I had anything left! With all the time I'd had out of the ring I was more than well rested. I knew I wasn't the same fighter I was, I knew my speed and youth had gone when I went back, but I felt stronger and had an inbuilt toughness that I lacked in my youth. Coming back, I was far more switched on and with me having a good job, I no longer needed to worry about the money side of things which I did all them years ago. Now I was ready to give boxing, my long-term mistress another shot at the ripe old age of 33. I was now wiser, and I didn't have the time to mess about so it was full steam ahead. All them good hidings in Teams Valley ABC had mentally paid off I'd like to think and made me stronger. I knew how the pro game worked this time and how the people in boxing operated. There's certainly slippery characters in boxing if you go in blind.

In my 3rd period in boxing I would have 6 contests all together and I won an international masters belt.

These days I know belts are flung around all over the place, but I wanted one of them to make it all worthwhile even coming back.

When I first entered the gym, I was 15stone which wasn't ideal considering I wanted to fight around 11stone 10lbs. I had unfinished business with my love of boxing and my better half Jen supported me fully 100% to give it another go. I will be forever grateful to her for letting me get it out my system once and for all. I know I must have been horrible to live with and bad tempered when I was making weight into fight week.

One thing I can say when I came back is I did it all properly, not like when I was a young kid and I'd cut corners for fun in my training regime. Coming back really wasn't for the money. I never made any real money out of boxing as a professional. At times I even boxed out of my own pocket because everybody knows how ticket deals work! You must sell 40 tickets normally to even see £1 and if you can't, you must pay for it yourself or not fight. I did it because I just wanted to box again. Many people in the North East used to call me the unluckiest boxer in the world. Many many times I was lined up to fight lads up and down the country, names such as Callum Smith from Liverpool when he first turned pro, a fight with him fell through. Chris Eubank Jnr knocked me back after it was made at the start of his career. He agreed then pulled out and ended up boxing some Polish fella who he blew away in a round. I'm not making out he was scared but the Pole was an easier night than he knew I'd be. Another fight I was offered was Dimitri Chudinov but at the time I had 2 broken ribs and had to refuse it. A couple of times a fight was supposed to be made with Liverpool's Rocky Fielding for the English title, but it never came off for one reason or another I don't know still to this day. Luke Blackledge and Scotland's David Brophy were supposed to happen but fell through. 2014 I was in the gym the whole year and only fought the once. At 34 this is the last thing you'd want! Many fights I should have had just didn't go ahead due to bad timing, injuries or just sheer bad luck or they thought I was too risky a fight for little reward. Many people knew I was a tasty amateur, but on paper as a pro I didn't look anything like as well as I was getting on. Many weeks my trainer ex pro Micky Duncan used to tell me on a Friday, "Stay by the phone wor kid", in case I got a call at short notice because some poor souls fight fell through. That's really how my 2014 in boxing went. John Pegg was managing me at the time and he would put my name out all over the country at shows. I would work all week, but I couldn't plan anything with the wife and kids just in case I would get a call to be in London, Liverpool or Manchester etc....

Boxing really has always took over my life since I started in it as a boy. Once this obsession started around 7years old it's just never really went away. At times it's been fading away, but it never completely went away. Even when I haven't been anywhere near a gym, I've, unbeknown to me, shadow boxed walking around and I don't even know I'm doing it. I've had this terrible boxing disease since I was a boy going to the shops to buy boxing magazines, then I'd put posters up on my walls on my bedroom. It got under my skin from that time and hasn't left me.

Now, I'm officially retired from boxing I'm still involved with the commentary side of things in the North East. I'm only watching boxing but many times I still get the urge to run in the ring and have a dance about. Boxing hasn't always treat me well at times, but I still can't let her go. I know one day if God spares me that I'll be 50, 60, 70 and I'll still whack a pair of gloves on or have a shadow box in the working men's clubs. I hope the Lord spares me, so I can go into boxing gyms as an old man and be a nuisance. I don't particularly train much anymore, but I spend a few nights commentating with Fighting Chance promotions who I ended my career with. I've also done other bits and bobs for Pete magazine and on Phil Jeffries shows in Sunderland at the Stadium of Light. I'm very well aware of the north east's up and coming prospects.

I totally screwed myself turning pro too early when I clearly wasn't ready. I'll always love boxing and I've had some funny times in my beloved sport. The time we went to Denmark to spar with former world champion Mikkel Kessler was a funny time I remember. I went over there for two weeks to be used as a sparring partner for Mikkel and former European champ Mads Laursen. Mads was training to fight Roy Jones at the time. Mikkel Kessler was a real gentleman who I got on really well with, he used to come and pick me up after training and take us around town for a bite to eat. It was on the last night Mikkel came to pick me up and we'd all go out for a drink because it was the last night of the fortnight we'd be there. My brother Paul was there as well as former British flyweight champion Londoner Francis Ampofo who had been there also and he'd been used for sparring. With me and my brother Paul being hard Geordies, we could handle or drink from birth. So, we decided to go across to Sweden and go nightclubbing. Me my brother Paul, Glenn McCrory, Mads Laurson, Mikkel Kessler and Francis Ampofo went out on the town. After a while I noticed Francis was drinking soft drinks. "Come on Francis it's the last night have a drink" we all said. His reply was he didn't drink and even if he did he can't handle it. I was laying it on thick and in the end, I think he had a drink just to shut me and Paul up. What me and my brother Paul did was sneaked to the shop and bought a can of special brew. This wasn't like the British special brew which is around 9%, this stuff was like 14% and it looked like tar that you'd lay on the motorways. It was like rocket fuel. Not only did we give him that but we gave him a double Jack Daniel's and coke and so while we partied inside Francis was to be seen fast asleep in the nightclub foyer oblivious and at the end of the night we had to carry him to the taxi which took us to the train station and while our party continued as rowdy Geordie parties do Francis was sat with his head in his hands trying to deal with his first ever hangover. Sorry Francis if you're reading this, it was funny at the time, but you'll think twice about drinking with sneaky Geordies again.

Another memory I have from my boxing travels was involving former British, Commonwealth and European champion Michael Hunter from Hartlepool. Many times, I would go down south to tournaments with the Hartlepool boxing clubs because it would work out cheaper. Newcastle and Hartlepool weren't a million miles apart and as our coaches knew each other it would make sense. So many times, I would travel to London, Birmingham etc. with say Michael Hunter, Terry Rowley and my old nemesis Dave Carter. Now I'm not putting a label on Hartlepool Boys Welfare ABC, but these guys were always in the thick of it. What I mean was every time our bus would pull over at a BP garage to stop for fuel, the Hartlepool crew lead by Michael Hunter would come in with bags full of goods unpaid for. They'd only been off the bus 5 minutes if that, then Micky Hunter would come back on laughing his head off with all the best sweets i.e. Ferrero Rocher etc.... These kids didn't mess about and only half inched the best! I'd be sat there naïve as owt thinking 'oh my God these guys are criminals' and we're gonna be pulled over by the cops and put in jail. It was the norm for young Hunter and posse and they'd rob anything and everything. Michael Hunter was one top shoplifter back in the day I'll give him that. Even at boxing shows there was so much thieving and normally there was an unwritten rule if you like of, don't rob on your doorstep.

Well the Hartlepool lads didn't give a fuck. I never had the balls to steal anything, but I often did profit from the Hartlepool lads ill-gotten gains shall we say (laughs).

People up and down reading this chapter might not know a great deal about me, but I'd like to think of myself as a boxing man through and through. I'm always willing to talk about boxing, that's the main reason I do the commentary. I'm always willing to get involved with new people in and around boxing regardless of age or levels in boxing.

It's important for people to understand that when you see a big name up in lights like Anthony Joshua, there's small hall shows and small names like I was scattered around venues all over Britain most weekends. These guys are the bread and butter fighters of the sport you don't get to hear about. We can't all be superstars in life! These young kids who want to go pro who think it's all glamorous let me tell you it's not. In all honesty it's a dirty, filthy business and I would say that to anyone who's wanting to go pro for money, because that's the bee all and end all in what it's about. Whether you're making it or losing it, promoters are making it that's for sure. I would say to these people you have two options, one is to be a big star from the amateurs and get signed with a big promoter and be able to sell tickets. If you can sell lots of tickets in boxing trust me, you'll go far on that alone. Or 2 if you're not a top star but you're a decent boxer then become a journeyman. Fight week in, week out month in, month out and get your money that way because boxing's a tough game. I never had any money out of it but luckily, I've got my health and my nose is still straighter than Jon-Lewis Dickinson's that's for sure!! I'd like to think I have all my faculties the same as when I went in boxing, but I know some lads who haven't, plus they've never made a bean. They've had their brains scrambled and had the piss took out of them by promoters who've never taken a punch in their lives.

Boxing is a very unforgiving sport and a ruthless game. When you're high and flavour of the month winning titles, people want to know you and you can be in the money. As soon as you're not and you've lost a few then people soon forget about you.

I love the game, I love boxing, I love getting in there fighting and I loved the people good and the bad. It's just a truly wicked sport at times and if you're not careful with boxing, it will have your pants down and your eyes out make no mistake about that.

I'm extremely grateful to anyone who has ever coached me, helped me or bought tickets to come and watch me fight with their hard-earned money. The biggest thank you I'd like to give is to my father Gordon Buchanan. That man raised me and my brother Paul and taught us how to be humble fighting men. Thanks dad, love you.

I'd also like to thank the Mrs. (Jen Buchanan) for letting me have another go at boxing. I know it was hard for you and the kids, I was a right pig dieting in fight week and the whole build up. Love you guys all the world.

If you'd like to get in touch with Andrew, you can contact him or follow his page @andrewbuchananboxing on Facebook and @andybee80 on Twitter.

"Boxing's a ruthless, unforgiving sport and it's up to yourself to get out at the right time. I wasn't going to let myself be a good name on some up and coming guys record. Towards the end of my career I was called out by fighters who wouldn't have came near me five years earlier".

Gary Sykes

Richy Horsley

Boxing and villainy has always gone hand in hand, right back in the early days of the 20th century when the mafia would involve themselves in many boxing scandals. I would say this is purely down to the nature of the game i.e. trying to punch to the point of unconsciousness. It will always draw the people from the streets rather than say Cambridge Universities. This is just how human nature works and we're drawn to the things that attract us.

Now I'm not saying Hartlepool's Richy Horsley was the biggest criminal in the world, but he certainly came from a background where the code was to never ring the police, you sorted it out yourself. By Richy's own admissions he hasn't always been the best-behaved fella in his past. Richy told me he had a strong conscience and had always lived by a code with strong morals, if there is such a thing in the criminal fraternity, but I totally understand were he was coming from. In Richy's world growing up, people didn't even consider going to the law with their problems, they sorted it out in-house. Or if they couldn't sort it out themselves they'd go find a man capable of performing these tasks. Somebody like Richy Horsley and he would be more than qualified to make these problems go away.

With me growing up in Middlesbrough, only 12 miles away from Richy's native Hartlepool (land of the monkey hangers) I often heard his name many years ago and understood what he was about. I heard he was a real fighting man, never a bully with it but he was a man whose name stood for violence. Richy's name commanded a great deal of respect and word had that he wasn't a bad bloke. My friends who knew him would tell me although he could handle himself, he was never a bully who would take liberties with people for the sake of it, like the kind of things Paul Sykes got up to for his sheer entertainment.

Richy himself wrote his own autobiography called Born to Fight published by John Blake books in 2005 and it was a huge success. I read myself around 2007 when I borrowed it from Berwick Hills library.

Richy also had a mini documentary filmed about him by Gangster Videos where he openly admits to almost doing a few life sentences because of people who swallowed tongues after he'd hit them. Richy says it was never him who started the trouble himself, but he just could not walk away from people blatantly taking the piss out of his good nature or taking liberties with his friends. Quite often on the doors he would be challenged by gangs of drunken youths, full of Dutch courage often wanting to test themselves and gain a rep by having a go at Richy Horsley. It tended to end up being a painful and invaluable experience for the perpetrators and an extremely harsh lesson learnt.

I caught up with Richy after spending a few weeks speaking via social media, I wanted to know how he got involved in the "hurt business" and at times became an enforcer to sort people's problems out in the North East of England. I wanted to find out how he first became interested in and found a love for pugilism and what he was doing now.

Richy said:

I'm 53 years old now and I grew up in the small town of Hartlepool. I've lived in Hartlepool all my life and I'm extremely proud of its heritage. I first got my taste of boxing being just 12 years of age. Many years ago, in the late 70s I would sit up and watch Sportsnight with Reg Gutteridge.

The first fighter that really got me hooked and I fell in love with was Davey boy Green, that fella was just all action and from the day that I watched him I would go on to follow his every move. When Davey Boy Green had the massive all British clash with John H Stracey in 1977 I stayed up late to listen to it on the radio. I really fell in love with Davey boy Green and I'd often get magazines just because there was a poster of him in it for my bedroom walls. At the time I was living in Seaton Crew and it was miles away from the nearest boxing gym, so I was snookered for starting up myself at that age. I would often shadow box in my bedroom and try copy the moves Davey Boy would throw. He was my first real memory I have when I think about how I became involved in boxing, me being just an impressionable kid in awe of this fighter who was all action and never took a backward step, I wanted to be him.

I never walked into a boxing gym until I was around 14 years of age. I was never pushed into it by anyone, my dad died when I was young, so I never had that backing that young lads need to become involved with things like that. It was the summer of 1978 and what always sticks in my mind is The Sun had a big piece in their paper of all the old boxers for maybe around a week. Fighters like The Brown Bomber Joe Louis, The Brockton blockbuster Rocky Marciano etc... I would read the print off the paper and I'd just think "WOOOOW" at what these boxing Gods did in their time. I'd already been hooked on Davey boy Green, but I never did anything about it but now I'd discovered the Marciano's, the Louis' in this spread that lasted a few days I knew I was gonna become an amateur boxer. Up until I'd seen this spread I'd always been too busy with the lads, not to mention I suppose it's fair to call me a bit or a tearaway at that point. Going to a boxing gym 3 times a week was just too much of a commitment and I wasn't prepared to take it on, plus it interfered with me dating girls etc... Until I got these Sun spreads I never gave it a second thought.

The lads at the time I hung around with all loved to fight don't get me wrong, but they liked to fight in the street. All were tough lads, but my friends weren't boxing people like I wanted to become. By this time, I was well and truly gone with this boxing lark, so I told them I was going with or without them. I went along to the United Services boxing club on Park road, Hartlepool, the building itself was just an old school, its well gone now. Some of my mates came for a few sessions but fell by the wayside. When I first walked in the gym and saw the lads skipping and, on the bags, it had a profound effect on me immediately. I was just in awe of the smell and everything about it. I was like a kid in a Toys'R'Us store, I never wanted to go home.

I managed to get my medical card and I had a few bouts and I was proud as punch to be classed as a proper boxer to all my friends. This high I was having of being around the boxing scene was cut short when I developed something called Osgood Schlatter's disease in my knees. I had to stop going to the gym for a good while and it broke my heart I was totally gutted to be missing out on this new-found love I'd found all by myself.

After what must have been close to a year I managed to convince my family to let me back in the gym, provided I wear these shoes that were built up by half an inch and wore supports around my knees. I didn't care if I looked a bit silly I was back boxing again and I loved it. I started competing in fights around 15. In total I had 39 bouts winning 31, quite a few of them by KO as well. I boxed the Leeds light heavyweight Crawford Ashley in the ABA'S.

Ashley was a real classy fighter won at least 4 national titles and boy could he punch. He was far more experienced than me and to be fair too good for me to be even in the ring with him at the time. People said I was flung in the deep end too quickly, but it was something I would learn from. He was a real classy operator. He actually hit me with a right hand in the throat that nearly removed my Adams apple. Another right hand he hit me with such force I could feel my knees go, I'll never forget the strangest look he gave me after that as if to say, "why haven't you gone down yet". After I boxed him I would follow his career and it didn't come as a surprise to see he went on to become British, Commonwealth and European champion.

A short time after I fought Crawford Ashley I had been matched with Consett's Glenn McCrory at his show. I'm not sure the reason that fell through, but I remember being pissed off for travelling to his show and not being able to fight. It was nights like that that would put me off boxing and I'd drift away for a few months being side-tracked. I would always come back to the gym and have many more bouts then pack in again. It would go on like this for many years because my dedication was poor. I made more comebacks than Frank Sinatra I'm telling you! I even toyed with the idea of going pro as I was offered to by the late Hartlepool promoter Gus Robinson.

Deep down I knew I wouldn't have made it as a pro because I had far too many distractions outside the ring i.e. girls, working the doors and coming in at all hours. I knew inside that I wouldn't have worked, and I'd been around boxing long enough to know that if you play at it you're gonna get hurt if you give it less than 100%. I declined Gus's offer and left it well alone and it was the right choice.

Many times, boxing as an amateur I would be boxing for 3 rounds and after the fight I would be goosed. So, doing that for 12 rounds was a real marker to think about! Also, for me I wouldn't have wanted to lose to someone who wasn't good enough to lace my boots if I was fit because I'd gassed out. Truth be told in many of my fights I relied on having the big punch, I'd always been able to wallop from such a young age and it tended to get me out of jail before I knackered myself out. It's not clever to say but it's the truth, I had a half decent boxing ability, but I never lived the life like a proper fighter should.

At the back end of my 30s, rapidly approaching 40 I did make a comeback in the white-collar scene and I had 4 bouts. By that time in my life though I couldn't be bothered anymore but I took the fights for the money. All the fights were on the Tel Currie London shows. I still had the attitude of, yeah, I'll take it and land the big shot in the first and it's all over. Of course, in boxing this is an attitude that you shouldn't have, and I was foolish to myself.

The last bout I had was against a guy called Gary Marcell and he could fight. He was hitting me with everything but the kitchen sink and I felt them all. The fight itself was on the Thursday, well I came down with the flu on the Monday so by the time I entered the ring it was right through my whole body and I was left weak as a kitten. It's not a nice feeling when you know all you can do is try to survive and try to hear the final bell. Even though I was bashed up in that fight I wouldn't go down and stay down. A lot of people in that situation would have thought "sod this" and took a knee but I got up and took my medicine and heard the final bell. As I said earlier, it's not clever to admit this but I didn't even train for that fight and approaching 40 years old I don't know what I expected!

Even now, these days when I actually don't do the art of pugilism any more, I still couldn't say no to when my close friend Kevin Bennett asked me to go in his corner on his bare-knuckle world title fights and I enjoyed being part of his team. I helped guide him to a world title belt and it was a real pleasure to work closely with someone as skilled as Kevin. I've been close friends with Kevin over 20 years now, I worked his corner amateur and professional.

Hartlepool town, where I'm from, has always been a little haven for boxing talent. Considering it's a small town we've always had at least five boxing gyms in the place. Not to mention good pro gyms like Neil Fannan's and Peter Copes' Gyms.

I still watch boxing on the telly and I keep up to date with the bare-knuckle scene with Kevin. Another good fighter from our town is former British, Commonwealth, European, WBF champion and WBO world title challenger Michael Hunter, I've worked Michaels corner in the past also and spent time coaching at the Hartlepool Welfare boys club. Alan Temple is also a product of the place.

Around 2003 time there was big talk of me having one last fight with Britain's most dangerous prisoner Charles Bronson. What happened was we were good friends at first, we'd often write to each other then he fell out with me over something stupid and we had an almighty argument. I wrote telling him "who does he think he is", that type of thing. Then he sends one telling me I'm not as tough as I think I am and I've only knocked bums out blah blah blah... I was then contacted by one of Charlie's promoter friends asking me would I fight him? I was told we'd both make real money and the interest in our fight would be huge, so I told the promoter yes straight away. The plan was to hold the fight in a big marquee in London but of course Charlie never got parole and it all fell through. If it was gonna happen it would have had to be then but it never, besides we're back good friends again now and we're too old. Another reason it won't happen is everyone who tried to make it happen are no longer with us, the main players have gone.

If I could go back and change my time in boxing, then I'd forget about all the distractions I had. I'd live like a monk! I would lock myself away and dedicate my life to boxing. Of course, it's all too late now, I wasted my best years doing stupid things, daft things that real disciplined fighters should never do. I wish I could have seen how far I could have gone, instead of sitting here full of regrets. The majority of times I did box I'd get in the ring half trained and knackered after a round and not doing myself justice because I'd been out drinking with the lads prior to the build-up living the crazy life. I had many fights away from the Queensbury rules and not in a ring. At times in my life I've had people come up to me, "Richy there's this lad in so-so town and he's the hardest in the town, he's going to do this, that and the other, if you sort him out we'll give you X amount of money". Sometimes I got involved in these things to make a living. To be truthful I have had a shit load of fights this way. I would do peoples dirty work making a living. Often people would just use my name and I wasn't even aware of it. People in establishments would use my name and they didn't even like me, never mind have met me, but they knew people would think twice about starting any shit in the pubs if they thought I had the door. Of course, the only things they'd heard about me was bad things such as wicked acts of violence and most of them weren't even true. These people would use my name as a deterrent and even play up on the stories that weren't true, add fuel to the fire to make me more of the bogeyman. The one thing I would like to make crystal clear in this chapter is for all the stuff I've got myself involved with over the years, I've never bullied people in my life! I've never took liberties with innocent folk and if I was prepared to have done half the things I'd been offered to do, well I'd be a millionaire now. I've always had a strong conscious. For me to do something really bad well they'd have had to of hurt my family etc... but in that way, so would any other bloke on the street. When I was younger I had a killer instinct and if I put a man down I'd keep him down because if that man got back up he could seriously hurt me.

These days I like a quiet life, I'm very much a family man with a wonderful wife Wendy who's my rock. I'm settled down, I go to work for a living on the cables and enjoy my grandchildren at the weekend. If I go out I tend to go for a meal with my wife, to be honest I've knocked the drinking on the head, just cannot be bothered with it anymore. I had enough of that shit with the years on the doors I did. I'm more content listening to spiritual music like Enya. I'm in a place mentally were its never been as good in my whole life. I'm 100% at peace with the world and nothing flusters me like it did when I was younger. I've also started doing a bit of writing a sequel to my book Born to Fight called 'Northern Warrior' which will be about my life also. I'll also be penning my good friend Kevin Bennett's book '30years a fighter'. The Kevin Bennett story is unique because he was ABA champion in 1999 as an amateur. He was then Commonwealth champion in 2004, then went on to become a world bare knuckle champion in 2016. To my knowledge I'm not sure anybody's done that before. Kevin had his first fight aged 11 years of age, then his last one at 41. 30 years a fighter, well the clues in the name so I'm looking forward to releasing that and doing my close friend Kevin proud.

Boxing has been a major part of my life for 40 odd years now and long may it continue. It doesn't matter how far you go from boxing, you can't turn it off once it's in your blood.

If anybody wants to learn more about Richy Horsley you can read his book Northern Warrior and Born to Fight, available from most book shops and Amazon. You can also contact him directly by his Facebook page Richy "Crazy Horse" Horsley.

"My girl summed me up recently when she said, "You're a good man who has done very bad things". That's all I can say. I was lost. My demons always stemmed from being a fat kid with glasses. I wanted respect".

Dominic Negus

Alex Morrison

Alex Morrison has been one of the instrumental figures in the British boxing scene for many decades. Particularly in Scotland where he's promoted many shows and also managed many fighters such as Cambuslangs three weight world champion Ricky Burns. I've found Alex to be a lovely big guy over the years when I've bumped into him and he has a sense of humour second to none, albeit very dry and his wit is very sharp. Alex has typical Glasgow humour, the kind of attitude that even when your life is falling apart he'd still have a smile on his face and laugh. The saying of "you've got to laugh, or you'd cry" always makes me think of him because I've heard him use it so many times over the years. I suppose being a staunch "Blue Nose" (Glasgow Rangers man) it's just as well for him.

Alex is now retired but is still very much around the boxing scene as he's Ricky Burns' manager, Alex told me Ricky is more like a son to him and when he talks of Ricky you can hear the love in his voice, you can always see "big Ecky" walking with pride when he walks Ricky to the ring on the big fight nights on Sky Sports. Alex also is still very much part of the famous Morrisons Gym based in Dalmarnock in the heart of Glasgow's East End. Head of the gym is Alex's daughter the lovely Christine Morrison, another bubbly, warm person with a cracking sense of humour. The gym is very much family run by the extremely large Morrison clan. Many posters are up on the walls of Scotland's greats such as Benny Lynch, Jim Watt, Ken Buchanan and Scott Harrison. It's funny because I would see Alex about a good few years before I got to know him, I always thought he was a big moody looking bastard and I wouldn't like to get caught stealing his milk from his doorstep. I would see him a handful of times when I lived in the East End of Glasgow myself in the late nineties. As I've got to know him over the years I now think I had him all wrong in that even though he's 6ft 1 inch and an intimidating man in the flesh, I now know he's just a big cuddly teddy bear, although I still wouldn't like to get caught stealing his milk from his doorstep. I've found Alex Morrison to be an articulate, downright funny and a warm gentleman who surprisingly can speak fluent Gaelic as that was his first language as a boy, as well as a great knowledge in other languages such as Indian, Pakistani and Italian. Alex became fluent Italian as during a ten month stretch 'inside' his cell mate who'd been caught for smuggling was from Italy. Alex taught him English and he taught him Italian. Alex also speaks Yiddish 'better than most Jews' as he has many friends in the Jewish community. Alex has also mixed in the same circles as crime Godfather Arthur Thompson Snr, Glasgow's Mr Big. Arthur Thompson died of a heart attack in 1993, age 63. Alex says, "Arthur hated drugs and drug dealers, His son Arthur Jnr got involved in drugs and his other son ended up a junkie, drugs were the downfall of the family. It was tragic".   Alex went on to say "There were a lot of lies written about Arthur Thompson Snr. It was once said Arthur was in charge of illegal saunas and had his pick of the girls. What a dirty lie. Arthur was a gentleman. He wouldn't tell a dirty joke or even swear in front of a woman. I remember one-time Arthur and I were having a drink in the pub, when this guy nicknamed champagne Charlie came in with some floozy on his arm, boasting, "Let me buy you a drink as my wife's just had a baby girl". Arthur asked, "why are you not at the hospital son?" Arthur called everybody 'son'. He then stuffed £20 in the girl's hand and told her to get a taxi then said to the new father, "if you don't get yourself up to hospital I'll smash that bottle of champagne right over your head". That's what type of man Arthur was. He had manners.

How I'd describe Alex Morrison is that he is a real man of the world although he often likes to tell me many times, "Jamie I used to be conceited but now I'm perfect". He's very open minded and always willing to learn something new. He's not your everyday typical knuckle dragging Rangers man that's for sure! I do enjoy his company though! I sat and had a chat with my favourite "proddie" and this is what he told me about how he became involved in boxing.

Alex said:

I was born in 1938 and raised in Croft with my brother on the Isle of Skye. Nobody pushed me into boxing I just started liking it myself. When I was growing up as a boy in the 40s I would often walk the four miles to a friend's house who had a radio, obviously there was no tellies in them days and I would often walk to my friend's house to listen to Sugar Ray Robinson.

Joe Louis the Brown Bomber, Jersey Joe Walcott and Sugar Ray Robinson were my idols as a boy, and me and my friends would get together and listen to the fights on the wireless. It's a far cry from folk of today watching the big PPV fights in HD isn't it! I would read so much about these great fighters in the paper as a boy and that's what sparked my interest in boxing really! I took boxing at school, the gym teachers used to bring gloves in and let us kids knock fuck out of each other. Teachers never used to bother about the same weights they'd just stick us in to maul each other. It wasn't really until I was 15 when I moved to Glasgow that I went to a proper gym. I only learned English when a cousin from Glasgow came to stay with us after being evacuated during the war. Before that I would only speak Gaelic.

I went to an amateur boxing club in Maryhill, Glasgow and that's when I started taking it seriously and competing. I joined the Dalmarnock amateur boxing club not long after then I also joined the Scottish national club. In total I must have had around 60 plus amateur boxing contests. Many of my contests were at light-middleweight which with me being 6ft 1inches I was very big for the weight. As I got older I filled out and I grew through the weights and finished at light heavyweight which was around 12st 10lbs in them days. I trained alongside Chick Calderwood, Johnny Caldwell, John O'Brien and John" Cowboy" McCormack as well, all very good pros from back in my time. Maryhill's John "Cowboy" McCormack was a very good friend of mine and I would often spar many rounds with him. Cowboy had 109 amateur bouts winning 103 of them and 51 by KO. He was some fighter right enough, a really good southpaw who represented the UK in the 1956 Olympic games in Melbourne, Australia. Another great wee fighter who I trained alongside in his gym was the British, Commonwealth and European champion bantamweight from Glasgow Peter Keenan. Peter was a superstar to the Scottish public and he used to put me on commission when I sold his tickets outside Glasgow's shipyards. Those were the days when top fighters were regarded as being on par with top football players. To this day I still hold the record of being the oldest Scottish heavyweight amateur champion at 44. Of course, that record will never be broken as you can't box over 35 in the amateurs. I remember I got picked to box for Scotland in Copenhagen, Denmark and when I got there they told me I was too old. There was a guy called John Brown who was Scottish heavyweight champion and he took my place and got beat. I was getting stick from John Brown after the fight saying the reason he had to step in for me was because I must have showed the boxing officials my pension book instead of my medical card for the fight. I boxed John

Brown after this on a show in Scotland and I give him a right battering with what he said kept in mind.

I never gave any real thoughts of turning over pro because I didn't live the life a boxer should, I just chose drink at the time like many of my pals. I would chose drinking over training, so I knew I didn't want to go professional myself. Back in the day when times were hard in Glasgow, one of the main reasons I would go to the gym was to get a shower. We had no bath and no running water in our house, just an outside toilet. The gym was only 200 yards from my house, so I might as well kill two birds with one stone and go get a free shower that was in with my sub money.

I married Annie my sweetheart when I was 20, she became mother of our 5 children. At times my life went out of control and off the rails through drink. I started drinking whiskey. I didn't realise it had such an adverse effect on me. It got me into a lot of trouble, fighting with the Police and stuff. I ended up inside a few times.

Regarding me as an amateur boxer I'd have to say my best moment was in the Western Districts and I faced David Summers. He was 6ft 6 and I beat him by unanimous decision. After I beat him he turned pro and I managed him as a pro for a while. David had 6 fights then retired undefeated. That was at the very end of my time as an amateur boxer, so it wasn't bad going as I was an old man compared to him in boxing terms.

When I decided to hang the gloves up I went into managing fighters as well as promoting them. I've been doing both these for 40 years maybe more. I've met a lot of slags in boxing let me tell you! I used to see guys coming to my show to box, and their managers pulling me to one side saying, "listen I've told my fighter he's getting such and such, can you give me the rest under the table". I never stood for that but occasionally you had to get the fight. I've had some wonderful highs though in boxing and none more so than in September 2010 when Ricky Burns became WBO Super Featherweight world champion. He faced the unbeaten murderous puncher Roman Martinez from Puerto Rico in the Kelvin Hall, Glasgow. Ricky was on his arse in the first round and I thought FUCK its all over. Ricky was a MASSIVE underdog and for him to get up off the floor was truly remarkable. That's unquestionably my best night in boxing, I'm really fond of the boy.

Me today, boxing doesn't mean as much to me as it once did. I've had a lot of good times in boxing and made a lot of money out of it also. I've travelled to Naples, Rome and Paris, all places I wouldn't have gone to if it wasn't for boxing you know. I went to New York with my friend Terry Feeley who was also a professional boxer from Glasgow. I'd beat Terry in the amateurs as a kid and we'd remained good friends. Terry had fought Joe Bugner, so we went to see Muhammad Ali V Joe Frazier, and I met Muhammad Ali in the Empire State building, when I was talking to him he asked me "what do you work as" I told him I was just a lorry driver from Scotland". Ali looked at me strangely and just said in the loudest of voices "WHAT, YOU CAME ALL THIS WAY TO WATCH TWO FUCKING NIGGERS FIGHT?" He was amazed!

In June 2000 I co-promoted Mike Tyson's fight at Hampden Park with Lou Savarese. The reason Mike Tyson was pictured in the Glasgow Rangers shirt was down to me (Alex laughs) I handed Mike the shirt and just said you need to wear that, he never knew the history in Glasgow between Rangers and Glasgow Celtic. I had Mike Tyson training in my gym prior to his fight but if truth be told, he never did any training! He just sat in the toilets smoking. He would occasionally punch the bags, but he did nothing to be quite honest. When his trainer had a go at him for not doing anything, Tyson got up, sparred with a couple of dummies he had had with him in camp and knocked them both out. Mike turned to his trainer and said, "happy now?" Then sat back down and started smoking again. I wasn't terribly impressed with Tyson as a person. He was always swearing. Then of course he did a jig on top of Frank Warrens car in a kilt. Tyson was a nightmare, to be honest. Before the fight I told him, he was 33-1 to knock Savarese out in the first round. Tyson told me to put my house on it. I think that's why he was in such a rush to knock him out. Afterwards he was saying, 'you'll be having a champagne tonight Alex' I don't think he believed I hadn't had a bet on him.

I've had Thomas Hearns in my gym I've had Sugar Ray Leonard in my gym. One guy I really did like was Roberto Duran he was a really nice fella.

In my opinion the greatest Scottish pound for pound fighter was Peter Keenan, he was better than Benny Lynch the lot.

These days I'm surrounded by my family, my daughters Katherine, Anne and Christine and sons Alex and Kenny as well as my many grandchildren and great grandchildren, they all help to run the haulage, boxing gym and promotions companies. For mine and Annie's 50th wedding anniversary a pal of mine sent Annie a gold medal and it said, 'you deserve this'. Without family there's nothing. That's my motto in life.

"The failure I have had to overcome is like the Titanic going through the iceberg".

Audley Harrison

Colin Hart

Since I first began to follow boxing my interest has always been predominately in the British domestic scene. When my friends were growing up raving about overseas fighters I was never that interested, maybe I lack ambition as a boxing fan! I was more interested in watching say Paul "Scrap Iron" Ryan versus Ross Hale as a fifteen year old boy when my friends were watching Oscar De La Hoya beat Jesse James Leja on the world scene. I always preferred the British pundits and boxing historians too.

For all the outrageous knowledge the legendary American Bert Sugar had, I was far more intrigued with the best Britain had to offer, and in my humble opinion the most well respected and well thought of was our very own Colin Hart from West Ham in East London. Anybody reading this that's followed British boxing like I have since 1990 would fully agree with me that our Colin is the "voice of boxing" on these shores! The man must have seen just about bloody everybody, and I was only too thrilled when he spared me a bit of his time to talk 'shop' with him.

Colin Hart was also the first British writer to win the prestigious Nat Fleischer award for "Excellence in Boxing Journalism" from the BWAA in 2011. Colin was also inducted into the International Boxing Hall of Fame in 2013 in Canastota, New York so he really is the 'big cheese' in my opinion.

I'd already had the pleasure of interviewing Colin for my previous book 'Further Agony' which is about the original boxing bad boy, the wild man of Wakefield Paul Sykes. This time I was more interested about where his love for the hurt business came from and how did he become Britain's most respected boxing pundit.

Colin told me: -

"I was born in 1935 in West Ham, East London. I first got the love for sport really from my old man and particularly boxing. How it was in the East End in them days was everybody knew everybody.

There were some great Jewish fighters such as Kid Berg, Harry Misler and Ted "Kid" Lewis, who my Grandmother knew well, and of course with me being Jewish I grew up idolising these fellas and their past brilliances from stories handed down to me by my old man.

The East End of London to this day is still the home of boxing and was then, so me growing up as just a lad I could never avoid boxing as it was spoken about by most people. The whole of the East End has always talked boxing none stop so that's where I got my love of boxing from at a very, very early age.

I started boxing myself at school and even in the youth clubs, but I quickly realised I wasn't very good at it. If you're not good at the game it's not like Football or Rugby, boxing isn't pleasant when you're eating right-handers night after night, so it can be quite painful and make you want to give it up a little promptly rather than stick about a tit, so I didn't take it any further.

I grew up during the war and was evacuated, then sent back to London in time for the blitz. As a child, I spent time on the London underground on the back stations to get away from the bombings. My area of West Ham had it pretty tough during the war as West Ham was the most bombed area across the country because of the docks. The Germans would come over night after night bombing the docks and of course this was a very densely populated area, so the civilian casualties were great. That's what my childhood was gravely like.

I left school and started work in a newsagent at the age of 17. I left there after a short while to do my national service in the R.A.F, I did two years which was compulsory in them days. After I had done my two years my thoughts were to become a foreign correspondent truth is told, but It just so happens that an opportunity came up to serve an apprenticeship as a journalist. I'd never given it any thoughts until then, so I joined the Daily Herald as a news reporter and became news night editor of the paper. I didn't become involved in writing about sport until 1962 when I joined the Daily Express. The fella in charge said, "Colin we want you to become our sports news editor", which I did for many years. I started writing columns in sport but gravitated immediately to boxing obviously just from my sheer love of the game and I've been doing it ever since.

I know a lot of people would say Muhammad Ali but the greatest fighter pound for pound of all time in my opinion was 'Sugar' Ray Robinson but I only ever watched videos of him, I may be old but not that bloody old!

The greatest fighter I ever saw in the flesh in my time following the sport was 'Sugar' Ray Leonard hands down, never mind ya bloody Floyd Mayweather, Ray Leonard would have beaten him with ease, Mayweather wouldn't have touched him.

If you ask my opinion who's the greatest British fighters we've ever had I have three for you, three fighters, and none before the other, as they were all magnificent fighters who could do it all. John Conteh, Ken Buchanan and Joe Calzaghe. Them boys could do everything and unquestionably the three greatest Brits we've ever had pound for pound! I love them all.

I must say we've not yet had anyone quite like the fella you interviewed me about for your last book, Wakefield's former heavyweight fighter/villain Paul Sykes. That fella was his own worst enemy and nobody could do anything with him, just like Tyson Fury. Paul Sykes was bad to the core and there's never been anyone as bad as him in British boxing, certainly not in my life time anyway! It's a shame because he had a personality and he could box, it's just everything he ever did outside the ring was anti-social. I've covered all kinds of fighters over many, many decades and seen them all. Maybe Michael Gomez was one who sticks out for being slightly crazy but none with the sheer nastiness Paul Sykes had.

"In boxing you create a strategy to beat each opponent, just like chess".

Lennox Lewis

Joe Maphosa

I'd first come across Joe Maphosa in early 2010 when he was just 15. I was helping at an amateur boxing club called Brambles Farm ABC at the time and we had taken a couple of boys to the Junior ABA'S in Durham and it was there that I was to see Joe box for the first time. My first impression of him was that he wasn't what you normally came across in amateur boxing on a daily basis. These days normally in the amateur scene you get taught to have your chin down, hands up and throw straight shots as they're normally the ones the judges recognise as point scoring shots. Joe Maphosa is very different to that style let me say! Joe prefers his hands down by his sides, he often sticks his chin over his front foot to lure his opponent into a false sense of security to think he was in range to land a shot, only for Joe to counter punch and score clean shots with his rapid hand speed almost Cobra like. I was very impressed the minute I saw him box and knew he had a bright future in the game if he chose to and didn't fall away like a lot of lads do at 17-18 years of age, about the same time when they discover girls/nightclubs/booze etc... I remember telling someone in 2010 that Joe Maphosa is the biggest talent in the Middlesbrough boxing scene.

I got to know Joe a little better when I went to take my stepson to Joe's Middlesbrough ABC club and saw in close quarters how much natural talent he had. Joe has a ridiculous amount of natural flair and his ability to switch hit, either way as good as the other, I've seen him make some very good boxers look like they've never put a pair of gloves on in their lives he was that good. I've seen him spar three lads at once, like Vasyl Lomachenko, and he still looked like he was getting the better of them.

As a person he's an extremely nice guy who's completely devoted to living the life to become a future champion in the professional game. I'd say the only fault I could say I've found him to have was when he came to my wedding reception in the summer of 2010, yes Joe I did see you dancing, your footwork wasn't so fancy that night!

I had a chat with young 'Smokin' Joe and I asked him when was it that he had the idea to start boxing.

Joe said: -

"I'm 23 years old now and I live in Thornaby on Tees with my partner Megan and 2 year old daughter Mia.

I grew up in a small town in Zimbabwe called Bait Bridge until I was 8 years of age. It was around maybe 8-9 that my parents moved to Park End an area in Middlesbrough. At the time I could only speak bits of English, so I had to learn to speak a whole new language all over again at just a young age.

My first memories of boxing were of watching Bernard Hopkins big fights when he ruled the middleweight division.

I was really into computers when I was younger and the games I would really play tended to be boxing games.

I'd never had anything to do with boxing myself and wasn't really sure if it was for me, so at first, I went to boxercise classes that had a lot of women in the class, I was only around 13 at the time. I stayed at the boxercise classes for a few weeks and that gave me the confidence to go to a proper club with some of my friends. That club was Middlesbrough ABC and was run by a man called Tony Whitby in North Ormesby in Middlesbrough. I liked Tony immensely straight away and I knew I wanted to get serious about this boxing game at his club. I would go on to have 75 amateur bouts for Middlesbrough ABC winning 60 in total. As an amateur I beat Haroon Khan (Amir's brother), fought Reece Belotti and lost a close decision in the ABA 2012 finals at the York Hall, Bethnal Green. Reece is the British featherweight champion now and is unbeaten as a professional. I also fought Michael Gomez Jnr in the unpaid code and beat him on points. I boxed the reigning flyweight world champion Joahnys Argilagos from Cuba in the WSB in London representing team GB. I lost on a split decision and there was only one point in it, it was very close. A lot of people there thought I should have had the decision.

Looking back on my amateur career I have won the NABC'S, the Haringey BOX CUP gold medal, won a gold medal in the Golden Belt international tournament for team GB and I also won a gold medal in the Round Robin tournament in Germany 2015 for team GB.

My most disappointing periods I'd have to say in the amateurs were losing two ABA finals against Reece Belotti and Sunny Edwards. I also got to the schoolboy finals in my first season but lost to Repton's Rio Wallace. I fought amateur boxing star Jack Bateson twice and he got both decisions. Tommy Ward from Birtley who is British super bantamweight champion now also beat me in the amateurs. I only ever lost to the cream of British amateur boxing, the top boys I suppose you could say.

My style is not something you would see a lot in amateur boxing. I would watch and study Floyd Mayweather and Roy Jones Jnr. I really liked the hand speed of both and it was similar to what I had in my locker, so I based my style on them guys.

The best I ever fought was the Cuban Joahnys Argilagos by far. That guy got a bronze in the 2016 Olympics at Rio and he's just won the world championships this year in Hamburg, so he's ranked No.1 in the world at the moment. The guys still only 20 years of age so he'll definitely be a superstar of the future in world boxing.

When I started training with team GB I was in Sheffield and still in my amateur club Middlesbrough ABC which I found a great strain to be honest. It just wasn't practical to spend half my week in Sheffield then in Middlesbrough, but I knew it would benefit me further down the line. The sparring I got with team GB was the best in the country, you only had to look at the people that I was training alongside like Nichola Adams, Mohammad Ali, Jack Bateson, Andrew Selby, Sunny Edwards and Khalid Yafai. I often sparred with top guys from other countries such as Ireland and Thailand and it got me the chance to travel the world. Of course, when you're on team GB you get funding based on your ranking or the medals that you've won. I was looking at the bigger picture!

In amateur boxing I only ever boxed for one club Middlesbrough ABC and I'd just like to say how much I owe Tony Whitby who's a fabulous trainer. That guy taught me so much and I'll always owe that man for what he did for me when I was growing up.

My best memories in the amateurs was boxing for my country and beating Haroon Khan because everybody said that I hadn't a chance before the fight. I was a massive underdog facing Haroon as he'd just won a bronze at the Commonwealth games for Pakistan in India. I beat him quite convincingly and that's what made folk like the Boxing News sit up and first take notice of me.

When I lost to Sunny Edwards in the 2015 final of the ABA'S I had one eye on going pro from then on. I felt rather than spend a few more years in the amateurs my style would be far more suited to the pros, the reason for that being is that I'd always fought like a pro. When I'd done 5 rounds in the WSB I felt really comfortable even though the rounds were longer. I knew it wouldn't be a decision I'd regret.

I was speaking to one of the North East referees whilst I was still an amateur and he told me that because of my weight that I'd fight at flyweight/super flyweight and that I'd fight for major titles after not many fights, meaning it wouldn't be a long road before I had a chance to fight for these big titles. When you hear stories like this from proper boxing people, it kind of made me really think about trying to make something of my life in boxing for me and my family.

I had already spoken to Imran Naeem a while back and he said if I was serious about going pro I'd be welcome to join his camp. Imran had been doing well with his lads Simon Vallily, Josh Leather, Chubbsy Asif and Mo Waqas. Imran's gym is in my hometown of Thornaby, so it was an easy decision of who to go with.

I went to Imran's gym and I liked his setup immediately so me and him sat down and talked. I haven't looked back and with the help of Imran Naeem I'm already on my journey and 3-0.

Promotion wise, Fighting Chance Promotions contacted me and offered me a contract as I'd already boxed on one of their bills, but then Imran got in touch with Frank Warren. Truth be told at first Frank was saying he's got too many lads on his books and I'm not sure he was ready to take a chance with me as it seemed to go on for a few months. Then one day Frank rang up and said he wanted to sign me so maybe he had heard something, or he'd watched footage of me, I don't know but I signed up with Frank Warren promotions. I think Frank Warren and Andy Ayling had done their homework on me and not just took the word of Imran. The good thing about being with Imran is we travel around for sparring gym to gym. I've sparred my old foe from the amateurs and current British super bantamweight Tommy Ward and Chris Woods from Darlington who's just fought for a Northern Area title the other week, so my sparring is with top quality fighters.

What freaks me out now is sometimes when I go out around Middlesbrough town people come up to me and say "Aah you're that boxer we seen you on the telly". It surprises me so much and humbles me that these people ask me for a photo when I'm just a normal guy. It's such a good feeling you know, and I quite often get inboxes asking for autographs on social media. It blows me away that these people spend their hard earned money to come and support me it really does. I'm from a council estate myself and I'll always have love and time for people who support me or just want to talk boxing with me.

As a fighter I'm always in the gym ticking over and I like to think I live the life a fighter should. Obviously in my down time I can relax and maybe have a drink but never in my training camps, jus at Christmas that kind of thing. To be honest I don't like beer that much I'm into fruity stuff or a couple of vodkas, not too much though! This time next year I'd like to think I'll have another 4 fights and maybe boxing for my first title.

I'm 23 now and the plan is to give it my best shot and have 10 years in boxing. I've always said I'm going to live right like a monk for the time I'm in boxing, and if I don't make it they'll be no excuses, but my plans are to become a world champion in a couple of weights. I know I have the right team so if they can steer me into the right path I know I can get there.

I'm really enjoying boxing at the moment and now I'm at the stage where I can use it to provide for my family, it's not just about trophies and medals anymore. It's not all a bed of roses though in boxing you can get hurt. I'd say the most hurt I've been in boxing was in the ABA finals against Reece Belotti, that guy was just freakishly strong, and he kept coming all night. There was a couple of times in that fight he hurt me, but I had to mask it, I had to pretend he never hurt me but inside I was in pain.

If someone was going to ask me what Joe Maphosa was about I'd say, good footwork, good fast hands and I can switch a bit as well I'm very unorthodox. As I move on to do more rounds as in 6,8,10 I'll start to put fighters away. I want to bring titles and the limelight to Middlesbrough my adopted town. I've always had a really warm friendly support from the Teesside folk, so I'd like to thank them by bringing good times to our town.

I'd like to thank my first coach Tony Whitby from Middlesbrough ABC. Tony kind of brought me up and he's been there for me when I've needed him. Also, I'd like to give a big thank you to Imran Naeem who's welcomed me into his gym. Imran looks after me not just in boxing but even outside the gym like a father figure. I'd like him to know I'm not going anywhere else and I just hope we have a successful journey in boxing together for the next decade.

Thank you to my support in Middlesbrough who've showed me love and affection in my time in boxing, I can't thank you enough.

People wanting to follow Joe on his journey can do so by following his page on Facebook @joemaphosaofficial and by Twitter @JoeMaphosa

"When you are around people who have money, you realise money isn't that impressive, it's about your class, morals and how you conduct yourself".
Anthony Joshua

John Spensley

As I was brought up in the town of Middlesbrough, John Spensley's name was a one I was very familiar with from around the Middlesbrough boxing scene. Being a very successful business man, and owning several pubs in Middlesbrough, he would often sponsor friends of mine who were young amateur boxers in the 90s.

Back in the 70s, 80s and even 90s John had been a top promoter/manager to many of the top fighters in the North East such as Dave Garside and Glenn McCrory.

When I was in my late teens I would often go into a few of John's pubs just to look at the unbelievable boxing memorabilia on display like signed Sugar Ray Leonard V Thomas Hearns posters etc...

I didn't really get to know John on a personal level until I interviewed him for my first book Sykes – Unfinished Agony as he was Paul Sykes' mentor if you like when he first went pro, but I've always been aware he was the guy who really brought boxing to Middlesbrough, kept it there for many years, and produced some big shows on Sky. Everybody's interest in boxing was to promote down South but John wanted to give the lads up North a fair shout. Paul Sykes says the exact same thing of John Spensley in his book Sweet Agony, from which I went on to do two follow ups.

I met up with John and his brother Jerry in the Golden Lion on Northallerton High Street and he told me how exactly he came about getting involved in the fight game at such a young age.

John said:

How I started getting a liking for the fight game was when my father used to tell me of stories of the Jack Dempsey V Gene Tunney fight in America 1927, he was at that fight was my old man. He would tell me stories as a boy and my eyes would light up with the excitement of it all with it being a million-dollar gate. I must have only been 7-8 years of age at this time but that is my first memory of any boxing that I knew about.

My dad wasn't a boxer, but he knew his stuff on the sport, a great deal of it in fact, and knew who was who in the game. My old man worked at Ridley's which was a bookmaker, so he was very good with figures on the race courses you see. In Ridley's office they had a speedball up and my dad used to lift me up on a chair as a kid for me to use it whilst I was waiting for my dad to finish work.

I started competing in boxing when I got to 11 years of age and I became Northern Counties amateur champion and my dad worshiped me for that he thought it was something great. My dad put a bag up in our shed and I made it into my own gym. All the other kids from the estate used to come in and we'd all train together in this little shed. One of Middlesbrough's top pros at the time Ernie Vickers used to live only 5 doors from me and I used to see him on the morning doing his roadwork. Ernie Vickers was always in the Gazette when I was growing up, so I suppose I looked at him as a bit of a superstar and looked up to him if you like. Sadly, Ernie was killed years after his boxing career had finished when the ship he was on, the Atlantic Conveyor, was hit by a missile.

I even used to promote as a kid in my street, I'd be around 14 and I used to match my younger brother Jerry who'd have been 11 up to fight kids in the street and charge everyone a penny to watch. I would make a ring up in an alleyway and we'd find gloves that were all knackered and used and I'd make all the kids in the street box and I'd charge. I would take my little brother around in a barrow during the day time telling all the kids our Jerry was gonna be fighting so and so and the time, then they'd all come around to watch my little promotions. I'd have loads of kids there on the night all punching hell out of each other with gloves that had next to nothing in them!

Myself, as an amateur boxer, I had around 70 contests winning near enough 60 of them. I was never knocked out, but I was stopped on my feet by murderous puncher Billy Walker in 1961 at West Ham baths. I'm proud to say I never had 10 counted over me.

There got to a point in my dad's life where, although he loved boxing, he never liked me doing it at all and he would try to tell me to wrap it in. My dad was an old Victorian and was very strict. My mother on the other hand used to go to lots of boxing matches with her brother and she was a better supporter to me boxing.

One day my dad took me in the car to see an old fella selling newspapers on the corner, this guy selling the papers was punch drunk if you like and dad took me to see this fella to show me what might lay ahead of me if I kept up with the boxing, basically "do you wanna end up like that John?". It was done to show me what happens to old fighters. This fella had been a somebody once upon a time and was a real contender but was now selling newspapers and he could hardly speak so this was done to shock me and to try and persuade me to chuck the fighting game. He even tried to stop me fighting at The Winter Gardens at Morecambe when I was an amateur for England against Wales. I was desperate to fight on this show as all the British Olympians from the 1960 games in Rome, Italy were there. What happened was that I had a rash from working at ICI and so at the time I was on pills, but you couldn't drive or drink on these pills and when he found that out my dad said "you're not boxing" even though I was 21 years of age. I'd just come out of the army, so he still thought he could stand firm and tell me what to do. I went anyway, and I boxed Robin Jones that night, who at the time was the Welsh amateur champion, looking back I wish my dad had stopped me because I got stopped on my feet again!

I was never counted out ever and, in all honesty, I made more money sparring than I ever made boxing. I was used by Brian London, Henry Cooper and his brother Jim because I was known as a toughie who could hold his own with a good chin. I sparred many many rounds with Henry Cooper because we were an identical build both being 6ft 2 and 13st 9lbs.

The reason I went pro was to make money, having a family and providing for my children. I was working at ICI at the time and I was needing time off work for fights, the foreman wasn't too happy about it, he'd say to me daily, "Well are you a lagger or are you a boxer make your mind up"? I wasn't happy with him putting pressure on me, so I thought "FUCK YOU" and packed in the job not long after to go pro.

I fought in the quarter finals of the ABA'S against Mick Cowen from Rotherham I beat him easy, but I had red shorts on and he had blue shorts on, but I was in the blue corner and he was in the red corner and they give the fucking decision to him! He'd been down 5 times. My trainer Bill Medhurst threw the towel at the referee and said, "HE'LL NEVER BOX FUCKING AMATUER AGAIN" and we stormed out of the building in disgust. I was 24,25 by this time and I'd had enough of amateur boxing, so I give the pro's a shot.

I turned pro and had 2 fights, but I used my dad's name and fought under Jack Spensley. My first bout was a no contest over 3 rounds and I won the second but of course this isn't on my record on BoxRec under my real name of John Spensley. Under that name I had 5 bouts between 1962 – 64. My first I lost on points versus the local lad Steve Walsh at The Old Liverpool Stadium and that was a very close decision over 6 rounds.

I went to Derry, Northern Ireland in my second fight and got a draw against Jim Monaghan which was like a win getting a draw away from home in the fella's backyard. After the fight the crowd were chucking money in the ring because we'd both been so entertaining. I got £50 so Jim must have got £50 also which was a lot of money back in them days. I was walking around the ring trying to pick all this money up with my gloves on.

After that I beat Mick Basten from Leicester at The Old St James Hall in Newcastle on points, then I knocked Dave Maxwell out in one round in Middlesbrough.

My last contest was against Feleti Fred Kaho from Tonga, who was a bit of a KO artist. Every fight Kaho won was by KO and he stopped me in the last round. I was originally going to face Jim Monaghan which is why I took the fight in the first place. They basically changed the fighter on the night and my manager at the time who was Jack Burns was in London, they never even notified him on this which should have happened. I'd trained for the fight anyway and I'd sold tickets as I was a great ticket seller selling them all to my work colleagues at ICI, so I just took the fight. When I went into the fight against Feleti Fred Kaho he was at least a good 2 stone more than me which wasn't in the small print, but I got on with it. In the fight itself I was boxing his head off then Harry Round who was in my corner said, "John you can knock him out here". So, I went out and tried to put it on him, but he caught me with the wildest swing anyone's been hit with, this fella threw punches from the floor honest to God, I hit the deck... I ended up hitting the deck 8 times in total I kid you not. After the fight the referee came up to me which was unheard of then as they must remain neutral "John, what the fucking hell did you do that for you were ahead in every round?"

On the bus the next day going to work, I had to ask someone on the bus how I got on last night! He'd hit me that hard I forgot like I had amnesia. After the fight I'd been ok and had a drink, but I just seemed to lose 12 hours of my life somewhere.

As I told you earlier the money I made in boxing was far greater being used as a sparring partner. I went to spar Birmingham's Johnny Prescott. I was flown out to Nebraska, USA to work as a sparring partner with Billy Nielson and I stayed with Billy for months training. They were gonna do all sorts with Nielson until Brian London flattened him in 4 rounds.

At times I was getting £10 per round and I was doing 6 rounds. If you want to compare it, I was getting £15 a week from ICI in them days. I did dozens of rounds with Henry Cooper and his twin brother Jim. I sparred with Brian London, but I didn't get a lot of money off him, he was hard to get money from.

When you thought I was only normally getting £15-£20 a fight in Middlesbrough, but in Ireland against Monaghan I got £100. Then when I was doing a few rounds with fellas and I was getting £30 for sparring from folk like Jim Wicks the boxing manager plus my lodge paid for, I could buy things for my kids. I wasn't on the breadline by any means.

Towards the end of my boxing I got a job as a bouncer on the doors in Middlesbrough and I was getting paid more for that. Plus, I couldn't go to the gym because I was working anti-social hours. Boxing kind of went on the back burner and I had a few years away from the game.

I had a complete break and cut all ties with boxing for many years, I needed it. I wouldn't even think about boxing until I went to watch an amateur show which my Son was on in Northumberland. It was a big plush dinner do and I thought I might try my hand at this, I knew I knew a lot of people and had kept my boxing connections over the years. I looked for somewhere for me to have my own promotions and I found the Marton Hotel & Country Club in Middlesbrough. Before I set my plans into play I got in touch with my old friend ex fighter Maxi Smith who was already a pro manager by that time, I told him what my plans were, and he said, "I've got the perfect fella I'll introduce you to", and that was Tommy Miller from Halifax. Tommy had been around the game for donkey's years and me and Tommy become great pals and he showed me the ropes. What people don't understand is, you must hold a licence for so long you can't just jump into it, so I worked my way up and did the correct procedures. I signed all types of fighters such as Beckenham's Kevin Lueshing and Barnet's Spencer Oliver. Tommy Miller became my matchmaker. The very first fight I put on was Terry Schofield against Charlie Malarkey in February 1978 for an area title. Terry went on to become a promoter himself in South Shields. I got Henry Cooper up as guest of honour for the show as a favour to me. At that time Paul Sykes, the notorious Heavyweight from Wakefield, had just got out of prison and moved up to my house to begin his professional career. Me and Tommy Miller had fought his corner with the board and he'd been granted a licence, so I had him in the ring at the interval saying what big things we expected of him. Tommy Miller was convinced he was gonna be the future of the heavyweight division.

The show was a huge success and the feedback was that I should do more of these shows. I think that night we had something like 900 people in there. Of course, it was restricted the next time because of fire regulations because the Marton Hotel & Country Club wasn't the biggest venue. I must have done the shows at that place for 6-7 years and we had some cracking nights in that place, I believe it's just closed down recently.

After the Marton Hotel & Country Club I opened up the North East Sporting Club at The Gosforth Park Hotel in Newcastle. I've put world title fights on in Scotland, I've put world title fights on in London. I promoted in Blackpool, Scarborough, Darlington, Sunderland, Washington and Middlesbrough many times. I put two world title fights on in Middlesbrough one being Glenn McCrory at Eston Sports Centre and the other being Alfred Kotey at Middlesbrough Town Hall.

I was putting shows on once a year for the Mayor of Durham in Durham. One year I did more promotions than Mickey Duff and believe me that must have taken some doing because he was everywhere in boxing let me tell you.

When I put them world titles on in Middlesbrough I'm proud to say people who didn't even like boxing came out, because I was a Middlesbrough lad. Even down as far as Leeds, nobody done a world title show were the local lad won a world title on it in them days but me.

Boxing's taken me far and wide working, places like Dublin for Steve Collins winning his world title against Chris

Eubank. It took me to Texas to see Billy Hardy fight for his world title and took my sons there.

Boxing brings the best out of people I've always found. Of course, you get the odd loon, but you do everywhere in life. I've always said the nastiest ones like Paul Sykes, when they get into boxing it calms them down. I never met anyone, and I've met tons of boxers, I've never seen any of them use violence in the gym. Of course, in sparring its fighting, it's a skill it's an art, but I've never seen anyone getting bullied or faced up against a changing room wall. Never did I ever hear, "I'LL SEE YOU OUTSIDE". The same fellas, put them in a pub and they'll rip people's heads off. In the gym the only violence I ever saw was in the ring and a lot of old school coaches will say the exact same thing as I've told you.

Boxing has always attracted characters like Paul Sykes, but I must say I always liked that fella. He was very quick-witted and one extremely funny man. He was the entertainment in my gym when he was there. You need people like him in a gym because boxing can be a very tedious boring sport at times. The long boring runs, the repetitive groundwork and he brought some great laughs to my gym when he was there. Taking the lads for long runs can be boring as fuck, well you were never bored when Paul Sykes was about! He was a comedian.

After the world title fight I put on in October 1989, Paul Sykes held court in my wife Linda's pub. People were in awe of him coming up to me saying "John where did you get him from? I've never met anyone like him". When I watch comedies with Ronnie Barker in and people say what a great writer he was, I put Paul in that category. If that man had had a different way in life, he could have written sitcoms like that he was very very gifted and by far the funniest man I've ever met in my life bar none!

I still have a gym at home in Cyprus and I still do a bit of bag work and speedball as I like to show off. Quite often I get a few of the little Cypriot kids passing by and they'll sit there amazed that I've this ball blazing away, quite often there's been a few of the kids over there who've asked me to show them how you do it or asking me questions on boxing. I suppose I'm what you'd class as a gym fighter, even when I was boxing I was better in the gym than I actually was in the ring. I used to suffer terribly with my nerves as a lad if I'm being honest.

Looking back the best fighter I ever managed was George Feeney from Hartlepool. That man had more skill than any other guy I looked after. Feeney should have won a world title but he was mismanaged after he left me and was told to go fight Ray Mancini in a non-title fight in Italy which he lost on points, they were never gonna give him a rematch after it being so close.

The lad I liked managing most was another Hartlepool lad heavyweight Dave Garside. Dave was with me all the way and you knew he would fight! He wasn't like some fighters who always complained of headaches, colds etc and Dave was a hell of a good fighter, hard as nails.

Neil Malpass the heavyweight from South Elmsall was another one of my lads who I'd like to mention. He should have beaten Alfredo Evangelista. Often Neil would never throw fights, but he knew what he was getting paid and he wouldn't take himself out of the comfort zone. He should have been more aware of how near he was to greatness. When he went to fight Mike Schutte in South Africa, Schutte couldn't stop him and he was knocking everyone over, but he couldn't get near Neil Malpass. Neil had one hell of a right hand I've never seen anything like it! He was like a heavyweight equivalent of Thomas Hearns. Long legs and nothing on him, but when he threw that right hand it went straight and fast like an arrow. When fighters have that leverage sometimes that's when they can really hit. People think it's the little squat fella's that hit hard but it's not, it's the lean beanpole fuckers that can hit. Perfect example is Gerard McClellan.

I've met so many lovely people in boxing in my life and I've got some wonderful memories. None more so than winning the Maurice Cullen award which I was voted for by a massive amount of people in the North East for my services to boxing. One of my other wonderful memories was meeting Muhammad Ali at the London Palladium at the weigh in for when he fought Henry Cooper at Wembley in 1963. I should have been on the bill but fought during the day and not on the evening, the press tipped me to win the £1000 heavyweight tournament.

I was in the dressing room with Ali and we're both getting ready for the weigh in. I was talking to him for quite a while and he was just like a normal man asking me how many fights I've had etc... He was the politest humblest fella you could ever meet and nothing like what I'd seen of him on the telly beforehand.

Anyway, the second he went out the dressing room he completely changed and started shouting "Henry's gonna fall in 5" ... The second, he stepped foot over the dressing room door he became mouthy, arrogant and playing up to the camera crew because it was all just an act like the wrestling. This was not the fella who I'd been chatting to in the dressing room for the last half hour I can tell you. He knew he'd created a monster and needed to get in his role and put his mask and cape on if you like.

I loved my time in boxing and the real people I've met. I've been to Mexico, South Africa, France and Germany. All places that I would never have went to if it wasn't for my life in boxing. Your normal lad off the Whinny Banks estate doesn't get to these places usually.

I did work with Cedric Kushner one of the great promoters from South Africa. I went to Trump Palace and met Donald Trump. Of course, I never knew that one day he was gonna be president of America then. The reason I was there was I went over with Glenn McCrory to spar with a peak Iron Mike Tyson around 1988 time. Bob Arum wanted to offer Glenn McCrory a 5-fight contract and there were offering 8 million dollars for it. Bob Arum and Donald Trump asked what I thought! My reply was "we're with Mr Kushner and I'm a boy from the sticks and to sit here and play with millions isn't me, I don't want to look a fool, I'll let Mr Kushner do the deal thank you very much" and I looked out the window to see the whole of New York lit up. Bob Arum said to me, "John, we all came the same way we've all been through it and started somewhere". It was quite tense to say the least. How many men from Middlesbrough have met the president of America?!

For a person like myself who's just an ordinary publican I've been all over the world and met so many great people. I've even been interviewed on American television when Lennox Lewis was fighting Evander Holyfield in the first fight in Madison Square Garden, New York. Cedric Kushner had arranged for me to go with some of my friends from Middlesbrough and arranged for free food and a free bar. He arranged for me to sit in the VIP box watching the fight which of course ended with a scandalous decision giving it the draw when Lewis won by a country mile. I've been to every capital in Europe and it's all down to boxing. Boxing's been very good to me.

"Boxing is just business with blood".

Frank Bruno

Francis Jones

These days in the North East of England Francis Jones is better known as Rent-A-Cop. Francis featured in a part fly on the wall television documentary plus a Christmas special on BBC3. The show in itself was a huge success and plans are underway for a second series at this present time.

Before Francis' television stardom he was well known for a different reason, and that was boxing. Francis campaigned at British title level and had a very respectable career with some good names on his record such as Matthew Hatton and Neil Sinclair. Very tragically Francis's career was cut short due to not passing the BBBofC brain scan level of expectations.

I'd heard of Francis Jones coming through the ranks as one of the up and coming British fighters around 2005 but I wouldn't get to know him on a personal level until 2014 when he would come to a few charity night events I used to organise with ex boxers.

I liked Francis immediately, as soon as I met him and in the last few years he's become one of my personal friends who often comes around my house to watch the boxing. In life I've always related to the underdog in life or people that other people might consider to be 'not quite all there', the people in life who don't look for approval and like being a little bit different. I think this is the reason I get on with Francis as we're both a little bit strange and usual.

I've been asked by my friends if Francis Jones is a real person as they thought he might be like Keith Lemon and just be playing a character. If you're reading this Francis, it's a compliment honest.

The readers who've watched the full series of Rent-A-Cop will fully understand what I'm saying. I didn't put my friend Francis Jones in the book because he was my friend, I put him in because he was a good honest pro with a winning record of 23 bouts with 17 wins, 6 KO'S with 4 losses and 2 draw's.

I had mad Franny around my house for an hour to conduct this interview one Friday evening when he was out on one of his security patrols for his company Sparta Security. I made Francis a coffee and sat back and listened to what he had to say on his fighting days.

Francis said: -

"I'm 36 years old now. I grew up in Lancaster until I was around 11 years of age. My parents were both teachers and they both got teaching jobs in the North East so that's how I ended up in Darlington.

Moving to Darlington unfortunately was the start of me becoming badly bullied for many years. From the ages of 12 years old right up until I became around 16 I was really abused. The reason I started boxing to begin with was because I was bullied, and I wanted it and needed it to just stop! I needed to be able to look after myself and stand up for myself once and for all. Lads used to bully me, girls used to bully me for fun. Verbal bullying, psychical bullying you name it I got it. It was an awful time of my life walking home from school being took apart. This went on until the day I learnt to box and look after myself and I got a bit of confidence about me.

The reason I was bullied I suppose was because I was different, some call it odd, strange a weirdo but that's the reason why people picked on me.

As a youngster I was pretty obsessed and addicted to football, football was my life and after school all I would do is be own my own kicking a football around practicing because I believed dedication, desire and determination got you far in life.

I used to go home and get the ball out and practice on different aspects of my game. I used to break the session up into 30-minute exercises. Sometimes I would practice corners for thirty minutes. I was putting the ball down somewhere on an empty field and then trying to hit the target possibly some 30-40 metres away. I would then run after the ball and do the same thing again. I would do this continuous for thirty minutes then go onto something else like dribbling then I'd do that for 30 minutes.

Those that knew me back when I was a youngster knew me as choppa. I was called this at Hartlepool united FC where I went onto do an apprenticeship for 2 years when I was 16 before being released at 18. I was bullied there also. You're probably thinking 'If he was that good why would Hartlepool release him?' and you're absolutely right, but it was consistency you see. When I was good I was good but when I was crap ……. well, you can fill in the blanks yourself, there is a but coming here, but when you are walking home from school at age 13 and a gang is after you it doesn't make you feel that good if I am honest. The feeling is lonely, scared and the nerves you feel seem not to be your friend. Well, see that feeling? That's the same feeling I felt sometimes if say my first touch wasn't very good for me in a soccer game . You see there's pressure attached to it . You can hear the negative comments and that didn't affect me positively. I reverted back to the feelings that I had at school, I reverted back to walking out into the school yard as the hardest in the school came over to fight me because I was unique, I was different. I reverted back to the sneers and jeering, I reverted back to Dave Luck who would be so excited that the hardest lad in the year was going to come over and beat me up and I couldn't perform playing under a cloud like that.

It is a queer thing isn't it? Life, I mean. Growing up on the streets of Tan Hill Drive Lancaster, when I was 9 years old I didn't know what bullying was, I was blissfully unaware. I was always popular at junior school, even when I moved to Framwell Gatemoor School, Newton Hall, Durham I was a popular character at school. I was popular because I was good at football. I was good because I used to practice.

Listen to me! No one did what I did, I used to practice and practice so hard. I used to be obsessed with football. I remember my cousin who was in the marines and my grandad who also possessed dedication, he possessed so much dedication did my grandad, well he said to me "to be anyone in life you have to practice , you have to become obsessed and just pursue and pursue" and he said "one day you will get to where you want to be" .

Make no mistake about this at all. I understand Hartlepool united FC released me at 18 years of age but listen when I was good I was exceptional. No one knew what I was going to do with that ball. They didn't have a clue where I was going to go or what trick I was going to do. They didn't know because I didn't know and if I don't know then what chance did you have of guessing where I was going but I will tell you this Francis Jones was an exceptional footballer.

But, see that bullying? See that walking home and the feeling so lonely and scared?

That made Fearless Francis Jones.

Those that watched that eight part show Rentacop didn't see 'Fearless' they saw a guy who they thought was probably a bit backward trying to help people and going that extra mile. I mean make no mistake about it that is what I do, I help people and animals. I honestly, despise 'man'. I know exactly what man is and how greedy and vile he is and how selfish humans are but that really is going off the point, 'Fearless' Francis is because of the bullying, Sparta Security is because of the bullying, that huge negative, well I turned into a massive positive.

You see when you bully a man who is dedicated and when you try and trample on him things are going to happen.

When you try and push down people with strong traits in their character other fruits or characters start to emerge.

Listen, I am no Lenny Mclean I am not saying look at me but I am saying ' Fearless' wasn't bothered about no man at all. I promise you faithfully and for those that know me I possess balls because I was pushed down with bullying so, in my British title fight with the commonwealth and British champion Kevin Anderson, he saw 'Fearless'.

Please watch the fight on Youtube yourself to understand. The point isn't 'look at me and look how good I was ', The fight is depressing to watch. The nerves I felt in that fight were unreal, honestly the feeling was really uncomfortable. The fight was in front of the Sky TV cameras in Scotland which was Kevin Anderson's home turf but walking out to the ring, honest in front of God Himself the feeling was like walking the Green Mile. If you were to say "Francis, see when you get to the ring you're going to die the most agonising death going" then the nerves would have been no different than the feeling that I felt then.

I remember the time like it was yesterday. I walked to the ring like a lion going to battle and the smile of gameness on my face where I couldn't care whatsoever who I was stepping into the ring with was a total bluff. The jeering from the fans was reminiscent of me walking home from school and getting set upon by the hardest person in my year when I first went to Branksome Comprehensive, Darlington.

Listen, some people work well with a kick up the backside and when they're shouted at but see me when I am sat on that stool and I walk back to the corner and you start being negative around me then you will not get the best out of me.

As, a boxing trainer it's not about your boxer doing hundreds of press ups and press ups and being the fittest out there. Fitness, is good don't get me wrong but see that mind that's the key right there to unleashing awesomeness.

So many trainers get their fighters in awesome condition but it's in the mind where the fight is won or lost, and mental rehearsal is a big part of the game which is overlooked so much.

For example, instead of getting a personal trainer to get fit and lose weight you find some music that gives you goose bumps and watch how that weight comes off and how much better you perform.

You want your boxer to train hard and run better? You've got to get to know your fighter. If you want the best results out of him then get to know him. Get to know what makes them tick. If they are competitive then stick them on a treadmill where there is competition beside them or make them run with someone they admire or who is better than they are. Are they too tired to train? You bring a girl into the gymnasium and get the girl to watch the boxers, especially them and see how fast their arms go.

The mind is the key to awesomeness, in boxing, in businesses, in finding the perfect partner ……. Understand how awesome you are!

I remember one time at Hartlepool United FC when we had trained so hard one day and all the boys came back to the football stadium for a shower. I was tired and physically exhausted but see this voice in my head, see this spirit that I have inside me the spirit sometimes needs a mentor who can tame it, which can be a coach or a friend or someone you respect that has wisdom.

This voice said "Francis, you want to be the best, don't you? Well, you get out there and go running .

You see all the boys were having a shower and doing their chores after a three and a half hour training session but see you 'Choppa' you get yourself out and go running!

So, I listened to that voice inside my head and I went out running. It wasn't much of a run because I was so tired but let's say if the lads found out at Hartlepool FC then it would be frowned upon.

It would be frowned upon because it would be different, and some derogatory name would be given to me. Like, we have been out training hard all morning and physically exhausting ourselves and then we come back to the ground to do our chores and then I decide to go running so when the word got around there I would receive grief from it and I got bullied .

I wasn't 'Fearless' then. As I've explained I was 'Choppa' Jones.

Like, I am a Christian, a believer in God most high and he says we shouldn't be ungrateful and when I see him one day I will ask him with the upmost respect and I will just say "Why, God?"

Going back to boxing though, it was wanting to stay alive and protect myself from the bullies that drove me to take it up. I did used to watch Prince Naseem Hamed a lot as a lad, I thought that man was awesome.

I first walked into a boxing gym when I was 16 years old. The gym was Larchfield ABC in Darlington. When I first walked in and seen all the lads skipping and punching the bags the same nerves came back that I had when I was getting my usual beatings in the school playground.

To be fair there was some impressive fighters in the gym at the time like Michael Mitchell who'd won many national titles as a junior. Martin Stead was another who was in there and he went on to win three senior ABA titles for the Army. Kevin Hope, Anthony Todd and Alan Hall all trained there too, and they were all successful amateurs. So, it was quite scary thinking back to me, a skinny big eared lad who didn't know how to fight. The only experience I'd had in boxing at that time was that I had a degree in being a live punch bag for my bullies.

Another of my first memories was getting Kevin Hopes glove in my face dozens upon dozens of times. Kevin was short, stocky and very good. When I used to spar Kevin I would try to be like my idol Naseem Hamed and box with my hands down my side, of course I didn't know how to even stand properly and it was usually a very painful lesson.

When I started off boxing I got myself a few more good hidings in the gym. They ran along nicely with my good hidings in the playground. If I wasn't so sick of getting pastings at school I think I'd have packed the boxing game in at that point, but of course it wasn't an option it had to stop, and I had to learn to fight!

I made myself a promise from 18, I would never be bullied again and having this mentality has turned me into the fearless Francis Jones that I am today.

After a while I began to really enjoy amateur boxing and I had 17 bouts in total winning 14 of them. I fought some good names as an amateur though, people like Martin Concepcion from Leicester who I lost to on points in the ¼ finals of the ABA's. I mean you might say ¼finals aren't that good and you'll know lads that have reached far greater heights but know this, one day I am being bullied and am nervous and scared and the next day I am knocking grown hairy arsed men spark out in the boxing ring. Like, I am a kid at 18 years I have blonde hair and eyes, I look like a kid and I am walking the ring so afraid, so nervous and then when the bell goes the loneliness I felt was really uncomfortable but I possess fast hands and I am quick and I used to knock grown men out week after week after week after week boxing and the feeling of success is good. Even, though that frightened kid lurks underneath that kid that the girls used to pick on, I found myself making quite a name for myself which complemented my success.

I'd rather talk about my life than talk about boxing, but I suppose I've been asked by Jamie Boyle whose writing this book, so I will answer.

The miracle is reaching the ¼ finals of the ABA's, the miracle was beating Mark McLean in my 3rd fight who was from Birtley ABC and he had 80-90 fights. Like, that is unheard of really. I think Mark got to the ABA finals or won them I am not sure, but I first walked into Paul Hamilton's boxing gym and then eight months later I am boxing English champions.

Now, as a man I look back and reflect on my amateur career and think would I have done the same thing Paul did if I had a kid under me now? At 4 fights I fought the Multi-Nations gold medallist and ABA semi-finalist Andrew Buchanan and lost on points, but I will be honest I disagree with putting me inside the ring with those men. You can't beat experience and a raw novice who eight months previously didn't know how to box should not have been fighting people who were experienced open class amateurs, even so, I am grateful for the techniques that Mr Hamilton taught me, but he lacked wisdom. I used to turn up at his gym and there'd be this professional boxer Andy Vickers and he would always want to spar me and every time he asked I used to say yes. I said yes because I was bullied at school and I made a promise to myself when I started boxing that I would not be bullied again.

Andy was a middleweight professional and I used to get done in time and time again at the gym. He used to try and knock me out and if I'm honest with you I hated it. I hated the feeling associated with going to the gym when he was in training and I didn't know when he was going to turn up then when he did turn up he would ask my trainer "Can, Francis spar? ". Paul did not have the courage to say "No" and the feeling was unreal really.

Have you ever met a person that accepts no blame? Nothing is their fault, they always have an excuse? These people live amongst us. I am sure you see them, know them, perhaps you are one yourself but my trainer is one of those people. All his good boxers left him when he was a coach in the U.K and non-of them want anything to do with Paul.

As a boxing trainer, oh boy you'll meet no one like him. Like, the physical activities he would have you doing would be so awesome and the shape he would get you in would be out of this world, but I remember boxing Andrew Buchanan in the ABA's and after the bout Paul decided it would be good for me to go and spar his middleweight brother at Gary McCrory's gym. Gary is the brother of Glenn McCrory the former world champion and Sky Sport's commentator.

Former ABA Semi-finalist and Multi-Nations Gold medallist Andrew Buchanan has a brother called Paul Buchanan who again would have won all the titles as a junior.

When, I was practicing football outside when I was 10,14,16 etc these lads would have been hitting bags as both were top notch.

My trainer Paul decided after I lost to one brother to go to Newcastle and spar his younger brother who was heavier and bigger. Like, I had been boxing eight months and I am not saying I wasn't any good because I was good but there's levels aren't there.

You will know kids at a boxing gym who are good but then that goodness isn't on the same level as goodness as the Buchanan brothers and never mind about that alone, but Paul Bucannon was bigger and couldn't half fight and add to that I've just had a fight with his older brother Andrew.

What do you think he would think about my trainer saying my lad Francis Jones wants to spar you?

I've just fought his brother and did well in my opinion to lose on points but now you've just asked the kid's trainer we now have your brother in our targets and not only that, but we are coming to your turf to give it you!

If, I was Paul Buchanan's trainer I would be saying "Give him it and send him back down the road the cheeky little shit". But, the thing is though I hadn't asked to spar nor did I want to spar. I don't know if you're understanding this correctly, but I had been boxing for about eight months and was a shitty arse kid previously getting bullied by everyone.

We went to Newcastle in the Paul Hamilton sign written car and pulled outside his gym. I walked inside the gym scared and frightened thinking in my sub consciousness "What on earth am I doing here?" I shook hands with him because I was scared and jumped in the ring and got absolutely battered. The spar had to be stopped and the punishment I could have gotten could well have been fatal.

I mean if that would have been in the street he would have got time for an assault charge, but can you blame him?

So, I learnt how to take beatings in my early days, which formed my character.

At 18 you're not a man you're a kid and that mind can be moulded so it's imperative to surround your child with wisdom as they listen to people at that age and their mind can be manipulated so YOU picking and advising their future steps and guiding them the best is highly recommended.

I never thought of turning over until Darlington's Argie Ward came to me in 2001 and put the idea into my head. At the time I was training with Howard Rainey in Sheffield quite a bit. I would often train alongside Dave Coldwell at Howards. Dave Coldwell has went on to become a very successful coach with Tony Bellew.

Argie Ward who himself was a Commonwealth champion told me to go train with Hartlepool's Neil Fannan who was doing things with Commonwealth champion Kevin Bennett.

I took my friend Argie's advice and I went over to Hartlepool for a chat with Neil Fannan.

I told my coach Paul Hamilton I was leaving and I went to Fannon's gym.

In life you meet people along your journey and at the end of life there will be significant people on that list.

See, Neil Fannon that mad one is one of those people!

The man is a trainer that takes charge of his boxer. He is old school, he is a fighter, and he is someone you don't mess with. He will fight any man going and if you go into battle then he has your back.

Just by standing next to you he will make you fight better if you know the man. Fano, is old school. Tuck your chin down and go into battle. He will train you accordingly and you will go into battle to fight. He knows the fight game inside out and its life skills, not just boxing skills that you get taught.

'Fearless' was because of Neil Fannon. I know I used to get bullied at school and I learnt to box but mentally I didn't have the ingredients. I've said to you before it's all mental. Fano used to say training is 90% physical and 10% mental but see on fight night it's 90% mental.

Going to Fano's gym was like a kid at school going straight into the army but with a general beside you every step of the way. Listen, when Fano is in your corner you turn into this superhero.

You learn along life's journey don't you? You make decisions and you do what you decide. We are all on a journey in life and we go down what path we think at the time is right.

Neil Fannon schooled me in boxing all through my professional career and I'd just started knocking people out and getting the RSC on my record 'Referee stopped contest' and I decided to leave the stable.

Life? "The bible says, 'who can know it?" Francis Jones is no yes man, I never have been a yes boy unless there was a female in front of me and I'd say yes to that, but I decided to leave Fano's camp when I was just coming into glory.

You see we'd worked our way up to this point, eight years to get ourselves to competition standard. I was 27 and I decided to leave the stable because I didn't think I was getting enough attention. We had Michael Hunter in our stable who won everything bar the world title and my head at the time thought I should be getting more attention in order to be a someone.

If you look at Chris Eubank Jnr today he knows how to fight. He is a man and knows the fight game. If I went into Chris Eubank Jnr's corner, then I'd be known as his coach but it's him not me that has to perform.

Fano, taught and schooled me and therefore it's like riding a bike he doesn't have to be there watching your legs go round and round on the pedals. He has taught you how to ride so just go and do what he says.

Life? Who can know it? I went back to my old professional boxing trainer Paul Hamilton who've I have told you is very good at getting you in tip top condition, but he lacks wisdom and would have you box Mike Tyson if you'd been in he's gym 2 days. Not only that he would brain wash you that you would beat Tyson so instead of you going out to fight Iron Mike to get the money and get a loss on your boxing record he would convince you that your power will affect Mike's chin and would send you out to knock him out.

Life, life though who can know it? I know God does but I'm not God because if I was I wouldn't have done the above paragraph and I would have been a British champion if Fano was in my corner.

Kevin Anderson was a really good fighter, bit of a puncher but I'd trained to beat him. Again, what played against me was nerves, but I had the ability to take him to the cleaners. In round 7 of that fight I was hit with a punch and it felt like a Butterfly in my brain. It was very much like when Rocky fights Ivan Drago and he could tell which punch gave him the brain injury, well I was the same. At times after the 7th it felt like I was floating, I didn't have a clue what was going on. I had no power in my punchers from the 7th onwards, that's how I felt. Then again if you watch the fight on YouTube I nearly knock him out in the 10th. It was in the 12th and final round Kevin caught me with a simple jab and my legs buckled. Often fighters get caught and they say I'm ok, well I was gone in the head although I was on my feet. I was dazed, and he came reigning in with his punches to finish me off. Kevin Anderson wasn't a one punch KO artist but he had fast hands and he'd wear his opponents down and he stopped me. If you look at Kevin Andersons career though, after he boxed me he wasn't the same fighter he once was, and I never won a fight again after me.

After the fight I knew something wasn't right with me in my brain. After the 7th round I really struggled in the Kevin Anderson fight but I choose not to give in, the reason being, I got bullied as a kid and nobody was gonna bully me again so I had this thing in me where I wouldn't quit!

The next day I was working on one of my doors in Hull, still marked up from the fight the night before. It was a strippers bar and something had kicked off and all chaos broke out, I ended up chinning this lad who'd come just to cause havoc. I still felt like I was floating like I'd been in the ring, this was 24 hours later. Even for days afterwards I was really struggling with the most ridiculous things like adding 5 plus 4 I was struggling and it was impossible for me. It was hurting me to even think so I went to the hospital about 7 days after the fight. The doctors said I had concussion and just gave me headache tablets. I let another week go past and my head still wasn't right so I went back to the hospital, they tried to buy me off with the same rubbish yet again. I said look something's not right here, watch the fight it was on Sky Sports for God sake. I ended up going back to my GP who then sent me to the MRI UNIT which I did.

From that day my boxing career with the BBBofC was over. What the doctors found was a bleed on my brain from the Kevin Anderson fight and that was me finished at the young age of 27. I was utterly heartbroken I'd had something I loved taken away from me through no fault of my own. I even went to America to seek another brain neurologist's opinion to say I could box again. I found two doctors and one of them was the best in the business. I had about five reports from this guy saying that I'm fine but of course they didn't wash with the BBBoC. It was so hard to accept that was me hanging up my gloves. Many years before that I broke my hand and the doctor said I'd never box again, I recovered and then I found a surgeon who wasn't gonna say no to me, I thought this would have been the same, but God had other ideas. My only route to box again after this was on the semi professional circuit, which I did for a number of years.

There is action to my walk. If I put my name to something then those that know me will know it's worth something as I have character to my bones.

It's the same thing with faith. Having faith is fantastic you know. Those that know know but with faith things grow. We can have faith in Father Christmas and so you know how faith works walking down those stairs on a Christmas day and seeing Santa has been at the Whiskey again really was awesome. It was awesome because we believed. We believed because we were told and we believed so every Christmas we walked down and the feeling was awesome .... Awesome until my 10th birthday and my sister told me Father Christmas didn't exist!

After, that point the faith died and the Christmas experience went downhill, downhill so fast that I actually hate Christmas. I hate all the 'Happy New Year' and then on January the 1st it's 'did you have a good Christmas?'

I mean you're not interested if I had a good Christmas or not. You couldn't give a toss. It's so annoying. People, come out the wood work like their your best pal on Facebook and send you images like 'send this image to those people you really care about but it only really works if you send the image back' so you get people that you hardly know sending you images of how much you mean to them and I am like 'I saw you the other day when I was walking home and you didn't even offer me a lift or acknowledge me and now we are like a proper family just because we are into the month of December.

I mean you get these Facebook messages from people you think really should know better but again life's life, who can know it?

Then these people see you and say 'Oh, poor lad he's been caught by them born again Christian doorknockers? He used to be a lovely kid. I remember Francis when he was chasing every girl in the district and now he's on the born again train, poor kid!'

People, who know me, people who don't. I promise you faithfully God is real.

If Father Christmas was real I promise you faithfully Christmas would be awesome and it would be awesome because of Faith.

You see Faith is believing before it's happened. Faith, is 'thanking' not asking. Faith is knowing, having a certainty what you are talking about is true.

Faith talks to God believing he is listening. Faith thanks God knowing he is hearing. For those that know me if I told you there was gold in a field not far from you then I suppose you would weigh Francis Jones up. If I am of good testimony from what you have known of me then you will go and dig for the treasure but contrary if my words are false and I tell you there is Gold somewhere then your action will reflect what you think of me.

If something is white I will not say it is black and versa versa so hear this.

The bible is the source where Faith lies and it has countless of prophecies which have happened and more which are to happen. One of the prophecies says one day we depart this realm and we go before our maker and we be sent either of two ways .

The source, which gives faith, states humans come into this world as sinners and for that sin there is a consequence.

God said Jesus Christ was sent into this world for the sin of man that anyone who believeth in him shall be given eternal life.

I'll give you an example, two boys were playing at home with their toys. One of the boys takes the other one's toy and starts to play with it himself. He didn't snatch it he just reached across and took it. He cannot ask because he doesn't know how to speak, and it wasn't as if his brother was playing with the same toy, he was playing with another toy but when he saw his brother playing with the toy which his mummy had given him he gets very jealous and angry and lashes out and snatches this toy back.

The lads are kids, still in nappies but the anger and resentment that the child displays where does that come from?

What about when a child wants something and you do not want them to have it then possibly they'll give a fit of rage, they will cry and go above what you have said.

The bible claims we have come into this world as sinners and Jesus 'blood paid the price for the sin we carry and if you put your trust in him then the bible claims fruits start to be produced by you such as helping people, animals, forgiving and being a better person.

It's all about love isn't it? Love is awesome; helping someone gives me satisfaction and makes me feel special, wanted and a benefit to society. I get job satisfaction with Christianity and I have seen answers to prayers many many times that cannot be just coincidence but God-incidence so if I know where solutions are, and I know you have problems then how can I not have a want and a need to tell you.

Does that mean that just because you know the source life is all roses and things happen to those special people that say they know the source?

Do champions start to cry when they get caught by a shot fighting?

I know I have learnt about Francis Jones when I have been in the valleys, in the gutter when I have experienced pain and I look up and say 'Oh, God where are you? '

If anyone is a walker on here then you'll notice that if you've ever been up on a mountain top there's nothing much that grows but heading up to the summit you'll witness yourself all the livery and plant and crop – things grow in the valleys so if you're in a valley in life just know that God thinks you are important and maybe you think he has given up on you, but just know that he loves you so much and wants a relationship with you.

His own son was sent into this world and he was crucified on a cross for your sin and mine and if you can reach out to him then I promise you faithfully you will enter that promised land and you will display actions of love whilst you're still in this realm.

The Rent-A-Cop business came about because I believed the doors were so much trouble. I am a boxer and I wasn't the best testimony for Jesus if I was attacked because I promise you faithfully I wouldn't turn the other cheek.

Women were my Achilles heels also. Oh, boy you can class them as God's best gift but I'm sure you'd change your mind when you split with them and they take you to the cleaners with money.

I haven't been screwed over as I write this. I mean I love my wife Rachel Jones but if we ever did split she'd inherit half of what I'd have and as I write this I'm in debt thousands, so I hope her new fella has some lawyer to bail her out. I tell her all the time that I am different, and your new fella will be nothing like me!!

So, I opened my security company Sparta Security. The Lord opens a lot of doors for you when you least expect it. Sometimes you're down in your life but that's when Jesus is working for you most. The Rent-A-Cop, The Sparta Cop I am, I was helping people. Many times, for nothing. All I was doing is following in Jesus' footsteps and if you do that, you can't not help people.

So, this film company got wind of this character called Francis Jones who's a little bit wacky and off the wall and they thought it would be good if they made a series on me so hence Rentacop was born.

After, the brain bleed I went southpaw and boxed southpaw for around 8-10 fights. I faced some good fighters, street fighters and half decent game boxers. I mean I changed overnight. I ended up living in the United States on and off for around 5 years . I went southpaw and started again. I was trained by Rodger Mayweather and Freddie Roach. Aye, you would think it would be awesome and I am not saying it wasn't, well actually I am. Yes, I am in Vegas, but I didn't half feel lonely. It's a queer one isn't it loneliness like you can be surrounded by people but yet still feel lonely.

I asked God to help me be happy and the next thing I am in a brothel in Vegas with a girl kissing me. Well, she wasn't kissing me. I was kissing her and I thought it was the same back but she was blowing smoke into my lungs. It's called a blow back. I didn't know at the time but she was blowing methadone into the temple.

I was off my nut. Literally off my face. I remember driving up the road on my scooter and there were bears coming at me on the roadside and then rabbits would jump in my path.

The Vegas experience is not going in this book.

Do you know the film what happened in Vegas stays in Vegas? Well, listen, my character would be tarnished if I told you the crack there. I've spent 36 years getting standards of my character to this respectable level and I am not going to blow it by telling you stories from Vegas.

I mean I am Spartacop. I run my town Darlington and keep trouble at bay and prostitution down to the required levels but there could be a film about my exploits in the devil's city which include a girl telling me she has HIV, seconds away from getting it on with world champion Andre Dirrell, running 6 miles down the strip off my nut on methadone and Badou Jack leaning over the ropes pointing at me and shouting 'I want to fight you!' And, that isn't even a warm up to my adventures there.

I was in America many times when Jesus told me to go southpaw. At times I'd be over there for three months at a time training in all the top gyms.

In America you really learn how to fight, take Chris Eubank Jnr for example. Neil Fannan was an awesome trainer, he was the best trainer I ever had and there's no trainer in America better than him, but I wished I'd have went to America when I was just starting out as a fighter. There's so many unbelievable gym fighters in America alone. I was once bust up in Gleeson's gym by a nobody, some guy I'd never even heard of give me a pasting! He was a 12-0 fighter and he was good because I am alright as a southpaw.

The level in America boxing is far greater than in Britain. I had many rounds of great sparring over there.

I trained alongside Zab Judah over in America for around six months. Zab was a phenomenal fighter.

I'm at a good place now in my life I was married only last year. I love Rach she's a star, you don't get many like that woman and she looks after me. If anyone watched Rent-A-Cop, Rach was my blonde secretary and we'd kind of been seeing each other for 10 years but I didn't take her seriously. I didn't have a clue that this was the woman for me until God opened my eyes and made me realise what I had. Its mental how life works out that's for sure. Although since I married Rachel I'm two and a half stone heavier and she's a qualified personal trainer so I don't know if that's a good thing for her CV.

Boxing is an art and also boxing's a business. If I was to train my son to fish, it's not about casting my rod in the water, you've got to make it a competition for them to bite the bait. Boxing's not about bravado and I'll fight anyone. Matthew Hatton had a sensible manager who certainly picked to box me at the best time for him, not the best time for me. The jabs the key in boxing and also body shots. You can make really hard hairy arsed men cowards if you just tap them with a left hook to the liver. Often you could come across a man who'll eat left hooks, right hooks and smile at you, but if you catch them with a quality shot to the body you can fold them like a deck chair. You break the body up and the head will fall.

I'm unsure if I will box again, I do not know. I am 15 stones as I write, I competed at British title level at 10st 7lbs.

I still think I could do it you know if say I got the weight off. I sit and think it's still there and trust me it is still there I haven't lost my sharpness I have just gotten fat but the weight can come off and my reactions are still some but it's that motivation isn't it?

Music motivates me. If you research a good play list what a session you can have."

If anyone wants to follow "Fearless" Francis Jones, his Facebook page 'Sparta Security U.K' and on Twitter it is '@ndthenew'.

"Mickey Duff hated everybody, but it was strictly business".

Steve Bunce

Matt Hamilton

Respectable boxing writer Matt Hamilton is 35 and comes from Cape Town in South Africa. Matt came over here when he was about 32 as he told me opportunities for white South Africans were limited in every aspect of society. Matt told me that 98% of his genealogy was British and he feels more at home in our country. Matt told me he considers himself to be British but with an accent.

Matt told me how he became involved in the most noble art of all.

Matt said:

My first memories, that I can recall, regarding boxing must have been from when I was around 5 years old watching Mike Tyson V Pinklon Thomas. My parents had these old VHS tapes of Tyson's fights, even though there was nothing in my background that would naturally bring me to boxing.

My father was very much a casual boxing fan, but he couldn't give you that much detail about the game. As a boy growing up I was never really into your Superman comic book hero stuff, boxing was my equivalent and Mike Tyson was essential to this as he was to lots of people just maybe not as young as five I grant you. I must have been the biggest Mike Tyson fan to up until 15-16 then eventually I learnt more about the sport and I understood that, although he was very good at what he did, he never came back from somebody with a victory over him and he lost most of his meaningful fights. I grew up and understood the guy was a bit of a mess basically. As I got older and more clued up on boxing I got a greater appreciation of defensive fighters and other skills, but certainly Mike Tyson flicked my switch and my love of boxing on.

As much as I loved boxing I never really wanted to do it and most people won't admit that, well I'll admit that. The theatre they create, the risks a fighter takes just wasn't for me. I'm way too much of a wuss. I'm friends with a lot of boxers or former boxers and I respect them immensely for what they do for a small chance of wealth, riches and glory but for me no never, I never once wanted to participate although I've hung around gyms forever, but I've never wanted to box myself. I trained in ju-jitsu for many years but that was purely for self-defence matters, I come from an extremely violent country. When I did martial arts, I was a high level purple belt. The reason why I choose ju-jitsu was a very small population of my country did ju-jitsu so the chance of me running into someone better than me at it on the street was very small. The ju-jitsu itself was a very affective form of fighting and defensive posturing and chokes. It was good for my confidence growing up in South Africa knowing you could tie a guy in knots if needs be, although I'm not a violent person. Ju-jitsu is about empowering the weak against the strong although it's kind of boring to watch I must add. My Dad was trained in everything with the Special Forces in South Africa and he also taught me a lot of stuff growing up.

I find Connor McGregor an inspirational figure because any guy who's gone from literally the dole queue in 2011-12 to go on to achieve what he has tends to be the main guy in his industry. The fight Connor McGregor had with Floyd Mayweather, which I didn't watch I thought was an absolute joke! I almost refused to talk about it but for what he brings to his sport of UFC, I wish him all the best. I think it's a sad state of affairs that that was the biggest fight in boxing in 2017.

The essential problem that I think boxing has compared to the UFC is the lack of competitive shows on the telly. For instance, if you go to a show on a standard weekend and try to do an 8-fold in the betting shop, you will do very well to find a bet that's better than 2/1, even though you've backed 8 contests. You do the same with the UFC and your talking down the middle on every fight and they are as close as they can be. In boxing, and through no fault of the fighters because they just want to fight, they think they can beat everyone and that's great, but the business and the way its handled, I say with respect, it is very wrong. I've been thinking about this today, take James Degale for example in his last fight, he lost his title to some guy (Caleb Truax) who I wouldn't know beforehand, and I wouldn't know afterwards. Occasionally these flukes happen, and it did to poor James Degale but now I tend to only watch fights that aren't predictable before the fight.

There was once a hall of fame matchmaker who said as much as I've said here. He was post-war time and he said anyone who has 3 brain cells knows Sugar Ray Robinson was a mile in front of anyone else at the time, but he lost 19 times. So, what do we dwell on, what he did or the 19 losses because in this era he couldn't have done that because they withhold the product and protect the fighter. They did the same to Anthony Joshua and Tyson Fury until they both became an inconvenience truthfully. I'm outspoken on drugs in the game but it's very interesting how selective the drug policy is implemented and how convenient it is for some people I tell you.

These days I go to a lot of fights in Birmingham because I have a lot of friends there. I'm also quite tight with Jon Pegg who is Sam Eggington's trainer and runs the Eastside boxing gym there.

Not long ago I went up to Hull to see Tommy Coyle V Luke Campbell and that was very interesting indeed. I went to do a bit of work and a guy on that undercard was Dillion Whyte when they were building him up for the Anthony Joshua fight. I remember feeling psychically sick, as I saw it, the Brazilian, Irineu Beato Costa Junior took a dive in the first round. I'm not saying he would have had a chance against Dillion, but it was clear there was only one outcome. There was no way Dillion was gonna be made to look bad when they were building him up for a PPV with Anthony Joshua.

Eddie Hearn, who in terms is generally good for British boxing as 85-90% of the time Eddie makes the right call because at the end of the day, Eddie knows what he's doing and if you look at the last year that Eddie Hearn wasn't involved in boxing, it was 2011, and British boxing is certainly in a better place now. I still have issues with Eddie over the 10-15% and I've told him this. When Matchroom put up fights that insult my intelligence that gets boring to me. If you ask me do I want to watch Anthony Joshua V Carlos Takam which turned out to me a good fight by the way, or rising star Sam Eggington V Frankie Gavin which was as 50/50 as you can get. In that fight there was one guy on the way up and one on the way down but the one on the way down had all the pedigree in the world and fights like that are about the changing of the guard.

A good friend of mine Ross Minter, well he has started what I regard to be the most competitive boxing league called The Queensbury Boxing League. A great quote from Ross was when he said to me, "Hey Matt, if you've got 2 donkeys against each other it's still a great race". It isn't the best of quality but it's not two guys in a nightclub fighting either and they make a hugely entertaining bout and there's plenty of them I must add. If you get a journeyman with a record of 100 fights, 95 losses but they've only been stopped twice, that tells me they've fought 100 times and only been stopped twice then that tells me they can fight! These are the gatekeepers of the 1-0 or 2-0 prospect and I do enjoy it when the 2-0 prospect loses. What people don't realise is fighters like Peter Buckley who had 300 pro fights and lost most of them boxed for England as an amateur. Delroy Spencer was another losing fighter as a pro but that guy reached ABA titles.

Brain damage is a real price that some people pay in boxing and I'd always encourage fighters to go and get this genetic testing first. For the last twenty years they've been able to do it and you can find out if you're in the 25 percent of heightened risk to develop Parkinson's disease. I think the BBBofC should make everyone have that test before they start a life in boxing. The brain is a very delicate thing, it's not meant to be punched and punched. What I will say is Michael Watson's legacy has been a very positive one as we went 15 years without a fatality. I know that sounds cruel but that in itself is an achievement of sorts. The access to oxygen once a guy's been knocked out, the heightened medical situation is there. Many times, the small hall shows, and small promoters suffer because they still must have two ambulances at the ready even at the smallest of shows, it brings something to it, but these guys should be respected as modern-day gladiators who put their lives on the line for our entertainment.

The three years before BT Sports entered boxing, it was pretty much a monopoly. You had the odd channel 5 show, but Eddie Hearn with Sky Sports was holding all the chips. Eddie Hearn could offer fighters whatever he wanted to offer, and you took it because if you didn't there was plenty of other fighters who wanted to get paid. Hopefully with the emergence of BT this will swing things into the fighter's hands essentially. What I would say now to these young fighter's is don't accept the first offer that comes your way.

When I was still in Cape Town, South Africa I got asked to run an American boxing website which I did for around five years. When I came over to the U.K the gentleman who sleeps about two hours a day I kid you not, who owned the boxing website company was very keen for me to get a foot hold on the same thing in Britain and initially I came over to do that. I came over here for only six months in 2013. At that time, I went straight to Johnny Eames TKO gym in Canning Town. Billy Joe Saunders, Frank Buglioni and Larry Ekundayo used to train there. I saw every aspect of it, I saw guys like Eric Ochieng who was very talented. I saw first-hand how the more talented guys who perhaps couldn't sell as many tickets didn't get the backing that the fighters did who could sell huge amount of tickets. A lot of people associate me closely with Eddie Hearn because they see me doing a lot of interviews with him. I must admit I find the guy fascinating to interview because there's literally not anything that you can't bring up. The guy never avoided a question in his life with me, not like another guy who I won't name but I'm sure you could take a wild guess.

Ambrose Mendy is another guy I'm quite close to and he said that Eddie Hearn has the energy that only comes with youth. Eddie Hearn is far less likely to ban you from going to his press conferences. You'd have to do something pretty bad for him to stop you coming to his press meetings. Eddie Hearn isn't a control freak like some in boxing are. It's a different era now with social media and the likes where people can say almost anything, I myself must be very careful as I've been threatened with legal action a few times, but Eddie isn't like that, he's more "of the time" should we say. Eddie Hearn has more of an attitude that he knows he can't shut down things just because he doesn't like them.

Two years ago, Sky Sports were running away with it, they had everything. Now they face a little competition and a few of Matchroom's fighters have jumped ship due to one thing or another. Boxing isn't about guys like you or I who are the hardcore fans, we're nice to have but we'll be there no matter what because we love the game. These television channels aim for fans who don't know that much, ok they know the Anthony Joshua's, Amir Khan's but they don't know the difference between a fight that costs a lot to put on, or some guy getting paid 5K. These armchair casuals are easily fooled and are 5% of the headache, us hardcore fans provide 95% of the headache.

One interesting scenario to watch closely in the next couple of years is the young London heavyweight called Daniel Dubois. He's already signed with someone, but I remember being at the David Haye/Tony Bellew press conference at the Dorchester and Daniels' dad was there. This was before he'd signed with anyone, his Dad was a lovely guy and I got talking to him. He asked me if he knew his son and I said of course I know who your son is we've heard all the stories of when he was still an amateur. Eddie Hearn that day had all the national newspapers there I mean this was as big as it gets. It was one of them press conferences where you had to apply to even get in to the place. Ambrose Mendy comes along and says to Eddie, "this is Daniel Dubois's father he'd like to have a chat". Eddie Hearn took himself away from the busiest day of his work year to have a coffee with this guy who he didn't know. That's how nice Eddie Hearn is and how he works. The story was from Eddies perspective is that another party offered him X amount of money and Eddie being shrewd said that's great go for it. Eddies thinking probably was that he was going to let someone else build him up and then in 18 months' time when he has his boxing education then he'll end up getting him back, very similar to what he did with the Frank Buglioni story, whether that happens or not remains to be seen. Frank Buglioni is a British champion now for as long as he lasts and Eddies reaping the rewards. I personally can see Buglioni losing his title sooner or later, if you can start at West Ham though and end up at Manchester United, then so be it. These fighters are offered a three-year contract usually so the big fights with Daniel Dubois down the line in five years will benefit Eddie Hearn. Whoever has got him now will only benefit for however long they have him for until there may be a switchover but, in my opinion, I think that will happen.

Let me tell you about Daniel Dubois and the things I've heard about him from very creditable people in the game. I've been told he's laid out Lawrence Okolie at The Peacock and I mean laid out and that he apparently also sparked Anthony Joshua in sparring in his teens. If you think this guy can do that at his age, he's' going to the top. In my opinion he's the biggest danger to Anthony Joshua's dominance in the heavyweight division than anyone else trust me. The guys frightening!

When I meet all these heroes of the boxing world I do get occasionally star struck. All the major PPV fighters have a different aura. I like to setup the first question to let the fighter know I know a little bit about them, for example Tony Bellew, I mentioned to him about his 3 ABA heavyweight title wins as an amateur, not every guy would know that. Stuff like this usually helps to get them onside.

One of my favourite fighters to interview is James Degale and when I first met him I was pretty star struck. I was at James' gym and that guy is 100% the opposite of how he comes across on camera. He's a really nice friendly guy who's very appreciative, likes to fist bump you a lot and make you feel at ease. At the same time James is highly charged especially if you mention his nemesis George Groves. If you're interviewing James, it's best to leave that topic alone. The needle is really that deep don't worry about that, the hostility is real. At the press conference of the second Cleverly v Bellew fight which Degale v Groves were on the undercard of, there apparently were derogatory remarks made by one person to another and it all kicked off and the security that day earned their money.

I've seen many fighters at the beginning who were likable fella's starting out, then they hit 15-0 and become different people. The one most talked about lately in that category is Ohara Davies. He has a lot of C celebrity friends and in my opinion, he shows how you can lose sight of things. I was speaking to Spencer Fearon about this kind of thing lately because he always likes seeing young fighters doing well. Spencer likes to advise them and offers them an ear.

I know Ohara Davies is hard hitting but, in my opinion he's not a greatly skilled fighter, I think he's technically limited and not rhythmically sound. When you get found out and damaged like he did against Josh Taylor last year you need to go back to the drawing board. I think Ohara may have a thing in his head where he's this great thing and really brilliant, perhaps he believes his own hype. He's definitely made a bit of noise though and I think he's tried to make himself a little bit of a brand like the Eubanks. There always seems to be controversy where Ohara Davies is and it's almost like he doesn't just cross the line he does a triple jump over it! He's still only 25 and maybe if he sorts his lack of judgement out he can come back, he's tried to run before he can walk in my opinion and needs to sort himself out before he ruins his career. I know there's a lot of boxing fans who'd pay to see him beat again so he has created interest albeit negative. He needs to focus on his boxing rather than on the loud bang he's trying to make on social media.

There's guys in boxing that go to a thousand press conferences and they say, "I've had the best camp ever der der der der der", but this isn't going to sell the fight! Dude being like Connor McGregor sells fights! He never goes into anything, he's just funny and joking and of course ripping his opponents to bits which is what people want to see. Sometimes though, take for instance Ricky Burns V Anthony Crolla, both lovely guys but that build up was boring to watch because they were both gentlemen. It's OK having one of them but you tend to need a little bit of an Ohara Davies type character in a press conference at times. A typical example of what I'm trying to say is that a friend of mine former British champion Darren Hamilton said to me on watching the build-up between Connor McGregor V Jose Aldo, "I know nothing about UFC, but I want to see that fight now". That build up is how you get 3,000 people to come to the press conference alone.

Considering I wasn't brought up in boxing and it's not in my blood, boxing is very much a way of life for me now. There's been times where I've wanted to walk away from it, but I can't!

Big things will change in boxing on the day that a Steve Goodwin or a Steve Wood, should they choose to, step up and try to stake a claim from being number 3 to number 2, that's when the waters will break. Then again, some promoters are happy where they are doing small hall shows, there not printing money like the other guys but their content. The future of British boxing is purely down to what Eddie Hearn has planned for the next ten years. A lot of fights he can make happen if he wants to he's that powerful. The era of Eubank, Benn, Watson etc that was down to terrestrial significance. If you want to include more fans don't do the PPV fights. At the same time a lot of the fights can only be made because of PPV so it's a catch 22 situation.

Me, personally, I would rather be a 50-year-old Chris Eubank than a 50-year-old James Degale because Chris Eubank fought on ITV for free and the whole of the nation watched him. James Degale on the other hand has fought in big PPV for example, his fight with George Groves in 2011 but that was PPV so if you compare the audience on who'll be most recognised there's no comparison on who'll be more of a household name when they reach midlife. Chris Eubank might have been paid less a lot of times compared to James Degale's where in one night he can earn a huge amount of money. Therefore, the brand Eubank has been hugely successful in his time.

The fact Britain has a genuine number one heavyweight now is great for Matchroom with the PPV'S, but the second that's all over he may have to rethink on it.

I must go on record though and say Eddie Hearn has done amazingly in boxing in such a short space of time. So, what he's capable of in the next ten years, well the sky's the limit. The thing with Eddie Hearn that sets him aside from every promoter I've ever read about is that he's the only one that I can sit down and listen to and he can analyse a fight or fighters, and you know this guy's watching! This guy understands about the actual fighting side of it. It isn't a business to Eddie Hearn it's more of a way of life, you could see that when he ran in the ring prematurely when Carl Froch stopped Lucian Bute. You could see that on his face when Eddie ran in the ring when Tony Bellew beat David Haye. Eddie Hearn would be in profit if all he did all day was bet on boxing. Whereas the other guys have been generally ambitious, genuinely come from nothing and have speculated to make something of themselves. Eddie Hearn is a guy who, from the age of 8 years old, spent every day at his Dads gym around fighters because he wanted to. He was already a wealthy kid so he's choosing to take this path, where others have had to do it to make something of themselves. Eddie is completely obsessed about boxing and from the age of 8 he could recite the record of any fighters around at the time. Don't forget it was his old man Barry Hearn who brought Chris Eubank and the razzmatazz of the 90s to our screens. Eddie as a little boy was exposed to this. Eddie Hearn was actually an amateur boxer himself and he had 3 contests winning all 3.

Boxing can be very intoxicating, it can be very addictive it can be very antagonistic. I would say especially for guys with kids and a family, they must look beyond that and think about their health first.

It's 100 times better to retire one fight too early than one fight too late. There's too many stories of guys going into a fight not 100%. When I say this, I'm thinking of Mike Towell and Nick Blackwell because these guys had persistent headaches beforehand that they would never have admitted to and it's lead to catastrophic consequences. If you look at the Nick Blackwell situation it proves it was an addiction because even after they took his licence away and the guy nearly lost his life, the guy was back in gyms again sparring. I'm saying you've got to think of your wife and kids that are involved you must look beyond boxing. The true question is, can you put them before you?

Boxing now, compared to the 1930s, there is a very small percentage of people doing it and the people who want to do it, well not everyone can deal with the elite no matter how much you love the sport. Boxing is a hurt business it's always been the hurt business so when I see fighters like James Degale or Darren Hamilton who are very good defensively, they are in the minority. Guys these days are less patient, so you get these that just go out and want to smash you up sort of like your Mike Tyson type, well we live in a world that's getting less and less patient. Any damage to your brain isn't good so put your health and family first.

If anyone wants to contact Matt and talk shop you can do on Twitter @matthamiltonLTD or his web page thekingmaker.me

"Someday I will have nothing left to lose. I can't wait".

Frank Warren

Alan Temple

I first heard of the name 'Alan Temple' around the early 90s. The reason being was that he lived 12 miles from where I grew up and was in the local papers quite a bit. He was the best lightweight in the amateurs Britain had.

I wanted to add Alan to this book for the very same reason I added my close friend Andrew Buchanan. That reason being that he was living proof that you can be the best amateur boxer around, but once you turn pro that guarantees you nothing! It's a complete whole new ball game.

Alan literally fought the best around in the lightweight and light-welterweight divisions British boxing had to offer. To say he was matched easy is like saying Adolf Hitler was a "little naughty". Alan was the perfect example of your model pro in how he lived, and certainly never turned a fight down regardless of which champion he was matched against.

It was an absolute pleasure to catch up with Alan and talk to him about his fighting days. Alan is the second "Monkey Hanger" in this book after Richy Horsley. It's a term for the lovely folk of Hartlepool.

Alan told me: -

"I'm 45 years old now and I reside in Seaton Carew near Hartlepool.

My first memory of boxing is back in the summer of 1984 when I was 11 going on 12. I went along to the Hartlepool Boys Welfare ABC. I'd recently moved from one end of the town to closer to the gym, this was down to my parents getting divorced, it meant I also had to change schools. It was my Mother that took me to a youth club type of thing and while I was in there I would hear all the commotion that a boxing clubs makes. All this noise made me have a wander in, just being a curious kid, I suppose.

That night I had a mess around on the bag and the coach must have seen me because he came up to me and asked if I fancy giving it a bit of a go? He asked me to bring a few of my mates and the next night I went down and that was me in boxing from there on really.

I had my first bout when I was 12 in March 1985. I was quite a quick learner taking to boxing. There was a fantastic number of talented lads in the gym at the time such as John Kelly, Chris Hubert and Kevin McKenzie. I would watch these guys with great interest and pick up little bits from their styles to put into mine.

I went on to have around 80 contests as an amateur boxer. I should have had a lot more but towards the end of my amateur days I only boxed in the ABA'S and for England. I just couldn't get matched in the club shows because I was No.1 in the country. I lost around 16-17 of my bouts and most of them were as a junior. I won the NABC class C in 1991. The year after I won the ABA'S at featherweight in 1992 beating Repton's Mark Ward. In 1993 I got beat in the semis to Edinburgh's Bradley Welsh and in 1994 I won the ABA'S again at light-welterweight beating R Edwards from St. Patricks ABC.

I didn't do anything in the schoolboys, the reason being I couldn't get past a young kid called Paul Ingle from Scarborough. Paul beat me twice and to be honest he was just levels above anyone our age. He beat everybody around and it just so happens he was my age and in my weight category. I was certainly a better senior boxer than

I was junior put it that way. I beat Stephen Smith from Repton ABC in the amateurs, he wasn't a bad fighter. Another Repton fighter I beat was Marlon Ward, big things were expected of him. Richie Edwards was another London lad I beat, he tragically ended up taking his own life. I beat Georgie Smith from Basildon also, he went on to become a decent pro himself.

I got selected to box in the Commonwealth games in 1994 but I'd already moved up to light-welter along with Peter Richardson from Middlesbrough who was a good friend of mine. He'd just come back from his injury as he'd been stabbed at a late-night blues party in Middlesbrough. Unfortunately for me, the space at light-welter went to Peter instead of me, I was pushed out if you like. Peter went on to win the gold that year, so it was obviously the right choice. There was an option for me to be part of the England team, but it was at lightweight which was 9st 7lbs, but I could no longer make that safely anymore.

I thought now was the right time to give the pro's a bash. I had a lot going for me at the time, I mean I was a double ABA champion and I'd boxed for England several times, so I turned over and it was the right time there's no doubt about it. Me and my coach at the time, Peter Cope, decided we were going have a look around to see what deal we could get. In 1994 our first port of call was to see Mickey Duff and Terry Lawless in Mickey's office in London. Meeting Mickey Duff was an experience in itself can I just say. As I was walking up the stairs to his office Lloyd Honeyghan was coming out. Now, I was only 21 and very much an impressionable kid a little bit star-struck. I was very naïve going in there with an old shark like Mickey Duff who'd been around in boxing forever. To be quite honest me and Peter wanted a signing on fee and went in there very much cap in hand if you like. Mickey was so dry and so straight, he just sat back in his chair and he asked if I'd brought any videos for him to watch! Looking back, I was really ill prepared for that meeting. He told me he wasn't going to offer me a signing on fee, then he pointed up to a plaque on the wall above mine and Peters heads. When I turned around there was this picture of all the stars he'd had such as John L Gardner, Jim Watt, Charlie Magri, John Conteh and Frank Bruno etc... He then said, "Listen, I don't have to prove myself I'm the best manager about, I'm willing to sign you up but there's no signing on fee boy" and that was that. I was a bit surprised with it all because he was pretty ruthless. Luckily for us we had a meeting with Frank Maloney later that day. I met him later in the afternoon and Frank was the exact opposite to Mickey Duff, he was just chucking money at us left, right and centre. Frank Maloney was the man at the time because he had a prime Lennox Lewis who was world champion. Frank also had Middlesbrough's Peter Richardson, so he must have been well aware of who I was. He also had Paul Ingle from Scarborough and Alan Hall from Durham. Frank threw money on the table for me and said he'd give me so much a fight and this was music to our ears. We went away very happy and I signed with Frank that day.

When I became a professional fighter I quickly realised it's a very different game to what I'd been used to. You've got guys in front of you who are just raw and want to have a go at you. For the last 5 or 6 years as an amateur I'd been up against the top European kids! Now, all of a sudden as a pro it's as if you're going down in class. However, what I will say is these guys I fought in my early pro days don't give a shite! All they want to do is take your head off and get a bit of money. If that win was by an elbow or head butt etc so be it these guys who are hardened journeymen if you like don't give a fuck.

The first guy I fought was at The York Hall in Bethnal Green in September 1994 against Stevie "Thunder" Bolt.

The fella wasn't the best, in fact he'd only had 6 amateur fights and this was his first pro fight. He was well over 6ft tall and like a beanpole. Obviously, the expectation on my shoulders going into that fight was great. I had a good 30-40 who'd made the journey from the North East and the fight was live on Wire TV. Stevie Bolt came at me with no style at all, very rigid. You could see he was pent up and wanted to spoil the party and he almost did because he put me down in the first round. I was coming off the ropes and he sort of just stuck his hand out and I ran into it like Road Runner "MEEP MEEP..." I found myself on the floor and this definitely wasn't in the script. I got up and finished the round. I come out for the second and by this time the crowd were finding it highly amusing because Bolt was throwing shots from everywhere trying to get lucky once again. Luckily enough I put him down in the second round and the ref stopped the fight. It wasn't the greatest of starts you know.

I would have three fights with Frank Maloney and three wins. In my fourth fight I was supposed to be on the undercard of the Lennox Lewis V Oliver McCall bill at Wembley Arena. How it turned out is that Frank put all the London lads on first and any leftovers were put on at The York Hall the following week. Of course, people know the outcome to Lennox Lewis V Oliver McCall and Lewis was knocked out in two rounds. Lennox Lewis losing totally made Frank Maloney's stable of fighters go tits up! All the money Frank had splashed out on myself, Peter Richardson and Paul Ingle was now a great strain on Frank's business plans. Basically, after I had had 3 steady wins, I boxed a kid called Everald Williams. What Frank had to do now was match all his own fighters up, which made sense in a business way. Everald Williams was a London guy and I boxed him yet again at The York Hall. This was still when the half point system was in, I thought I beat him 4 rounds out of 6 to be honest but they give it to

Williams by half a point which was a hard one to take. It was a really bitter pill to swallow to get that first loss on my record by half a point.

After that loss that's when everything changed because Gus Robinson approached Frank Maloney. Both were quite pally anyway through Dean Powell. Dean had been close with John Westgarth who Gus had a lot to do with back in the day. I spoke to Dean on the phone over it and he advised me to change over and go with Gus. At the time I didn't fancy it because Gus Robinson wasn't really the big time in boxing no disrespect, he was more of a small hall show promoter. Gus, I think knew what my thoughts were and what he did to win my confidence was give me a job outside of boxing. Funnily enough I still work for the company to this day. Gus Robinson gave me the security, basically what any other promoter/manager couldn't.

From September 1995 I turned pro with Gus Robinson and my first fight was at the famous Borough Hall in Hartlepool. I was to take on a guy called Kevin McKillan from Manchester. He was a decent enough kid as he'd been in with some good fighters and I got the victory over him on points in a 6 rounder. That was me back onto winning ways.

Gus co-promoted a couple of shows at Newcastle Arena in 1996. The first one was Nigel Benn Vs Sugar Boy Malinga in the March. I beat Hull's Tony Foster on the undercard. In the next show I fought County Durham's Micky Hall on the undercard of Naseem Hamed Vs Daniel Alicea. I stopped Micky due to a cut over his right eye. From there I travelled to Scotland to take on the unbeaten Scott Dixon from Hamilton. I lost the fight on points but it was a bad decision. I'm not being sour because Scott went on to become the Commonwealth champion, but it was definitely a hometown decision. I had to put it behind me, at the end of the day you go to Scotland and you know you've got to knock them out to salvage a draw. After the fight Scottish boxer Gary Jacobs came over to me and told me that in his opinion I had won the fight, which was nice of him.

Alan Hodgson the referee was in my lift after the show, I asked him what fucking fight had he been watching because he scored the cards, it wasn't on the judge's scorecards. He told me I was ducking too low and he hadn't liked it. I told him it didn't matter what I was doing as long as he hadn't taken points off me which he hadn't, he couldn't count it. Yet again I had lost a fight by half a point.

Billy Schwer when I was an amateur was someone I looked up to. I used to watch him and dream of even sharing the ring with such a fighter. I remember working in the pub at the time, I used to run Gus Robinsons pub for a year or two when I first joined up with him. So, I got a phone call off Gus telling me he's had an offer from Mickey Duff for me to fight Billy Schwer. Immediately I jumped at it and screamed yes down the phone at him, this was something I was never going to refuse. "Are you sure you want this Alan?" Gus said. I'd only had 9 fights at the time and Billy had been British, Commonwealth, European and been over to Las Vegas to box Mexican Rafael Ruelas and only been stopped on cuts. Without doubt Billy Schwer was world class 100%. I took the fight and that was that, so I was training away, until we got another call from Mickey Duff telling me he doesn't want the fight. Gus told me to stay in the gym and tick over, almost like he had a sixth sense. Sure, enough a fortnight later it came, Mickey Duff calls up saying the fights on. This is boxing and it happens all the time these sneaky tricks go on. Luckily for me I'd been in the gym 8-9 weeks at the time. Mickey Duff must have thought I was going to drink beer for the fortnight, but I lived in the gym, always did do as a pro fighter. 12 years I dedicated my life to professional boxing, so I wasn't going to get caught out napping by that crafty old Devil.

My fight with Billy itself was a very close call over 8 rounds. I lost by one point to a world class operator so that gave me huge confidence, especially as the Boxing News' write up said "Temple will get stopped in 4 rounds, Schwer is a different class all together". I was a huge underdog but there were times in the fight where I was backing Schwer up. After 4-5 rounds I started thinking when is this going to turnaround! This guy in front of me had been spoken of so highly in the boxing fraternity for so many years I couldn't quite believe it. Of course, things were going too smoothly and of course Billy upped his game in the 7th and put me down, so it was that knock down that lost me the fight. Mark Green who reffed it told me afterwards "If you hadn't of gone down in the 7th round I'd have given you a draw". Dennie Machini in his corner gave me a wink after the fight as if to say you did really well there lad.

The people around ringside never expected a performance from me like that, it was a great fight. To be quite honest that loss didn't do me any harm whatsoever and it actually brought me a British title eliminator facing Glasgow's Tanveer Ahmed in a 12-round fight at the Kelvin Hall, Glasgow. The fight itself was a complete war! I had him almost out in the second round. By that time, I was being trained by George Bowes before Peter Cope re-joined and got me back to my boxing. So, George was training me, and he was one of them trainers that expected you to be very brave. He demanded I get stuck in and have a tear up which wasn't really me in truth. I ended up losing the fight in the 8th but that was a hell of a spectacle for the boxing fans there and it was fight of the night.

Next up I was to come up against Bobby Vanzie from Bradford in another British title eliminator in Seaham. I had Bobby on the floor in the first round, then he put me down in the third and finished me off. Before the fight I was looking at Bobby and thinking fucking hell this fella's massive at the weight, he had a huge physique. I'm not making any excuses but when I took the Vanzie fight I'd had a full year off, barring a day. To have a year off then go into a British title eliminator after having a British title eliminator was pretty tough for anyone in boxing. My attitude at the time was that I had to take these opportunities with both hands.

Another loss followed in 2 rounds against London's Michael Ayers which took me to 3 losses by KO. I managed to turn the corner with wins over Alan Bosworth and Ivan Walker, I had to get up off the floor in the 6th against Bosworth to win. After my back to back wins I was put in with the highly rated unbeaten scouser David Burke. Burke had represented Great Britain in the 1996 Olympics in Atlanta, Georgia but I lost the fight 72-79 so I was well beaten. I was still fighting under the George Bowes style which as I mentioned earlier didn't suit my style at all. I'm not blaming anyone as I took the fight. In the fight itself David Burke was a clever boxer and I must have gone down 4-5 times in the contest. It wasn't much fun for me being in there, but it must have been great for the fans to watch on the safe side of the ropes.

Even though I had a fair few losses in my career it never seemed to affect my career because although I would lose, I would lose very graciously and next up for me was an opportunity to take on the current British champion at the time West Ham's Jason Rowland. Jason had been out for a bit and he basically took me on as a bit of a warm up fight over 8 rounds. Before I was about to go out and face

Jason his team came in my dressing room and said will you take it over 6 for the same money? I said yeah fine let's just fight and I lost on points. Maybe I shot myself in the foot because I lost to Jason by one point. In the fight there was a point where I knocked Jason down with a jab, but the ref never classed it as a knockdown. At the back end of the fight Jason went on to put me down. I've seen Jason over the years many times going down to London and he told me he and his team were sweating in the corner. His corner told him he hadn't done enough to win.

One of the funniest stories of my career was travelling over to fight Eamon Magee for the Irish title... even though I'm not Irish! I'd say taking on Eamon was my hardest fight. That man was utterly ferocious, absolutely ruthless and he was the only guy who ever knocked me clean out ever. Eamon Magee was the first one to put Ricky Hatton on his arse and he lived up to his nickname which was 'The Terminator'. Believe it or not but I was beating him over 3 rounds, but you could see he was just waiting and biding his time. It was a very cagey contest with us both being southpaws. After the first round Eamon's nose was bleeding as I'd been catching him with some good solid jabs. After the second round I got back to the corner and Peter Cope said to me, "Alan that's fantastic you're doing brilliantly he hasn't laid a glove on you". What I said exactly to that was "you better keep a fucking eye on the ref because somebody has". Eamon caught me flush right on the last second of the third round, we actually caught each other at the same time but his left hook knocked me out before I hit the deck then he finished me off with a massive right hook on the way down for good measure. It was like something out of Mortal Kombat. I hate to say it, but it got voted one of the best knockouts of 1999. To further humiliate me when I was down Eamon stood over me and done a bit of an Irish jig and spat on the floor. I thought what an arrogant bastard when I was told what he'd done. After the fight Eamon Magee was a gentleman and we've come across each other over the years, even though he can be a bit of a nuisance when he's had a drink Eamon's a right character and his trainer John Breen are good people.

The late Gus Robinson was a character himself and before the fight he said to me, "You've got a bit of Irish in ya haven't ya Alan"! He knew I was related to the Linighans who were footballers David and Andy were my first cousins. So, I said "yes I have". Now, Gus before the Eamon Magee fight was making this big thing of how Irish I am, so the fight could be for the BUI Ireland title. Before we flew over there he asked me to bring my I.D which proved that I had a hint of Irish about me if you like. I never thought anything of it and just did as he told me to, but I certainly didn't think I was Irish or was even going to box for any Irish titles. The fight was made at 10st and that was a little bit big for me in all honesty. Getting there Gus made a big thing of wanting to see Eamon Magee on the scales. What happened was our plane from Liverpool to Belfast was delayed by an hour so when we got there Eamon's already been on the scales and he's stood there smiling with a sandwich in his hand and a bottle of pop. So, as I'm getting on the scales the officials are saying how much of a proud Irish man I was. Gus must have given them some story and the Irish belt was already there for this title. I'm thinking this has to be some fucking joke because I've never been Irish. Frank Maloney was stood there laughing, he was in on it with Gus, laughing like schoolboys they were. I'd been well put on the spot by this time. Up until then really I'd had no idea this was going to be for the Irish title because I'm not fucking Irish. After the fight when Eamon had knocked me out, the ref put his hand up to "and the new Irish champion". Even to this day on BoxRec it says it was for the Irish title.

From my "Irish title" loss I went on to beat Steve McLevy from Glasgow by TKO in 6 rounds. Steve was a really good Scottish fighter and he was knocking them all out. He was supposed to be facing Tanveer Ahmed put he pulled out, so I got the call to go up to Glasgow again at 3 days notice to step in. The fight itself was one-way traffic and he was pretty cut up and he couldn't continue.

I went on to beat the useful former British champion Wayne Rigby after that which led me to face world class operator Souleymane M'baye known as 'The Sensation'. He was unbeaten going into the fight and tipped to be a world star but without a doubt I'd trained to beat him. I have taken on some of the elite in boxing around in my time and on every occasion, I went in to win. Before the fight one of the pundits described me as a bit of a journeyman and maybe my losses can vouch for that, what I will say is I never had that journeyman mentality where you see these Polish taxi drivers taking knees for fun. I went over to Spain to beat Souleymane M'baye and if I did lose at least he was going to know he'd been in a fucking fight. M'baye before he took up boxing was a former French kickboxing champion and you could tell i.e. he had a very wide stance. In that fight it was the first time Peter Cope wasn't in my corner in some capacity since he joined my team. That night I had Gus Robinson in there with me. Gus was nice and calm and knew what he was talking about. I could see M'baye was getting frustrated and waiting for the big shots very much like the Eamon Magee fight. M'baye couldn't handle my southpaw stance he was really struggling with it. By the end of the 6th I was 2 rounds up and even Steve Holdsworth who was commentating on Eurosport was giving us most of the rounds. If you watch that fight on YouTube, you can see M'baye deliberately stuck the nut on me at the end of the 7th which opened up the tiniest of cuts above my left eye. Gus tried everything in the corner and we only had one more round to go and we could have battled through it. That was until the referee came over and had a look, squeezed it a bit to see if any blood come out. Nothing came out and you can clearly see that on the video but he waved his hands and stopped the fucking fight! It was absolutely disgusting! Whether or not I'd have got the decision away over in Spain I don't know, but to stop the fight going into the last round I thought was appalling. He went on to go and win the WBA title.

Another title loss came after the M'baye fight when I was beaten by the unbeaten Essex boy Steve Murray for the IBF Inter-Continental lightweight title in 2 rounds by a TKO.

That brought me to another top fighter at the time in Norwich's Jon Thaxton on the Ricky Hatton V Tony Pep bill at the Wembley Conference Centre March 2001. I'm going to try not to be disrespectful to Jon because he's a top lad, but he wasn't the hardest person to catch. Jon was so gung-ho and in your face that he often left himself in range. The fight itself was a bit of an insult to both of us because it was only a 4 rounder and it was initially going to be an 8-round fight. Frank Maloney was trying to keep the taxman away by keeping things at low purses. The fight just wasn't long enough for me to get a win and Jon took the decision 39-37. Frank told me afterwards he thought I could have got it so that was another one of my 20 losses that could have ended up either way.

A month later I took on the decent Gary Hibbert from Oldham. Gary had fought for the Commonwealth title, so he was obviously a championship level fighter and I beat him on points over 6 rounds.

Then I was to come up against a fighter in the form of his life and that was Junior 'The Hitter' Witter and after his loss against Zab Judah in April 2000 at Hampden Park, he went on a 21-fight unbeaten streak. I took the fight with Junior over 6 rounds and I have to say in all my career he was the hardest to lay a glove on. He was so clever on his feet. I was known to be clever on my toes, but Junior was really nifty, he picked his shots well. He wasn't a devastating puncher he was more of a thudder. His gym, the Ingle camp, were all limbo dancers, so hard to hit and he wasn't any different. Junior put me down in the 5th round, I got up at 4 but the ref waved it off. I was a mile behind, so I can say the right decision was made.

I would lose my next fight to WBU champ Colin Dunne in the 7th which led me to having a rematch with Gary Hibbert who I'd beaten the year before. This time Gary Hibbert was a different fighter to the one I'd beaten quite comfortably. In the first fight he gave me too much room and allowed me to do what I wanted to do. In the rematch the guy did a demolition job on me plain and simple. He flattened me 2 minutes into the first round so I can't complain. To be quite honest he caught me in the first 10 seconds of the fight and it could have been over then which would have been embarrassing. He bullied me and pushed me around and I lost to the better man.

I wouldn't fight again for 6 months and when I did I took the fight at 2 days notice against Leo O'Reilly from London. O'Reilly was unbeaten in 11 and spoken about very highly around the boxing scene he was one of Barry Hearn's young guns. I was simply being used as a trial horse a bit of a test for the lad before he went on to better things. Leo's style was made for me he was just an aggressive come forward fighter. If he had any boxing skills he didn't show many of them that night. He was continually trying to take me out with the big right hands and I found him easily enough to read. The fight itself was stopped due to 2 bad cuts he received. One from a bad clash of heads and one from just my jab. If it would have went the full 8 I'd have beaten him anyway because I was ahead by quite a bit. He was just made for me very much like Wayne Rigby. When I beat Wayne Rigby he was using me as a warm up fight for his IBO challenge against Michael Ayers, but that was one of my easiest fights, no disrespect he was just a big strong come forward type and I always relished them fighters.

I would then lose to Darren Melville on points then I beat Silence Saheed due to him punching me when I was down, so I got the win by DQ which isn't ideal. No boxer really wants to win like that I know I certainly didn't.

I would go on to face my old foe David Burke yet again to lose inside 4 rounds by TKO. My career was very up and down, and you can see from my record that was I never really hit a winning streak. I found it hard to sustain a winning run but of course I was matched with the top guys fight in fight out so of course it's always going to be a hard one.

One guy I did beat who was a bit of a legend was Birmingham's Peter Buckley. That guy went to have 300 professional fights which is quite remarkable, and he boxed for England as an amateur, people won't realise this from just looking at his record.

You've heard some of the people I shared the ring with but facing Ricky Burns who is a 3-weight world champion and sharing the ring with him was a real honour. I took Ricky on in another short notice job in Glasgow. When I fought Ricky, he was 12-0 and he'd just beaten Luton's Graham Earl which was a great scalp to have at that stage of his career. I'd asked Frank Maloney many times for the Earl fight because he was looking after him, but they didn't want it. I would lose to Ricky over 4 rounds 37-38 and that was a close fight again.

It was a funny situation before the fight because I saw Ricky at the weigh in and he asked me who I was fighting, I told him "you"! Dean Powell was the matchmaker at the time and Ricky wasn't happy at all. He told me there must be some mistake and off he went to have a word with Dean Powell. I'm not saying Ricky was scared but he wasn't happy I could tell that. He told me he's wasn't fighting me and off he went to speak with his team. By this time, I'd been on the scales so if they didn't want the fight I'd done my job and I was getting paid regardless. After what was a bit of a discussion Frank Maloney came up to me to tell me the fights still going ahead as planned. The fight was in Edinburgh on the undercard of Alex Arthur's bill. I accepted Ricky was going to get it if it was close and that's what happened.

One of my best victories came after the loss to Ricky and that came against Stokes former English champion Scott Lawton. Scott was quite a nice technical boxer and it was more or less on his own turf, he was expected to go on and brush me aside quite easily, but I beat him reasonably comfortably.

My last ever professional fight was against my old mucker Jon Thaxton and it wasn't to be a 4 rounder like the first one. This was scheduled for 8 rounds which I was happy with. This fight was the same as my second fight against Gary Hibbert, meaning he'd learned from his mistakes. What I should have learnt in my career was never face anybody twice(Alan laughs). Jon had done his homework and he stopped me in 5 rounds. Jon told me afterwards he didn't want the return fight he didn't want to see me in a boxing ring again after the first time. Jon Thaxton told John Ingle his matchmaker, "whatever you do, don't get me Alan

Temple again". It actually says this in someone's book, but I can't recall whose. John Ingle went back to him and said we've got you Alan Temple Jon, we couldn't get you anyone else. After the fight Jon Thaxton said he was glad to put his demons to bed because I'd been a little bit of a bogeyman for him. Jon Thaxton was definitely a better fighter by far in the return bout. I hit him with everything that night, I did think I was going to beat him because the first fight was so close. I did make my mind up that night that if I lost that was going to be me out of the game, I was 33years old at the time.

Looking back on my boxing career I don't have any regrets at all. If you're going to ask me who the best I ever faced in a pro boxing ring was I'd have to say Billy Schwer. As an amateur Andy Green from Middlesbrough's Phil Thomas School of Boxing must be up there. I beat him in the finals of the North East ABA'S. Then the next year he went on to win it down in the lightweight division. I become great mates with Andy and I'd like to give him a mention. Also, Steven Smith from the Repton and Basildon's Georgie Smith deserve a mention and the Scottish kid who beat me Bradley Welsh were all up there as my hardest amateur fights.

I'm still heavily involved in boxing. Since Gus Robinson passed away in 2011 I took over his licence and for the last 5-6 years I've looked after a couple of the fighters. I train the lads alongside Peter Cope and I'm in the gym 3-4 times a week. It's never going to be what it was when I was competing. I don't walk about shadow boxing like I did as a kid it's all gone. Besides I don't think I took that many punches to be walking about shadow boxing these days (Alan laughs)

Hartlepool has always been a little hotbed for boxing its part of the history going back to Teddy Gardner in the

1950s. There's always been a right good few amateur boxing clubs in the town. Of course, Hartlepool is a working-class town and it brings along tough kids. We're not the best footballing town but we're not bad in the auld art of pugilism shall I say. I won two ABA titles so did Michael Hunter, Kevin Bennett and Ian Cooper won one. I hope the town carries on the tradition for many years to come yet.

"This boxer is doing what is expected of him, bleeding from his nose".

Harry Carpenter

Dominic Negus

Thinking back to a quote boxing royalty Mickey Vann said to me in one of my other books, "Boxing needs characters". Well they don't come more colourful than East End hardman Dominic Negus.

I was first made aware of Dominic around 2002 before he was to face the unbeaten Olympic gold medallist Audley Harrison in that summer. Watching Dominic in the build up to that fight it was impossible not to like him. Like Kevin Mitchell and Matthew Burke, he is another seriously Cock-er-ney geezer and he has the gift of the gab as well as an infectious sense of humour.

Many years later the BBC showed a fly on the wall documentary on Dominic's life around 2005 which I watched a few times. This was very much in the same style as the cult classic Paul Sykes At Large, I also bought his book 'Out of The Shadows' which was published in 2007, Roy Shaw wrote the forward to Dominic's book.

I don't mind admitting I was hugely intrigued with Dominic and would often Google the guy from time to time to see how he was getting on in his life away from boxing.

In 2008 Dominic also featured on Danny Dyers Deadliest Men in which he was seen telling the East End Cockney wide boy Danny about the time when a gang of hoodlums broke into his gym in balaclava's and armed with axes shouting "DOMINIC" and then attempted to murder him. I found it so interesting that Dominic told Danny Dyer if he knew who those men were he'd shake their hands as that was the wakeup call for him to change his life.

Over the years when you watch all these top press conferences or weigh ins in boxing, when it gets heated and the fighters are on the verge of kicking off, the rather imposing figure keeping them apart with a cheeky grin in Dominic. One such incidence off the top of my head was Tony Bellew's "LETS DO IT NOW YA FUCKING RAT", episode at a conference with Nathan Cleverly, it was only stopped by Dominic and his band of merry men. I remember Steve Bunce on his show The Bunce Hour saying, "Often fighters start it and Dom and the boys finish it". I actually bumped into Dominic and had a chat with him at the Ricky Burns/Kevin Mitchell weigh-in in Glasgow 2012. I found him a jovial down to earth guy and I asked him about his bout which really brought him to the public eye in the first place with Audley Harrison. I also interviewed Dominic for Sykes – Unfinished Agony as there were a lot of similarities with the way Dominic once led his life to how Paul Sykes had let his i.e. debt collecting/Neanderthal behaviour.

Dominic does have an extremely good sense of humour and he's very good with his one liners. The one that sticks in my head from my Sykes book is, "If you wanted a row you'd want people like me and Paul Sykes by your side. If you wanted a nice party with nice people you'd keep us under the stairs".   I'm sure when you go on to read Dominic's chapter there's another couple in there that will bring a smile to your face whilst you're reading this.
I caught up with Dominic and I asked him how he first developed an interest in the world of boxing and what he's doing now. Dominic said:

I'm 47 years of age now and I was born in Bethnal Green, but I was brought up in Woodford Green, Essex so we were quite lucky really. Dad worked on the print and with the Times newspaper all his life.

My Dad used to wake me up in the early hours to listen to fights like Marvin Hagler on the radio. I was always interested in boxing from the early 80's and one of my hero's growing up was Leicester's Tony Sibson. My Dad was my hero and he did a bit of boxing in the army. That was where I got earnt my respect from my Dad in the end when I won the Southern Area title as a boxer myself. My Dad wasn't the kind of fella who'd dish out compliments, but I remember the next day my Dad went to Clapton with the belt in the bag proud as punch. When I would give him a cuddle and say I love you Dad he'd kind of just shake it off and say get off soppy bollocks. My old man was very old fashioned and if you ever showed him love he'd hit you sort of thing in a playful manner. The boxing brought me and my Dad very close in the end and he was like my best mate.

As an 11-year-old boy I went along to the boxing gym to make my old man proud of me. I was a little fat kid who looked like the Milky Bar Kid, jam jar glasses and I got a punch in the mouth and decided boxing wasn't for me. To be quite honest as a boy I just wanted to sit at home and watch the telly and that was me with boxing finished till I was about 19. I did look up to the likes of Roy Shaw and Lenny McLean growing up that was my thing, them guys were utter monsters in a fighting sense, I sometimes think how was I ever going to be any different to how I became to be when the people I grew up looking up to were Roy Shaw and Lenny McLean. I was never going to become a dressmaker, was I?!

I'd say I was destined for doom from a young age and that was nothing to do with my Mum and Dad because they were the two best people in the world. Me and my brother were so fucking lucky to have had the parents we had, and I still miss them fucking dearly even now. The only reason I'd say I even went near a boxing gym again was because

I used to do door work. Before I started boxing I knew I was a game fucker and I could have a fight but boxing of course was only going to do me the world of good in my line of work. I started doing the doors with proper fella's like Terry O'Neill and John Camp in a company called Top Guard. Terry O'Neill who lives in Australia now said to me, "Dom you're wasted here on the doors, you need to get back into taking up boxing properly".

I didn't really start competing as an amateur until I was 20. At the time all I wanted to do was fight, I loved fighting. So many people who I boxed with as a young teenager ended up in prison. I was doing the boxing to stay in shape for the door work. Back in the early days I was working in some shithole nightclubs and in them places you were scrapping quite a bit so boxing added to my arsenal for my security work. When I got to about 24 I won the North East division. I ended up getting to the London semi-finals and I got beat by Rick Clark on points. The next year in 1995 I went on to beat West Ham's Stevie Lukas and Repton's Everton Crawford in the North East division. For a kid like me boxing out of the Five Star gym beating the fighters from the calibre of places like west Ham and Repton was a great achievement. I was to knock Lukas out in the last round and Crawford I beat him in Bethnal Green unanimous. You had to beat a kid well when you were taking on a Repton fighter it's a little bit like a fighter going to Germany it's very hard to get a decision.

My amateur career was nothing to rave about compared to some fighters, but I did win two England vests. I also boxed for London versus the RAF. A name people will know of who I beat as an amateur was Billy Bessey. Billy was a great fighter and his brother Chris was a bit of an amateur boxing legend winning six ABA titles. Me and Billy were one a piece in the amateurs, he beat me once at Finchley's show and I gained revenge in my second from last fight in the amateurs when Billy was boxing for the army.

In total overall in the amateurs I had 35 contests winning 27 of those. My most defining moment in the unpaid code would have to be against a fella from Barking called Marcus Lee. Marcus had already beaten me twice but then he'd moved on to the Repton ABC. You could say Marcus had been my bogeyman and in my last amateur fight the chance of redemption came around when I was to face him once more. Well you know what, that's the only amateur fight I promise you I trained for. I know that sounds bloody bad, but I never took the amateurs seriously. It was only to polish my tools of the trade for the security work. Well I really bloody put myself through a proper regime because I had a bee in my bonnet about him. Of course, he'd beaten me twice, but both were way of a split decision. In the build up for that fight I'd done all my training with British title challenger Mark Potter who of course was in the same gym as me. I gave myself a great camp and I went out there and knocked Marcus out in the second round and it was the easiest fight I'd ever had. That day I learnt the difference between being a fighter and being a trained fighter! When the Marcus Lee 3rd fight was in the pipeline I wanted to turn pro, but I told my coach if I can't beat Marcus Lee I'm not turning pro because I'm not good enough. When I went on to do a proper number on him it made me realise I was bloody good enough and I started to believe in myself a bit more. I did so much sparring with Brighton's Scott Welch. I consider Scott one of my very good friends but he's probably one of the most spiteful people you could ever meet in the ring. Outside the ring you couldn't meet a nicer bloke, but he taught me so much. He showed me that when you get in that ring it's a business and we're not mates, doesn't matter if you're fighting your Mother. Once the bell goes it's over and you leave it in the ring, go have a laugh and a cup of tea.

I turned pro in September 1996 with Frank Maloney (now Kellie). I had a good start to the pro's winning my first five contests. I'd earned a shot at the BBBofC Southern Area Cruiserweight title against Tottenham's Chris Henry at Grundy Park Leisure Centre. We were the only contest on the bill and it was a cracking fight. I knocked poor Chris out in the 10th and final round and he suffered a blood clot because of our fight. I don't care what people say, you can be the hardest fucker out there but when you're involved in something like that, it does mess about with your head a little bit. Afterwards I sparred with Harry Senior, Lennox Lewis and Garry Delaney and it was really strange. Even the next fight after mine and Chris' fight in the draw with Birmingham's Trevor Small it took me a few rounds to get going because it was in the back of my head is it going to happen again? I had to really ask questions of myself, am I gonna be a fighter or not! You've got to accept that things like this can happen, but we are in the fight game and time to time this does happen.

I gathered myself and my thoughts together and put the little box of troublesome thoughts away. Besides, what else was I gonna do! Fighting was all I knew, and it had to be done.

I had a KO victory in six over Kostiantyn Okhrei which got me back on the horse then next up I was against the hard-punching Bruce Scott who I lost my title to in the 9th round. It was only my 9th contest compared to the vastly experienced Bruce Scott. I was a young lad with an attitude of 'I don't give a fuck I'll fight anyone'. Going into the fight he'd had more KO'S than I'd had fights, the geezer could punch like fuck. Talking about my career now looking back in hindsight, we should have swerved that one. I was very green in the pro's and still a baby but of course I knew better. Before Bruce stopped me in the 9th it was a very close fight. How the end came about is Bruce caught me with a lovely uppercut and he managed to split the bottom of my eye with it and the fight was stopped. The referee Frankie Black (God rest is soul) said to me afterwards, "Dom I was gonna stop that fight because Bruce was fucked". It was an unbelievably hard fight for both of us. Many years later Bruce Scott did an interview and went on record saying, "My hardest fight was Dominic Negus because every time I hit him he just laughed at me". Bruce didn't hurt me that much but afterwards I knew I'd really been in with a class fighter, but I'd given him such a scare. Before then I didn't really realise I was up there as a close second to him.

When I was growing up my Dad would say to me, "You got to train hard son because there's someone always better than you out there". My reply would always be, YEAH BUT I'LL BE THE CLOSEST SECOND THEY'LL EVER FUCKING HAVE!

After the fight with Bruce Scott I had so much respect for him as a man and a fighter. Even though it was my first loss I'd turned from a boy to a man that night. The Bruce Scott fight was a bit of a game changer because it made me realise I can compete at that level as I'd said earlier.

Looking back its fair to say I had a bit of a hit and miss career being involved with a bit of skull duggery outside the ropes. I neglected my training at times and I'll be the first to admit it to anyone reading this, the name Dominic Negus will always have a hint of controversy. You go and ask Steve Bunce he'll tell ya. There's always a story to be told regarding me. I like it straight forward, but a lot of the time people aren't straight forward are they you know what I mean.

From the invaluable experience with Bruce I was to take on London boy Kevin Mitchell 'The Outlaw' and I fucked the fight up well and truly. I'd already bashed Kevin up in sparring and I took him for granted. I just couldn't get out of second gear and that night was his night. In the build-up I didn't do the weight properly and I was pulled out by my corner at the end of the 5th round with dehydration because I'd fucked about. It's that night alone that makes me get on my boys' cases in the gym to not do what I did that night. Listen I know what it's like to cut corners and get caught out like a rabbit in the flashlights.

I'd get the chance to take on The Outlaw again only four months later. This was really a DO OR DIE fight for me. I was under so much pressure because every person that bought a ticket off me I told them if I lose this fight I'll give you your ticket money back! I'd trained so hard and I give poor Kevin such a fucking hiding blacking both his eyes. I put him over in the 6th with a body shot but fair play because he stuck it out and full credit to him for hearing the 10th and final round. The points score was 98-94 and I was back BBBofC Southern Area Cruiserweight champion and back up there for the time being at least.

It would be another seven months until I was in the squared circle again. This time facing Chris Woollas from Lincolnshire at the York Hall in my birthplace of Bethnal Green. This fight would be an eliminator for the British title. The year was 1999 and that probably was my best year of boxing. Mentally I was good and keeping away from a lot of stuff. I was away from stupid relationships and was focused like a fighter should be. I don't mean to be disrespectful, but the Chris Woollas fight was the easiest fight I'd ever had in my life and I took the decision 99-91 over 10 rounds. The reason I made it easy? Because for once in my life I listened. I can still remember it now, everything I did that night was off the jab and I really enjoyed myself in there it was more like a glorified sparring session I was that fluent. Even a week later Boxing News said this fella Dominic Negus is going to be hard to beat after this performance at cruiserweight. That was one of the best write ups I ever had in boxing but what did I go do after the fight?! I got myself back in all the shit again didn't I and I didn't fight again for exactly a year. When I came back I took on Tony Booth from Hull and I lost on points in Bristol. I'm not just saying this, but it was a terrible decision. I'd like to go on record now and say Tony Booth is one of the best fighters we've had in this country to never win a British title and on his day, he'd beat anybody, and I mean that. Dean Powell used to say Tony was always willing to fight anybody and was a slippery boxer. Where I just wanted to punch you in the face and then they could punch me in the face, but he was a bit more talented.

I was to face West Ham's Garry Delaney the month later at the Maidstone Leisure Centre who I'd already done quite a bit of sparring with through the years. Me and Garry had such a fight that night. Garry wasn't hurting me, I mean you could have bounced a brick off my head that night. In the first few rounds my trainer was nearly wetting himself in the corner, "DOM YA GONNA STOP HIM" were the cries. I was really bashing him up to the body big time. Then in the 3rd round he started saying to me, "IS THAT ALL YOU'VE GOT? I THOUGHT YOU'RE MEANT TO BE HARD"? This would get a little argy bargy and Ian John Lewis ended up taking two points off me which lost me the fight. Garry Delaney didn't beat me I beat myself but there you go.

The following season I beat poor old Paul Fiske in a minute then a few months later I beat Eamon Glennon of Blackpool at The Elephant & Castle Centre. Eamon was a tough boy but yet again I stuck to the perfect plan and out boxed him over six rounds. My problem a lot of the time was I would be too busy trying to knock people out but of course you don't always have to get the KO. As long as you get the win that's what's important in boxing.

In the December of 2001 I got a shot at the vacant WBU continental Super Cruiserweight Title against Eddie Knight from Kent. Eddie was quite slippery for the 1st round until I was to KO him with a left hook to the body which almost broke him in half. I thought he'd shit himself. Eddie had a lovely jab and Dean Powell read me the riot act in the corner after the first. I'm sat there thinking his fucking jabs bloody really hurt! Dean tells me he's open to the left hook to the body, so I've went out and TA TA he was gone. I always was a good body puncher, so I put him away.

A month later in January 2002 I was put on late at The York Hall and I won every round of the four against Paul Bonson. Bonson was another fucking hard man and he's got a head like a robber's dog, what a lovely fella though.

It was in the summer of 2002 that I was to take on Audley Harrison and really that was the fight I'm best known for regarding my boxing career. I'd already been offered the Audley fight before but I was suffering from stomach pain. When I took the fight with Audley I wasn't given a load of notice, but it was enough to pack a load of weight on. In my preparation to the fight I thought I was gonna beat him. Talking to a few of my friends beforehand, the conclusion they came to was Audley was gonna steam roll me because I was only weighing around 14st 8lbs and he was around 17st plus. I'm gonna be honest although it's embarrassing to say this, I went on a course of juice (steroids). Up until then steroids were never my thing because I was a fighter but in about two weeks, OH MY GOD. Everything was so different. I was covered in lumps and bumps and I was throwing the weights around with ease. It was an amazing transformation. I know the reason I've got a bit of weight on me today is because I took the steroids even my doctors told me that himself. He told me all the years of me boiling down to 13st 6lbs and then taking the juice has me blown me up now. He said to me only now does my body realise how much it was starved and of course I'm a big boy. What fucked me with the Audley Harrison fight and I should have used my head a little bit, was that I got on the scales at 17st and when I'd boxed in my last fight against Paul Bonson I was 14st something, I was on the scales with my T-shirt on, Audley's team then started shouting "Take your top off"! When I took my top off I looked like Arnold fucking Schwarzenegger. You should have heard all Audley's team screaming like little girls. His manager Colin McMillan and Audley were going mad. Audley after the fight actually paid for my piss test himself out of his own money and that's what got me a lifetime ban with the BBBofC. If I'd have beaten Audley that night I'd have never deserved to win that fight. If Audley had never paid for me to get piss tested as a matter of urgency it would have come out somewhere along the line. I'm a very straight up person and anyone who's read my book 'Out of The Shadows' will know that. A winner's a winner and a loser's a loser and I did cheat. The better man did win that night. Maybe if I'd have gone in there naturally I could have moved around him a bit quicker. With all the bulk I'd put on I was tired from the 4th round onwards where normally I could do 10 rounds standing on my head but carrying the extra bulk didn't agree with me.

All the people over the years saying oh that Audley Harrisons shit! Well I'm telling you now he wasn't you know that geezer was not shit! You don't get Olympic gold medallists who are shit. A good big un will always beat a good big un and when I boxed him I thought he had tremendous hand speed for a big fella. What struck me the most facing Audley was his footwork. He hit me with that big left hand of his right down the middle and my head was looking at the ceiling, I had a tefal head. Of course, the talking point in the fight was in the 4th round where I nutted him. If you watch the fight carefully you see he caught me with a half decent shot and I went down. Then as Audley walks away he walks back and hits me as hard as he could in the side of the head when I was down and that's when I got the hump. I jumped up and my attitude was 'you wanna fuck about with me I can fuck about with you' and I nutted him.

The referee that night was Ian John Lewis and he grabbed hold of me, marched me to the corner and calmed me down. I'd say the fight changed then and he went on to beat me 55-59. I was the first one to give Audley a proper fight, I brought him into the trenches a little bit. After the fight, what really upset me was I took my Dad in his wheelchair to see him in the dressing room and he blanked me and my old man. Normally what happens after a fight it all gets left in the ring and you shake hands or go and have a pint but not Audley. That's why I've always had the needle with him for the last 16-17 years. I know he probably had the hump with me because I stuck the nut on him but like I said the fight was over. After the fight I myself received a little bit of fame and it hugely raised my profile. Of course, because of what I was doing outside of the ring it made me more known to the Old Bill and caused me a great deal of misery.

After the Audley Harrison fight I lost the plot a little bit. I was going into pubs like the Lee Duffy from Middlesbrough character and if people looked at me funny I was knocking them out. My biggest weakness has always been my strength and I could have a fight and I was a dangerous man. I'm around 20 odd stone at the minute. I might not be as fit as I once was, but I can still fight for five minutes. If I punch you I don't care if you're Bruce Lee or Jackie Chan you're going for a kip. I was knocking people out when I was 15 stone so imagine now I'm 20 stone I punch like a motherfucker. I've always said to my boys in the gym, whatever I teach you one of those things will definitely be how to punch but it's got me into a lot of trouble in my life at times.

When my boxing career was finished I went and had a stint in Tenerife and absolutely blitzed the gaff. The thing with Tenerife 15 years ago is that it was like the Wild West anyway. Sometimes, I was fighting day and night, I was like a pig in shit out there. I had a lot of very well-known people out there and there looked after me. When I came back to Britain I very quickly realised there was no chance the BBBofC were ever going to give me my licence back and that's when I turned to the dark side shall we say for about 10 years.

If I was ever going to fight again the only option that I was gonna have was on the unlicensed circuit. I would have 37 unlicensed fights winning 34 of them. The three I lost to were Chris Bacon, Danny Williams and Carl Barwise. Carl Barwise I put right as I managed to get the return, but it took me two years of chasing him. I ended up ironing him out pretty good. The time I lost the fight to Barwise I'd never said anything, but my Dad was in hospital. I went up to see Dad in hospital and he died the next day. I couldn't have given a fuck about that fight because I was so worried about my Dad. When you're getting psychical pain it was taking the mental pain away and I was a broken man in the build up to the fight itself it was awful preparation. Me and Chris Bacon were supposed to fight again but nothing became of it. Chris was one of the hardest people I've ever met. I phoned Chris up the next night after we fought, it was a little bit like something out of Rocky and I was upset I lost. I asked him what it was like facing me. He said, "Dom you don't know how close you were to beating me". Chris caught me good in the second and all I could see out of my left eye was just white and my corner pulled me out. Chris said to me he needed to go to hospital after our fight with broken ribs, he also said I nearly made him shit himself I've never been hit like that in my life. Out of everyone I've met in my life Chris Bacon is one of the few people I've got true respect for and the toughest bloke I've ever faced. The Danny Williams fight happened in Danny's last ever unlicensed bout and I was well finished by then anyway as it was only around four years ago. My biggest regret in boxing was me pissing about with my career. I should have stopped being a prat and fully concentrated on the boxing, but I mucked about.

I used to spar with Lennox Lewis, alright Lennox could have beaten the fuck out of me if he wanted and he may not even remember moving about with me, but I wouldn't have been put in there in the first place if I didn't have anything about me.

Another top name I was used for sparring for was American Montell Griffin before he went and boxed Dariusz Michalczewski for the world title. Dariusz' team fucked me off after two rounds saying I was too mad. Dean Powell had arranged it, but they fucked me off and paid me all the money for only two rounds saying, "You're obviously mad mate we don't need that kind of sparring". I was on him like a fucking dog I smashed him, absolutely smashed him that day in sparring. I was in the gym constantly at the time in 1999.

Looking back, I wish I'd have stepped up my game after the Chris Henry fight because I got a bit one paced. I'm always on my boys' cases in the gym and I say to them if I feel I can't teach you anymore, I'll take you to someone who can because this careers too short. I tell my fighters if they're loyal to me I'll be loyal to them. I never got stuck in it and lived the life as a boxer I wanted the party life as well. That's why I say I'm lucky because I've got a second chance as a trainer. With my contacts in boxing I've made some good friends who've helped me out travelling about for good sparring etc…

I think I was good enough to be world champion, but I fucked it all up because I didn't live for boxing. Some days in my gym I scream at the boys, "DO AS I FUCKING TELL YOU", then I get the odd one who says, "Yeah but Dom you didn't blah blah blah". In one respect boxing's saved my life and it's been good because of all the people I've met along the way I don't think I've got a lot of enemies. The one thing I'd really like to do is sit down with Audley Harrison one day and have a cup of coffee with him. That's one thing I would love to do. It totally gutted my Dad after our fight when I said to him, come on let's go see the champ and he shunned us. I'm not even sure Audley is aware I had my Dad there he told his team he didn't wanna see me and that's why I've had a lot of hostility towards him over the years. Maybe to him I was just about twenty minutes at Wembley Conference Centre but to me he was a lot more than that and I'd like to find out how life's been treating him and make him aware that I had my old man there that night in his wheelchair when he shunned us because I don't think he's aware. I'd like to hear that from him out of his mouth.

If you're talking about hero's in life well my old man was my hero. He was the straightest person I've ever met, and he worked every day of his life and that was only for Mum, me and my brother. Even when my Mum and Dad weren't together she was looked after until the day he died. That's what my Dad was all about so if I can be half the man in life my old Dad was I'll be doing well.

Boxing these days is still my life massively. It brought discipline when I needed it most. It's not always the nicest people you meet in the game though. All this handshaking at press conferences isn't worth a wank and you've got to have your blinkers on. I've always been a loyal person and people know me know that. I'll always be straight with people and I want people to be straight with me, but you don't always get that in the boxing business.

I don't live like a king by far but boxing still to this day provides for me and my daughter. My Mum and Dad are gone now, and I hardly speak to my brother so my focus apart from my daughter Annabella is the boxing. My two boys in particular Boy Jones junior and Mike Sakyi keep me going. Boy Jones in particular is a good kid and he'll be in the mix for titles very soon so if anyone's reading this go check him out on YouTube. If anybody wants to contact me on Facebook, you can do so on Dominic Anthony Negus. I had to use my middle name because I've had some nutter on there pretending to be me for the last six years.

These days I've turned my back on the skull duggery and that's down to my little girl Annabella. That little girl saved my life and also, she saved a lot of other people's lives. Before she came along there was only two ways I was gonna end up and that was dead or doing a life sentence. I know because of the things I did years ago I'm very lucky not to be doing a long time in somewhere like Wandsworth or Pentonville. The day my little girl came into my life I realised how selfish I had lived my life until then. Nowadays I can walk out of the house and smell the grass or feel the rain. Before Annabella came along I was so blinkered and selfish I did whatever I wanted to do, and nobody could tell me anything. If I'm being brutally honest with you back in them days I thought I was above the law in this country. When this little baby came along I thought

FUCK THE LOT OF IT! I've got to look after this little thing now. Most of the times these days she looks after me and tells me what to do and she's only 13. She's my diamond and I'm truly blessed to have her in my life. I owe her so much and I'd like her to know that.

"I was prepared to get knocked out myself trying to knock him out, because then I could sleep at night knowing that I'd given my best".

Carl Froch

Peter Richardson

Peter Richardson is arguably the greatest amateur to ever come out of the wonderful town of Middlesbrough. I could hear an argument for John Pearce to contest that as he won two ABA titles and a Commonwealth Gold Medal only for peter to go that one bit extra and go to the Olympic games in Barcelona 1992.

I'd always been aware of Phil Thomas' School of Boxing's Peter Richardson growing up in the Middlesbrough boxing scene, as he was the towns elite, forever in the Evening Gazette for winning this medal or that title. I suppose he was someone I looked up to and I personally would always make a bee line for him in the Madison nightclub when I first started going out with my fake I.D as a 16-17-year-old. The man won absolutely everything in the amateur game and in 1997 Barry McGuigan tipped Peter as the fighter of the year to watch, this was ahead of a young Ricky Hatton.

A man with Peters talent he should have gone on to become one of the greats. Known as 'The Craftsman' who came to the ring to the classical Tchaikovsky's The Nutcracker, Peter was heading for the high heights of professional boxing, so where did it all go wrong? I had to find out and hear it from his own mouth myself and I caught up with the likeable lad from Berwick Hills, which is the same area as I grew up in.

Peter said:

I'm 47 years old now and I grew up in Berwick Hills in Middlesbrough. My first memories of boxing were watching a Muhammad Ali film when I was around 10-year-old. In the film Muhammad Ali won the gold at the Olympics then went and threw it in the water over a bridge and I just remember thinking how crazy he was. A short time after that a lad I knew at school was training in Joe Walton's Youth Club in Berwick Hills. The place had its own amateur boxing club ran by Topsy Lowe and Ronnie Cave, who still runs the club today under the different name of The Phil Thomas School of Boxing. The gym later changed its location to the over the border area of Middlesbrough but it's very much the same club. If I'm gonna be brutally honest with you I wasn't really a natural. I remember one-night Topsy Lowe was going up and down in the gym picking kids out saying, "You're not good enough, don't come back tomorrow", because there were that many kids in the gym the place was overflowing with kids and there wasn't the space. I'll always remember he picked me and told me I wasn't good enough so don't come back tomorrow. So, the next day I went back of my own accord even though I was told not to. I'd been going a few weeks by then and he obviously didn't think I was improving but I wasn't going to be deterred. I keep forcing my way in and continued to be there and I remember watching a fellow boxer called John Green winning the North East school boy title in his first season as a school boy. In the first year you don't go all the way there's only your area which is normally one fight. Well I was watching John win this as an 11-year-old thinking "WOW" this is a big thing and I wanted one of my own. To me, at the time, it was like winning the WBC championship of the world. I must have rapidly improved because the club put me in and I won the North East title and I was on cloud 9. I made a pact to myself to stay dedicated to the sport and I was gonna win the full thing the year after which I did. I went through the full five rounds and won it which I was so proud of myself for at the time. Not many kids in Middlesbrough had gone on to do that apart from maybe Anthony Hoe and Steve Davies.

After the first year of winning it I wanted to win it four times which is all you can enter. I failed on my target winning three but still, not a lot can say they went on to do that as a schoolboy.

I would go on to have 165 contests winning 150. I won three schoolboy titles. The one I didn't win I was ripped off in Chorley with a really bad decision and he went on to win the full thing. Apart from that everything I went in I won in Britain.

I won one NABC's title, Junior ABA'S twice and I was boxer of the year in them both and the only person ever to do that other than me was Liverpool's John Conteh. I would go on to win two senior ABA titles the first one of them it was all of Britain and not just England, so it had Wales and Scotland in it and I was only 19. I won the Commonwealth gold medal in 1994. I won the Canada cup silver medal, I won a silver in the Acropolis cup in Greece and a gold medal in Finland and the St Georges cup in Liverpool and a tournament in Germany as well as many England vests for my country. I would have two fights with American Vernon Forrest who was tragically killed in 2009 in an exchange of gunfire after he was robbed at a gas station in Atlanta. He was only 38. I was to beat Vernon in the Olympic games in 1992 but I would go on to lose to the American Thomas Tate, he went on to fight for a few world titles. I fought Andreas Zulow in Australia, he was the Olympic gold medallist at lightweight in 1988 and was voted boxer of the year that year. I beat him very easily.

I never set off wanting to become a professional fighter but at the time there wasn't much money in amateur boxing like there is today. I'd have had a field day if I was boxing as an amateur now because the funding goes by what medals you've won so I think I'd have been alright. I could have just boxed as a day job.

After the Olympics I came home, and I was gutted I never won a gold. I sort of forgot about boxing and didn't live the life for a short while and just started going out for a few months. I had no interest in boxing at that point. I didn't care if I never put a pair of gloves on again. I completely went off the rails. After beating the favourite Vernon Forrest, I thought I was sure to go and win the gold. I didn't realise at the time it was all experience and I was heartbroken, but it was very foolish to think like that, but I was a young lad.

When I went on to win the Commonwealth Games in 1994 in Canada at light-welter I realised it wasn't about burning myself out. Rather than run about like an idiot like I had in the Olympics two years earlier, I would spend my time resting by the pool all day when I wasn't training. After winning the gold in the Commonwealth I was asked to stay on for the next Olympics in Atlanta 1996.

Repton coach Tony Burns offered me money to stay amateur. My thoughts were if I stay till the Olympics I'm not guaranteed a gold and of course I had distractions out of the ring which wasn't ideal, so I thought I'd give the pro game a go. Before I turned pro I went to meet Mickey Duff on two occasions. Mickey Duff was aware already of who I was because when I was in the Olympics he was there with legendary boxing promoter Jarvis Astaire looking for new talent. After I boxed in Barcelona Mickey Duff shouted me over and gave me his number so here I was meeting him to talk pro terms. What Duff offered wasn't worth my while, so I looked further afield. Duff was good at what he did, but he wasn't offering enough money. When I spoke to him after the Olympics he offered me a signing on fee, then when I met him he failed to mention it. Mickey Duff told me I'd have to keep my job if I was to go with him and I thought I don't want that I want to be 100% committed to the pro game. I'd served my apprenticeship to high standards in the amateurs and I think I'd deserved it. It would have taken me a long time to earn the big purses with him. I was also to receive a call from Frank Warren. Frank had got in touch with Robin Reid who I'd been to the Olympics with in Barcelona, Robin had signed up with Frank. When I went for the meeting with Frank my instincts screamed out not to trust this man so I back heeled him on his offer. At one-point Frank asked me to leave the room while he discussed things which put me right off! Why did he need me to leave the room to talk about me, my Dad was also with me and he said it didn't sit right with him either.

A short while later Frank Maloney got in touch with me. As soon as I met up with Frank Maloney I thought he was the best out of them all and I liked him immediately. When I was sat talking to Frank I felt I could trust him not like the others I'd spoken to. If I could compare the two Franks, Maloney was genuine, and Warren came across as a bit of a snake and had a look in his eyes I didn't trust. Frank Maloney was offering me decent money, so I signed with him that day.

I had my first fight in February 1995 at the Elephant & Castle Centre, Southwark against Nottingham's John O'Johnson. It took me a little while to adapt to the pro game and I found it awkward. I was training in the famous Peacock gym in London and I didn't know anyone. It was like starting from scratch again in the Joe Walton's Youth Club. People get involved in amateur boxing because of the love of the game, people are involved in professional boxing for one reason only and that's money and things for me had changed. I was this young 24-year-old having my eyes opened to what the sport was really about.

Every time I went in the ring I was super fit, but it was cuts than ruined my boxing career. I had 17 professional fights winning 14 and 8 by KO. The three I was to lose were all through injury. I was to lose to Rimvydas Billius and Michael Smyth through cuts, then I lost to Dennis Berry due to a damaged right shoulder popping out in the first round. I boxed on till the third round with one arm until I couldn't take the pain and stopped and turned my back, I couldn't take any more. My skin type wasn't made for the pro game I mean even as an amateur I was cut 3-4 times which is virtually unheard of, even in the Olympics I got cut across my eye. I was even getting cut in sparring with 16 oz gloves on it just wasn't meant to be for me it had nothing to do with my ability.

When I lost to Dennis Berry in February 1998 I came back over two and a half years later to beat Costas Katsantonis and all that was just because I didn't want to go out on a loss. I was 29 by that time and I wanted to see if I still had it, but I think I knew I'd seen better days. At the time I wasn't with very good trainers I needed somebody like Jim McDonnell. He kept his lads super fit and he's fitter than most boxers today.

If I had any regrets at that time it was my trainers I should have been with someone who taught the hit and not be hit game which of course was what I'm about. When I first went pro I was trained by Darkie Smith, but he shot off and left me. He was too busy with the big Croatian Zeijko Mavovic who fought Lennox Lewis for the world title. Darkie was more for him and his son Stephen, so I was left in the background, that's how it felt. At times I was taken over to Germany for sparring, but Darkie was shooting off and I was being left trained by different strangers over there.

For long periods I went and lived in London to escape the silly things I was doing in Middlesbrough. London's the place to be for any young boxer because the place is packed with good trainers who know the game well. In the East End people just live for their boxing and of course the Repton is the best club ever, no doubt about that. The Repton have got amazing contacts and are a very wealthy club so they can look after you if needs be. The Repton staff were good people who lived for the game it's their lives. Thanks go to Tony Burns as if it wasn't for him I wouldn't have got back in the England team when I was coming back from being stabbed. Tony sorted everything out for me on that front and spoke to a few people. When I'd been stabbed nobody would touch me. It wasn't until my mate Paul Lawson rang me up and said Tony said you need to move back down here to the Repton. It was Tony who got me my first fight back on, a London select versus Irish select amateur show. When the Irish fella found out he was boxing Peter Richardson he wanted to pull out, so Tony Burns gave him a few quid to fight me. I owe that man a lot and that's how I got back on the England team, so I'd like to thank Tony Burns he's a lovely man.

My old club in Middlesbrough, The Phil Thomas School of Boxing, was a great gym to be in. It was the best and still is in the town to this day. When you think of the champions the clubs produced like myself, Stephen Swales, Guy Corbyn, James Donoghue, Mark Thompson, John Mett and the Green brothers it's been phenomenal.

People over the years in Middlesbrough have often compared me and the Wellingtons John Pearce. The difference between me and John Pearce, who is a top guy, is that I was doing that level at 18-19 whereas John's huge successes came when he was 26,27,28 he was a mature man. John's rise in boxing came really when I was finished so I suppose we were like ships in the night passing by.

I boxed for England at four different weights, not many people can say that. My biggest regret though is not staying amateur for the '96 Olympics in Atlanta which at the time I thought time was against me being 26 but it wasn't. If I'd have won the Olympics I could have very well been a millionaire. When you look at what it did for Audley Harrison, Amir Khan, James Degale and Luke Campbell's careers it would have been a terrific start for me in the pro's. I don't think I'd have had to haggle with the likes of Mickey Duff put it that way they'd have flocked around me and I'd have been hot property.

Things are all very different now compared to back then. What I mean is these boxers live in the TEAM GB headquarters in Sheffield on a full-time basis. Back in '92 I would have one week in Crystal Palace then come home, maybe do a month at my amateur club then I'd have another week back at Crystal Palace. I think we would only have six training camps a year and you can't really train like that if you're a top world class boxer, can you?! When you look at TEAM GB'S set up today they're flying around the world getting different techniques from various coaches. It all came too late for me and my generation of boxers I'm afraid.

These days boxing doesn't mean anything to me whatsoever if I'm being truthful. I don't even watch the sport. I still go on the odd jog but if I punched anything now I'd be suffering with my hands, I do have a lot of nerve damage from my neck and arms which I must take medication for from my doctors. Quite often in the gym I'll try go on the bags but within five minutes my body falls apart and it's too painful, so I stick to my running machine.

I think you could say I've fallen out of love with boxing. I don't mean to sound big headed, but I underachieved for the ability I had. At the very least, as a professional, I should have been a British champion, but my body wouldn't allow it, that's the harsh reality of it all. When I was doing well everybody wanted to know me, then when I was finished and riddled with injuries nobody wanted to know me. I'd been boxing from the age of 11 and by the time I was 30 my body had had enough.

Sometimes I look back and I think I should have done it all different with a top coach. I did have one chance of going to America which was brought up by Frank Maloney, how I wish I'd have taken the chance and made something better of myself.

Boxing in the professional ranks I always found a very serious business, in the amateurs it was much more fun.

One of my funniest memories was in Australia with Robin Reid around 1992 whilst we were representing England. I'd lost my first of two fights with Vernon Forrest, so I was a bit pissed off so went for a few beers on the night. Scarborough's Paul Ingle wouldn't come out, so it was just me and Robin and we went in this bar which was a hive for transsexuals, but we didn't know. What happened was what I thought was a girl bent over in front of us, I turned to Robin and said look at the arse on that! As she turned around we realised it was a bloke and he started abusing me because he had heard what I'd just said. I stupidly enough shouted, "At least I'm not wearing a dress!" With that he took its high heels off and blew a whistle to this army of transsexuals who all then took their high heels off also and started chasing me and Robin Reid around cars. They chased us all the way back to the hotel which was a good thirty minutes from the bar we were at. When we got back all the lads were taking the micky out of us, even the coach Ian Irwin had a good laugh at our expense we never lived it down for the whole time we were out there. Another storm in a tea cup I caused was when we were sent home from the Olympics early in '92. It even made the News of The World and the News at Ten. We'd got into a fight with some Iraqi wrestlers. What happened was me, Paul Lawson and Stevie Wilson went out for a few beers when one of these Iraqi wrestlers stole my bum bag with my money in. The fella who'd stole it was throwing it about and wouldn't give me it back, so I stuck one on him. Looking back, it probably wasn't the brightest thing to do as they were only three of us and about twelve of them. The next day everybody was saying to me, "FOR FUCKSAKE PETER OF ALL THE PEOPLE YOU HAD TO START A FIGHT WITH IT WAS WRESTLERS WHY DIDN'T YOU PICK THE SWIMMERS"! When the media got hold of that story we were called complete disgraces and told that we'd let Great Britain down. God, they went to town on us. Even when I arrived home in Middlesbrough I was having the paparazzi knocking on my door sniffing for stories. I was offered £1,000 to tell my side of the story. I told them I had nothing to say. The next day our face faces were in the paper calling us all the names under the sun you could think of. The funny thing was though what they actually printed was very inaccurate and I took them to court and sued them and won. We were all paid damages and received a public apology in a little tiny column.

These days I live on the outskirts of Middlesbrough. I'm very much a quiet man, I just do my work and come home, and I enjoy living the quiet life.

"I've a problem with my legs, they just can't walk past a chippy".

Ricky Hatton

Josh Warrington

I was first aware of the name Josh Warrington in March 2011. The only reason being was that a lad I was quite familiar with at the time Chris Riley had had his fight with former British, Commonwealth, European champion Rendall Munroe fall through. I remember being told from Chris "I'm boxing Josh Warrington who's already beat our John" (brother). That night I went home and watched the DVD of Josh Warrington V John Riley and my firsts thoughts on Josh were that he was nothing special. He just looked like a skinny twerp of a lad, but he had the work rate of an angry wasp whose nest had been disturbed. Also, he didn't have a great deal of meat in his punches. I was convinced Chris Riley would have had too much for Josh. Chris Riley himself had won a few national titles as an amateur, so he was no mug himself. The fight itself was at The Rainton Meadows Arena on April 9th which was my 31st birthday. I recall a pink haired lady who sat in front of me, she that would go on to become the lovely Mrs Natasha Warrington.

Josh Warrington V Chris Riley was put on the undercard of Darlington's Stuart Hall V John Donnelly. Watching the fight Riley won the first round quite clearly then seemed to have shot his bolt, or Warrington wouldn't let him fight his own fight. Warrington was a clear winner 59-56 and the fight was shown live on Sky Sports as the chief undercard.

It was around two months later that I would meet up with Josh and his Dad 'Papa Sean' at the Middlebeck gym in Pallister Park, Middlesbrough. A good friend of mine who was a good amateur, Michael Debnath had signed pro forms and was about to go pro, so he needed some top-quality sparring, so his trainer had arranged for Josh Warrington and County Durham's Martin Ward to come for a good auld punch up. Michael did four rounds with Martin Ward and broke a rib in the second but continued to do the full four rounds with Martin then four rounds with Josh. I remember hearing the crack from outside the ring as Martin Ward caught Michael with a peach of a body shot. It's a real shame Michael's marriage broke down only weeks before he was to make his debut against Eddie Meskry from Bradford. He'd have made a good pro. Josh and Martin Ward went hell for leather for a few rounds also. I spent a bit of time chatting to Josh and his old man and I liked both immensely. Turns out 'Papa Sean' grew up in the same part of Middlesbrough that I was brought up in, it's a small world indeed.

I'd always paid close attention to josh after that and would read about his journey in the Boxing News whenever he was in. The most likeable aspect about him for me is that he has a lot of time for the boxing fans. Never once have I read his social media status's and thought you're getting above your stations pal. The stuff he does for charity and his community can only be commended. Of course, he's a charming young man with a great sense of humour, Josh has labelled me 'Buffalo Bill' because in his words from around 2012 he said to me, "I like you Jamie, but you remind me of that weirdo in Silence of The Lambs", so it's kind of stuck. Even to his lovely better half Natasha I'm 'Buffalo Boyle'. Thanks Josh I take it as a compliment, honestly!

Over the years I've been to support Josh watching his fights and weigh ins, it wasn't really until I was there in Hull to see him win the Commonwealth title against Samir Mouneimne in November 2013 did I really sit up and take note of his boxing ability. Yes, I knew he was a game young kid who would come forward all night but what impressed me was his body punching. I think this played a big part in stopping the previously unbeaten Mouneimne in the 12th and final round.

Since then it's been a bit of a whirlwind story for the proud Yorkshire man. After a few weeks of stalking Josh and his wife by text Buffalo Bill style I was thrilled that The Leeds Warrior spared me a bit of time to talk to him about his rise from the council estate of Leeds to becoming one of Britain's finest stars in the game.

Josh said:

I'm 27 years old now and I'm born and bred in Leeds, boxing came from my Dad really. My old fella was a big fan of the sport and all his friends would come around our house most weekends to watch it on the telly. Not only that but my Dad would always be talking about boxing and watching his old VHS video's, so I think they are my earliest memories of boxing.
My Dad did a bit of boxing but nothing to ever really talk about only really a few unlicensed fights, though he had plenty of fights on the cobbles don't worry about that.

I was always an active kid and full of energy. When I was little I always liked to play-fight with my younger brothers and kids in the street. I went through the stage that every lad does of watching kung-Fu films and that lead me on to joining karate at around 7 years old before I took to boxing. To be honest I didn't even get past the white belt, it wasn't physical enough for me. At times it was when we'd be throwing people over our shoulders it was good then and the kicking parts I would enjoy. Many times, in the karate class I'd be stood there punching thin air in a line or doing the kata. My auld fella picked up on this and said, "Come on I'll take you to the gym". Dad took me when I was still seven to the old bingo hall which people know as The Star building on York Road facing the Irish Centre, the gym was East Leeds ABC. When I was walking up them steps I could clearly hear that there was some sparring going on. I remember that distinctive smell of the sweat and leather of the bag. When I saw some guys sparring away I just thought to myself 'I want a bit of this like'.

My Dad always said to me from day one if you're gonna do it don't piss about at it because at times from the age of seven I was stopping and starting. Dad was always telling me, when I got frustrated that, I'd only get better and that I'd learn because I wouldn't be Mike Tyson overnight.

Dad used to drop me off at the gym and that'd be me training for two and a half hours for three nights a week. If I didn't go to the gym for a few weeks, it would register that I missed it, so I kept on going. By the time I'd got to eleven I was fighting for East Leeds ABC. I wasn't a natural, I got beat up by lasses in the gym. If I could say anything positive about me back at the start it would be that I had a natural hunger.

By the time I'd got to eleven I had to win everything, I had to win the sparring sessions, runs, bag sessions I had to be the fittest there I had this hunger to win. If we were sparring and I got hit on the nose, I'd have to hit them three times. If we were having a 'ding dong' in sparring I wasn't gonna be the one to take a step back, I would just keep going forward throwing my arms, some people say I haven't changed. I think beside skills and talent, it's things like that that you can't teach.

In my time as an amateur I was desperate for an England vest. I remember going around boxing shows all over the country and I would look at these kids with England vests on and badges of what they'd won all over their shorts and I'd think 'fucking hell I wanna be like them'.

In my first year I won the North East counties but that's as far as you could go. It wasn't until I won the full schoolboys in my last year at school that I thought I'd climbed the top of the tree, I'd done everything. In my mind it was like a Tony Montana moment in Scarface where he gets to the top and knows he's made.

Growing up through the juniors, my problem was that I was too light, I mean the schoolboys I won was at 38KG and I was 15 at that time. When I was younger I was always baby faced, when all my mates were starting to get moustaches I was far from that. Many times, I would spar a fully-grown man and although I only looked a boy, it was like I was the man in the ring.

People around the Yorkshire boxing scene at the time will remember me for just throwing loads of leather.

When I was 16-17 I had a bit of a growth spurt and started putting a bit of weight on. There was a lot of politics in boxing and I remember going down to the Junior ABA final 2007, I'd already beaten some decent kids to get to that position like Kid Galahad in the junior ABA'S and that was on his home show in Sheffield. In the final I boxed a guy called Billy Morgan from West Ham. I still have the tape of it somewhere it's absolutely disgraceful! In the last round I was only given a point but if you watch the fight you can clearly see I scored more than one point. That junior ABA title was taken away from me that year and for a short while I'd lost all interest in boxing. When I went back to the gym I'd made my mind up I wasn't going to box for England, even if I got called up. I won that title and the fuckers had robbed me it was a blatant robbery.

The next season I carried on boxing not thinking of any England call ups. Half of my mind was already set to go pro.

Before I was going to turn pro I would give the senior ABA'S a go, bearing in mind I was still only 17 years of age. When I went in the first round, which was the Yorkshires, I stood on the scales and the official says, "Josh your over 57KG, you've got to come back in a bit if you want to enter featherweight". I was past caring with amateur boxing and I told him to just stick me in the heavier division of lightweight which is 60KG. In the amateurs there wasn't a super feather which was 9st 4lbs, so I said put me in lightweights, bearing in mind I was a tad over 9st, so I was giving away a lot of weight. That year I won the Yorkshires and the quarters, then in the semi-finals I boxed Liverpool's Tom Stalker. He was 60KGS dead I was 58.2 and to be honest he towered above me. Tom Stalker was a seasoned GB squad member and he had Terry Edwards from the England team sat ringside and Frankie Gavin all there supporting him, so he was heavily supported. I won the first round 6-4 then the second was level. Tom went on to take the third not to mention I had a point taken off. After the fight that was me done with the amateurs I'd had enough of this shit and I was fully focused on turning pro. All together I had 45 amateur contests winning a total of 35, although in my head I lost one.

From the age of 15-16 maybe even younger I'd always had my mind on the pros. When I was still at school my Dad would take me down to Huddersfield to spar with Dale Robinson when he was preparing for a British title fight at super flyweight. Of course, being that light at times it was hard to get sparring so that was perfect for me to go along and use him like he was using me. Dale said I was the perfect come forward pressure fighter he was training for at the time.

At that point in my boxing that's all Josh Warrington was about, I'd just run forward bombarding my opponents till they give up. I also did quite a bit of sparring with Nottingham's Jason Booth when he was British champion as well as Dewsbury's Gary Sykes who was also British champion at the time. This really gave me great confidence because all these boys were fighting for titles and I was holding my own with them. The last couple of years in amateur boxing I enjoyed, when I didn't think of getting on the GB squad or picking up England vests, I knew everything I was gaining was good experience for the pros.

Before I went pro I had a few offers in and around Leeds but my Dad kept saying to me the worlds my oyster and that we needed to have a good look about. My Dad approached Steve Wood and the rest is history from there really, I was always comfortable with Steve I got good vibes from him.

When I started my professional career, it was an eye opener. I'll never forget going to Huddersfield to spar with a pro and for two minutes of the round I was busy as a bee unloading loads of punches, then in the last minute he came alive and I was fucked then. He beat me up for the last minute and this was happening a lot around that time in sparring. One of the best bits of advice that I was given was when someone told me to learn to go, then learn to pace myself. I wasn't really mature for an 18-year-old. Sometimes you see these young fighters turning over and they are men, they've got muscles on top of muscles, well I was a skinny boy. When I turned pro I was mixing with proper men like the likes of Dougie Curran and John Riley. When I boxed John Riley, he was a 30-year-old bloke and I was just 18 so I couldn't afford to get in close because I didn't have the strength.

In the early days I would stick to being busy but using some boxing ability and moving my feet being clever. I couldn't have traded with them because of course I didn't have the strength at that time.

It's well known that I used to be a dental technician and at that time I was working 9-5 in the lab, as well as studying at Leeds university to get a qualification in the business. I was training every day and on my days off I was going out and trying to promote myself, often spending hours putting fight posters up in working men's clubs and pizza shops trying to drum up as much support as I possibly could single handed.

Looking back on them days it was so tough. Inside the gym on the way up I sparred many rounds with Carl Johansson in a dingy little gym taking heavy shots. I was of the age where most of my friends were all out living the party life. At times I would get so frustrated and wonder if it was all worth it and I wanted to go do what they were doing. Them feelings changed a couple of years later when I was 21, I remember selling tickets to one of my pals who used to not be a bad boxer himself. I said to him I bet you're having a right old laugh going around town in all the bars! He turned around and said, "You know what Josh, it was alright at first but now we're doing the same old shit for the last three years I wished I'd have stuck to my boxing like you" and I've never forgotten them words. He told me he wished he was in my shoes and he'd trade everything to be where I was. I think that was what gave me a boost at the time, that coming from another young lad my age.

When I got to title level it came very fast, ever since I turned pro I'd wanted the big nights and they were here quicker than I had thought. Professional boxing's all about timing and you've got to be 100% ready. When the titles came I won the English title then defended it twice against Jamie Speight and Ian Weaver, so I knew it was time to step up again against Samir Mouneimne. I was to win the fight against Samir winning the Commonwealth title. I defended it once when I retired Rendall Munroe in 7 rounds. The fight after that I won the British title against Martin Lindsay then the fight after that I would win the vacant European against Davide Dieli so it all happened in the space of 18 months which is remarkable considering I still had time on my side.

I don't think my team planned on moving along so quick, I'd have loved to win the Lonsdale belt outright, but you don't turn down these opportunities in boxing. I'd gone from fighting in front of 1100 in Leeds Town Hall to fighting at Leeds Arena in front of 7,000 it was crazy.

Around that time Matchroom were tipping me to be the next big thing people were saying I was the next Ricky Hatton. Also, I had WBC international titles I had Vinny Jones walking me out and the national press flocking around me, radio stations ringing me asking me to go on their shows, I spoke to my team and said we have to put the brakes on somewhere.

From day one its helped me immensely having my Mrs, Natasha, by my side. She's a pain in the arse sometimes but she's been by my side since before I turned pro and you do need that rock, that stable influence. In our early days Natasha didn't really understand why we couldn't go out and eat and go out all hours partying but she soon got to grips with it. Natasha is right by my side before the fight and through the hard times when I'm starving myself. People think it's all glamour in front of the huge crowds and you're a hero when you put a performance on but it's not like that. People don't see the times when you've had an awful night sparring, or you've fell in shite out running in the rain. Sometimes when you walk through your front door you need that lift up and that's where she's been a massive part of my life and I'm so grateful that she's my wife she's my best friend and she's also a bright girl is Tash she's got two degrees so I don't know what she's doing with me, it must just be my good looks!

From an early age, in terms of boxing I've always said I wanted to put Leeds on the map. I aspire to encourage other kids in Leeds to join boxing and say you know what I wanna be like Josh Warrington. Leeds, in my opinion has never been classed as a boxing city like Liverpool, Manchester or London etc... I want to leave a legacy in the city that I love and I'm proud of and to be the first world champion, well it will go down in the history books and nobody can ever take that away from me. It will be massive for me and I tell you what we'd have a big old party afterwards with an open top bus. It's not just for me because there's so many people who've been on this journey with me from the small hall shows right through to English, British, Commonwealth, European and travelling to all these places with me even over in Germany. Now, I'm staring down the barrel of a world title it's for all those people as well as me.

I was actually still working as a full time dental technician when I was European champion, its unheard of. So many fighters win titles then they turn into celebrities instantly, but I was never gonna do that, I'm just a lad from the council estate in Leeds. I know now boxing's a long and painful business and it takes a long time to get there. When I started as a pro I thought just aim for the British title. Then when I beat Martin Lindsay I thought you know what, I'm far from fucking done here I'm not even out of second gear.

With my old fella bringing me up the way he did he's kept me really grounded. We come from a council estate and I've seen the lads walking about full of themselves because they've got an older brother who's the cock of the estate. I used to think fucking hell you're no bigger than any of us. Another memory I recall was being in the gym as just a young boxer and this boxer came in holding a belt, and he was walking around the gym like he was a God and had no time for anybody. That isn't me man. My attitude is that if you can make someone's day by having five minutes of your time or posing for a picture then you've done something fucking decent haven't you.

Boxing is my life I mean I was only in the gym speaking to Femi Fehintola and he was telling me he's still ticking over at 35. Femi told me boxing's a worse drug to give up than heroin is, and he can't leave it alone.

If they can't compete in the ring most fighters still have a little involvement. Deep down if you've loved the sport from the start it's hard to give up. I really haven't got any idea what I'll do when I retire. My plan is to win a world title, unify the featherweight then go to Las Vegas, take all the Leeds lads and smash a few casino's and I'm gonna retire with my marbles intact that's the plan.

My routine these days is to train twice a day and have one day off. I've always felt that bit more advanced than any of my opponents in the ring and I'm fully focused on bringing that world title back to Leeds.

I'm a lad from the estate who had a dream and worked hard at it. I wouldn't be where I am without my old fella 'Papa Sean' behind me so I'd like to thank him for the love and support he's shown me in my life. Also, my wonderful wife Natasha and the army of fans who've always turned up to support me in any way i.e. purchasing a ticket or just sending me good luck messages. All the love I've received has all gone in the bank and it's all helped me in my boxing career.

If you want to follow my journey to the top get behind me by following me on:

Twitter @J_Warrington
Facebook @JoshTheLeedsWarriorWarrington
Instagram @J_Warrington

and my website is JoshWarrington.com

MARCHING ON TOGETHER... ALL LEEDS AREN'T WE!!!!

"Sure, there have been injuries and deaths in boxing, but none of them serious".

Alan Minter

Jon Lewis Dickinson

In boxing if you look closely you can see a lot of bad professional boxers. Many of them you wonder how they were even granted a boxing licence and entry into a British ring.

How many times have you watched a fighter from overseas coming to box on a British show and look to take a knee from the first half hearted clip that glanced the top of his bonce.

Then he'll stay down, take his fight purse and go back to Lithuania or somewhere like that to continue his life as a taxi driver, until his 28-day boxing ban clears from being KO'D, so he can come over again to repeat the same thing.

Well there's a saying in boxing, you may well get bad boxers in the sport, but you don't get any bad British champions.

The British title, also known as the Lord Lonsdale, very much like the F.A Cup in football, is the most famous and oldest title of its sport. Jon Lewis Dickinson wasn't only a British champion, he defended it three times meaning that he gets to keep it outright.

There's been many top British champions in this country such as Wayne Alexander, Esham Pickering, Gary Sykes, Curtis Woodhouse and Darren Hamilton who've all shared the huge success of being British champion, only for them not to manage to defend it three times and win it outright. Not only did Jon Lewis win that beautiful belt but he also picked up the Northern Area, English, WBC International Silver Cruiserweight as well as competing for the

Commonwealth Title. Jon Lewis also won Eddie Hearn's Prize-fighter tournament in 2010 when he was really just a novice pro at the time.

I'd always followed Jon Lewis' and his younger brother Travis' careers from the start of their journey's, with both of them being from Stanley, County Durham it's not a million miles from Middlesbrough. I'd had the pleasure of meeting Jon Lewis a few years back when I did a charity event in Saltburn which was An Evening with Hartlepool's Michael Hunter. It wasn't one of my best ideas to get a photo stood next to Jon Lewis with him being 6ft 4 and me only being 5ft 8. I caught up with Jon Lewis and I asked him where his journey in the toughest sport of them all begin.

Jon Lewis said:

I'm from Stanley in County Durham and I'm 31 years of age now. I've been retired a couple of years and away from the game. I first started training when I was really young about 5-6 years old. My Dad used to take me down a boxing club called Chester Moor ABC. To be honest it was my Dad doing his training and me and my younger brother Travis would get brought along to run about in the gym and punch things. Me and Travis would be happy spending hours punching others lights out. From until Travis learnt to walk, me and him fought all the time and that continued until I was 17 and he was 15. The reason it stopped was I'd learned to drive, and Travis started using his head thinking he could get lifts everywhere. Me and him seriously used to kill each other like badly.

When we were young my Dad used to have horses, so he would take me and Travis to the stables, what me and Trav would do is whilst we were in this barn we'd lock the door from inside so the other one couldn't escape, then we'd spend hours kicking the shit out of each other basically. There were no gloves involved it was just bare fist. We'd be there for hours until my Dad or Grandad would come along and find each other totally busted up.

I wouldn't have my first proper contest for Chester Moor ABC until I was 11 years old, I'd just started secondary school. I stayed with the Chester Moor gym until I was around fifteen, I had 13 bouts for them.

Boxing I would say came easy to me, although I had my first proper contest at 11 years old, I'd been scrapping with Trav since as long as I could remember. At times me and Trav would fight our Dad when he was on his knees, so I suppose you could say fighting was in our blood. There's not only me and Travis there's four of us in total. I have an older brother, that's who's two sons Mark and Jacob are doing well for Birtley ABC now. I also have an older sister and me and her used to fight like hell also. Saturday nights entertainment would always be someone fighting in our house. It wasn't until I joined Birtley ABC when I was 15 did I move up a few levels.

The reason I decided to leave Chester Moor ABC was there was no sparring for me there, I was on my own in terms of my weight. At the time I needed to be around lads who were a level above, no disrespect to my old club, but Birtley ABC already had it all so it was an easy decision to make.

When I went to Birtley I spent a lot of time sparring with Mark McClean, Gary Barr, Andrew Buchanan and Paddy Ward. To be honest the place was packed and there were so many people I could look up to and learn from and Ronnie Rowe was and still is the best coach in the business. All in all, I had around 55 amateur contests. I boxed for England in the four nations twice, I boxed in Germany a few times also. I didn't do very well for England

I must admit, although both my fights in Germany were against a European Bronze medallist and the other was world silver medallist. On that record was two junior ABA titles and an NABC'S title. I reached a schoolboy final also as well as a getting to the senior ABA final in 2005, but I lost to Liverpool's Tony Bellew. My fight against Bellew is on YouTube if you type in TB v JLD if any readers want to watch it. It was the first time I'd ever been on telly as it was covered by Grand Stand. I was only 18 and I was in the final of the ABA'S with some nutter by the name of Tony Bellew. If you watch that fight you'll see I was trying to kill him because I fucking couldn't stand him, I absolutely hated him. The needle started at the semi-finals of the ABA'S and he was being his usual gobby self letting his mouth go. At the time this was all new to me, I'd only come up from the juniors. I'd never seen anything like Tony Bellew before. In the build up to the ABA final with him I couldn't sleep at night thinking about him, but Tony done a job on me even before the fight because he got in my mind. He made me want to just go and kill him and forget about my boxing and I left myself open being wreckless.

The year after I would go on and win it beating Mark Redhead from Kingfisher ABC. I beat Dale Youth's James Degale in both of my junior ABA final victories.

My brother Travis actually knocked George Groves out in the 2006 junior ABA'S, that's also on YouTube.

Another quite decent guy who I beat was Kent's Tom Dallas, I stopped him in 4 rounds as an amateur.

I was to beat David Dolan from Sunderland twice in the amateurs and as a pro. David was a very talented fighter and underachieved for the ability he had. I have so much respect for David he was a tough fella and a nice bloke so it's a great shame.

In 2008 I found myself really losing interest in the amateur game. One day I was reading The Chronicle (Newcastle paper) and in John Gibson's column I'd noticed it said Frank Maloney (now Kellie) was coming to the North East to sign some fighters. The article had a number, so I phoned it and was put through to Frank, then we just went from there really.

When I began my professional career the thing that hit me instantly was these guys were a lot tougher than the amateurs. Of course, I fought a few journeymen to begin with and all they are is tough men. No skill whatsoever but what is clear in abundance was in the pro's, people really wanna hurt you. Amateur boxing's a bit like a game of tig, you know you score points, but these bastards are there to really hurt you, so you mustn't switch off or its lights out.

In April 2010 there was an opportunity for me to be on Eddie Hearn's Prize-fighter that was coming up. At that time, I was 5-0 but it wasn't interesting enough fighting these journeymen for me. I found it so bizarre that I'd been mixing it at a high level in the amateurs, then suddenly, I'm facing cavemen with no skill, so I rang Frank Maloney and asked him if he could get me in the cruiserweight Prize-fighter that was coming up! Frank, at the time didn't want to put me in, saying it was too early for me because Herbie Hide was in. I told him I was sick of pissing about with journeymen all the time, with that Frank put me forward to be in and I was selected. At the time I was training with Newcastle's ex pro Micky Duncan because amateur trainers couldn't work with pro's but other than my stint at Chester Moor, I'd only ever been with Ronnie Rowe.

Of course, around that time they'd changed the rules to amateurs can train pro's if they seek a professional licence, Ronnie gained this, and I was much happier because that meant I could go back to Ronnie, I was so familiar with him and I wasn't travelling to Newcastle every day I was in my own area.

The Prize-fighter really gave me something to focus on and was what I'd been lacking. I was out running every morning as well as training twice a day. When I'd been fighting the journeymen, the times I should have being going for a run I couldn't be bothered. Towards the Prize-fighter I was absolutely flying, sparring was going so well.

I'd been over to Ireland to spar a few of the Cubans who were over there. I was really ready for the tournament and I think it showed on the night in my three victories against Leon Williams, Mark Krence and Nick Okoth to take the 32 grand prize money and the Prize-fighter Cup.

I retired aged 30 and if I had to give you the biggest reason why I retired, I'd have to say it's the area where I'm from. There's just not enough big shows! There's a lot of small hall shows in the North East but the money's not there in them. The promoters on these small hall shows force you to sell tickets if you're to gain a bit of a wage and its shite. If you're gonna fight you need the telly involved for a kick off.

Maybe one day it would be nice for Sky and BT Sports to putt shows on up here, but I can't see it. Everything like that is in London, Manchester, Liverpool etc…

My last fight was May 2016 on a big Sky Sports show against Belfast's Tommy McCarthy on at the SSE Hydro in Glasgow on the Ricky Burns undercard. I lost the fight on points. Straight after the fight Eddie Hearn came up to me saying "Jon I wanna put you on in September". I was thinking great I'll get a good camp because they'll be a few quid in it for me and my family, you know what it never happened! Wasn't even close to happening. My fight after that was forever getting put back and I just thought, sod this I'm out of here I've got a wife and child to support. If you look at the big city's Eddie Hearn has his shows in, there's a big show every three month and you need to be on them to live in boxing from my experience. If I was from one of Britain's big major city's I'd still be boxing now for sure I'm still only 31.

I'll always love boxing, the training and getting myself fit but it's the politics in boxing that put me off. I was never going to get put on a Manchester show when they could stick a Manchester lad on who'll sell a load of tickets that's the harsh reality. It will always be the same in boxing unless you're a massive name who's come from the amateurs or you've won Olympic medals etc... Any young lad who wants to turn pro, you must do what you can in the unpaid code before you turn over. I tell my nephew Mark Dickinson who's just getting on the GB squad to get his head down, get funding and do something internationally because that's were you get your platform to start in the pro's, without that you're pissing against the wind.

Winning the British title outright was my biggest achievement in boxing, not many people get to keep one of those.

My best night was winning the Prize-fighter because it was all new, I'd never experienced anything like that before and of course I wasn't one of the favourites.

Even though I was a professional athlete I never missed out on anything. Say for instance the lads were going on holiday to Ibiza every year, I used to go. If I could have dedicated myself more to boxing it would have been nice to see how far I could have got.

When you look at the likes of Anthony Joshua who train, train, train then train some more, I wish I'd have had the mindset like that but that was never me. I was very much like Ricky Hatton was, I'd have a fight, go partying and eat a few kebabs. I loved drinking and eating shit and having a good time which isn't part of boxing is it?! I wish I could have been like an Anthony Joshua but that wasn't me. Who knows, if I'd have missed all that crap out I may have gone further but I've done it now so there's no point going back its negative.

These days I'm happy. I married a beautiful lass called Kate. We have a little boy Joseph Lewis who's two, he's a little JLD also. I work for myself and I run my own business. These days I am not involved whatsoever in boxing, I can see myself becoming a trainer in a few years but for now I'm just enjoying my retirement and getting fat.

If anyone wants to contact Jon Lewis, you can by messaging his Facebook business page JLD Groundworks & Grab hire and also by his Twitter account @jonlewis_D

"Mr Cooper, have you looked in the mirror lately and seen the state of your nose?"

Henry Cooper

Bradley Welsh

It would have been 2008 when I first heard the name of Edinburgh's Bradley Welsh as he was featured on 'Danny Dyer's Deadliest Men' a documentary which aired on the Bravo channel.

It's fair to say Bradley's had a really colourful past running with the Capital City Service(Hibernian football casuals),becoming a gang boss in the hard city of Edinburgh and serving a lengthy prison sentence which was inevitable considering his extracurricular activities.

Before he got side tracked with that though he was one of Scotland's top amateur boxers. Anyone who has seen the footage of the southpaw Bradley training on the Danny Dyer program can see he was a really tasty fighter back in the day.

Speaking to Bradley I could tell he had a love for amateur boxing, but his voice often changed when he would speak of the professional game as if it had all left a bad taste in his mouth.

Bradley took me back to the start and told me how he became involved in boxing, and how still to this day he's using it to keep the youth of Edinburgh off the streets and on the straight and narrow.

Bradley said: -

I'm 47 years old now and I've been involved in boxing for around 40 years. Most of my time spent in boxing has been around the amateur game although I did turn professional myself in 1994. The reason that a lot of my time was spent on the amateur scene is that I'm quite anti-pro boxing and I have my reasons which I'll explain to you along the way.

Any young boy who's got aspirations to turn professional and wants to become champion of the world is entitled to follow his dreams, but for me I know it's a very unfair playing field. Professional boxing is a business and I've now distanced myself away from that. In the last four years I myself have put on the biggest amateur boxing shows in Europe in Edinburgh with thousands of spectators watching on any one night. What Bradley Welsh is about now is going around Scotland opening gyms to entice kids to participate in amateur boxing. Over the years I've had lots of kids in my gym but the moment that they've said, "I want to become pro "I won't have anything to do with that and I've walked away and put them in touch with somebody who can take them on that journey.

My earliest memory of boxing was in 1977 and I was 7 years old. My older brother Sean took me to Meadowbank sports stadium to go to karate. When I was there I wandered into the room next door to see everybody in the boxing gym. I stood there staring as a nosey wee boy. Looking back that was an extremely pivotal memory for me because I chucked the karate and started boxing, which I took to right away. The feeling boxing gave me was fantastic and I just loved it and I never stopped loving it. I boxed all the way through from 1977 right up until 1998, till I had my last professional bout. In my time as an amateur I won maybe 9-10 Scottish championships as a junior. I went in the Army and won the Army championships. In that time, I must have had around 200 contests, boxing was a way of life for me. When I drifted away from boxing it was only then I fell by the wayside and of course the environment I was brought up in lead my down a criminal path and on to becoming a football hooligan.

When I had the focus of boxing I was kept away from that life, it was only when I lost the boxing I fell into that. The darkest times of my life was when I received an incarceration of 4 years. When I was in prison completely down in the gutter, I was given a chance to start boxing again and that saved me once again and led me to travel the world with the Scottish national team.

On leaving Polmont prison, it was only by chance that when I was transferred to Dumfries prison in the H unit, that I met Ian Black a Prison Officer who was on the Scottish National team.

The screws who ran Polmont segregation were animals. They would put a hose under my door for their sheer entertainment. Today there's a big civil case going on because of the brutality suffered by prisoners in there.

Ian was a really good guy and not like some of the animals who worked for the prison system, and he offered me a wee olive branch to behave as I was on hunger strike at the time. It was down to Ian who cajoled me back to normality and he got me to start my boxing again. After a year of behaving myself I was moved to an open prison where I could compete in the Scottish championships which I won. 12 weeks after that win I was fully released from prison and went on towin the lightweight British ABA title in May 1993 for Leith Victoria ABC against Vincent Powell(Army). From winning the ABA'S I spent the next seven months going to Italy, Canada and France with the Scottish national team. At around that time boxing had changed to the point scoring system and it made me really disillusioned about amateur boxing. Also, I was still public enemy with the Edinburgh Police, so I turned professional.

Looking back, I must have only been one of the very few to ever have been let out of prison to box, then be brought back to the jail in a prison van. I even boxed for my country against Italy whilst I was in prison, boxing really gave me back a dedication that I'd lost for the last few years and now it had saved me from lying in a cell in a straight jacket covered in blood.

I had a lot of problems inside prison and people wanting to fight me because at the time I was known all over the country for fighting on the terraces at the football. On many of them dark nights I'd be laid in my cell when I would hear a chorus of, "You're getting it in the morning Welsh", I would have to fight constantly and be on my toes.   I used boxing as a vehicle to get me out of prison and It was my saviour, just like when I was a young boy and boxing saved me because I was born into deprivation.

I grew up in the ghettos of Edinburgh and my mum was a single parent, I didn't have a Father, so I wasn't brought up the easy way. In my youth I would use boxing as my expression. To be quite frank I started getting that good at it I started using my talent outside the ring and on the streets of Edinburgh. For many years I was maybe nine stone getting into fights with grown men. I was a fearless wee kid with huge confidence and I could punch!

Getting back to me turning professional, I had five contests with Glasgow promoter Alex Morrison. The environment I was pushed into wasn't great. At the time I had no trainer and I was travelling back and forth to Glasgow from Edinburgh everyday on my own. It was a real eye opener into the hardest sport in the world, in fact it's not a sport it's a business. The boxing game takes nothing but total dedication and I have nothing but respect for any young man who takes the journey and devotes his life to boxing because I know how hard it is. Myself at the time I was getting really pissed off, so I did what I thought I had to do and went and sought better training and found a way to get out Edinburgh. I secured a promotional and manager deal with a company called USC(United Sports Corporation) based in Edinburgh. They paid for me to go and live in America. I went over there with a friend and I went on a scouting mission for gyms in New York. I lived there for around eight months. I trained at the famous Gleeson's gym under the watchful eye of the famous Ira Becker who'd coached at the world famous gym for around 40 years, I lived in Harlem at the time. I then moved to Detroit and trained with the late Manny Steward at the famous Kronk gym, but I only last two weeks there because I found them to be very racist towards white people.

I was only starting off my level of education as a pro and I could fight, but I wasn't anywhere near the level of the people in the gym who were mainly all championship fighters. From there I went to Miami and trained with the legendary Angelo Dundee at his Hollywood gym for three months. Something that happened there was pivotal in my mind and I told this story on Danny Dyers program when I was featured. What happened was that one day I was training away and I overheard Angelo Dundee talking about some guy who'd sailed from Cuba to America to seek a better life for himself and become a professional fighter. His boat had sunk along the way and he ended up swimming the rest of the way to Angelo's gym. I heard Angelo speaking to somebody saying, "Ooh we can make a lot of money from him". That to me sums up what professional boxing is all about and hearing him say that kind of sickened me. People like him are making money off these young kids who are just chasing their dreams. These guys bastardise young boxers in order to make money! Just because that's the way it's always been doesn't mean it's right.

I left Miami and went to stay in Los Angeles for almost two years. I would come back to Edinburgh maybe every four months. At the time I was just as paranoid as I was before I'd left the city. I was constantly looking out for the police fitting me up once again like they had a few years previously.

When I was in Los Angeles, I hooked up with Freddie Roach. I had the opportunity to train with a hell of a lot of good fighters such as John David Jackson who was a middleweight champion. He was out of this world to watch training and when I spoke with him I found him to be a really placid guy. The top American middleweight James Toney was also there but he was another racist, me and him had a bit of a scuffle in the gym, he was a total arsehole. I was never impressed with James Toney's attitude. I had one fight whilst there and I boxed a guy called Jesus Valdez over 4 rounds, and I was absolutely terrible. The fight was a war and we each received two warnings. It was a complete and utter swinging match. That was my first and only loss as a professional boxer in nine contests. I have always told people over the years the only person to ever beat me was Jesus...

I came back home from Los Angeles and I signed with Tommy Gilmour. I had three contests with Tommy and won the three in 97/98. I'd got to the point of my life where I was really getting sick of professional boxing, it was an insidious sport and I was disillusioned with it all by now and chucked it at only 28.

The potential I showed as an amateur, winning the British ABA'S I should have been out fighting for a British title, but it was my input that let me down. I can do anything I put my mind to I'm that kind of boy, but I didn't see why I had to get my face punched, and these promoters and managers were sitting ringside making money from me. All the pressure was on me to provide, whilst they're sat there and doing fuck all! I didn't fall out of love with boxing, I fell out of love with professional fighting. I didn't see it as boxing I saw it as a business. The amateur game is totally different I did that for years for nothing but a trophy, medal or a certificate.

When I left boxing I stuck my head in the sand for about 4 or 5 years. I had nothing to do with the game I was sickened by it for a long time. I cut myself out of society to tell you the truth. Then once again for the third time in my life, boxing was my saviour! It was my saviour when I was a 7 year old child in the ghettos with fuck all, it was my saviour when I was lying in a cell in a straight jacket covered in blood being angry at the world, now in 2005 boxing was my saviour once again and I opened up Holyrood Boxing Gym with a view, not to put kids into amateur boxing, but to use boxing as a media to get kids involved in sport and give them opportunities that I had as that 7 year old boy.

Over the first five years I've built up probably the biggest amateur gym in Scotland. At one time our club had 70-80 competitive boxers in the amateurs. We have classes at all times of the day. We have maybe 400-500 people a week easy through our doors and it's still those level of figures to this day.

In 2011 I started working with Boxing Scotland and I put on some huge events with them. I put on an Edinburgh V London amateur boxing show and that was the biggest amateur boxing show in Europe. We had 3,200 people in attendance and it was sold out. I had a wee fall out with Boxing Scotland due to the government stopping the funding. It wasn't just that I didn't like what they were doing not giving too many opportunities to the kids so me and Sam Kynoch set up our own amateur organisation. Myself and Sam went and opened 20 gyms around Scotland in 2012/13. We must have had something like 400 boxers involved in the project and that was going great, until Sam decided to fuck off to MTK because he likes professional boxing.

To cut a long story short, I just continued to look after my gyms in Edinburgh, as well as opening Castle Boxing Gymnasium. Castle Boxing Gymnasium has turned out to be the biggest boxing gym in Europe. The place has 7 boxing rings and 200 punch-bags in it. I'm also the chairman of a registered charity called ABA Limited. One of the purposes of the charity is to open boxing gyms to engage with kids and give them an opportunity to participate in boxing. Even now I'm constantly scouting for gyms in and around Edinburgh to keep the kids off the streets, I'm a community organiser but I don't get paid for it. I also run food banks and do football initiatives from my gyms. It's all about engaging with my community for me these days. Boxing's the vehicle I use. The same as I once used boxing as a vehicle myself to get out of sticky situations, now I use boxing as a vehicle to help other people.

Last year I did free football training for over six thousand kids. This year I'm doing free boxing training for around the same. Just to let you know now I've joined back with Boxing Scotland and we're going to be doing kids events and taking boxing into the communities of Edinburgh and Glasgow.

These days I'm married with two children. I have a wee boy and a wee girl and I'm very settled. When I came out of prison 25 years ago I turned my back on crime and I've never been back since. It's taken me 20 odd years to cast off my reputation. Of course, I played Mr Doyle a bad guy in Trainspotting 2 and I've had other movie offers, there's plans for a Trainspotting 3. I'm good friends with Irvine Welsh and Danny Boyle who wrote the Trainspotting films.

It was me who took them around Edinburgh in search for the locations of the film. The boxing gym in Trainspotting 2 where Spud goes to train was the Castle Boxing Gymnasium.

My passion now is working in boxing gyms with kids I'm in a gym working with these kids every day. My gym Holyrood Boxing Gym turns over 100 people a day pal, on average I may do between 60-70 rounds of pads a night. Freddie Roach taught me something and it was, you can't be two things, you can't be that guy wanting to go in there sparring with your kids on the pads who you're training, because if you hit them you're a cunt! Then if you don't hit them they stop listening to you! Does that make sense? Well that's how I run my gym in a place for 6 year olds to 16 year olds. I'm probably running the busiest gym in Scotland but what I won't do like a lot of other gyms do, is only spend time with the best kids. Well I'm the opposite to that, I've created an environment and a platform for kids to come, who have free expression to practice with the right guidelines. It's up to the kids to push themselves with the right support no matter how good or bad they are at the sport. I have no aspirations to have championship level boxers in my gym and if I did I'd move them on elsewhere to the right people.

One of the really good things I did, and I'm in the Guinness book of records for it, is I did a thing called pads for charity. I hold the record for doing the most amount of pad sessions in 2015. I did 360 x 3 minute rounds of pads for charity in 24 hours none stop. I did it in memory of my mum Patricia, some of the cast of the Trainspotting films come and did a few rounds with me in support.

Bradley Welsh can be found daily at the Holyrood Boxing Gym, 146 Duddingston Road West, EH16 4AP. working with kids and adults at all levels of ability. Bradley wants to introduce people to amateur boxing and the benefits it can have, psychically and mentally. Bradley is a very friendly guy and his gym is very much a community gym. You can also find Holyrood Boxing Gym on Facebook and on Twitter @holyroodboxing

"I train the same way as I've always trained, even before I was a champion. That's the difference, I train like a challenger".

Joe Calzaghe

Nick Manners

I was to stumble across the name of Leeds man Nick Manners in my research of the first Paul Sykes book I did. Reason being, of all the forums I read, many of them said reference to Nick's well known clash with the wild man of Wakefield Sykesy at Elland Road before he was about to box in 1992. When I asked a few on the Leeds forums what happened, peoples response was always, "You better ask Nick yourself". Me being my nosey, pushy self I just did. I managed to track Nick down via social media and I asked him about the incident with Sykesy I'd read so much about. "Oh you must mean before I boxed at Elland Road then? Send me your number and we'll have a chat", was Nicks response. To be quite honest id never heard of Nick Manners before I came across him, I'd heard of his brother Colin Manners but only because he fought Cornelius Carr in 1995 and I grew up in Middlesbrough so I followed Cornelius's career in the local papers. When I think of Nick Manners I can't help but think of what boxing royalty Mickey Vann said to me a few years ago at a charity talk night I did with him in Redcar. He said boxing needs characters! Well Nick Manners is a character alright. Over the last few years I've got to know Nick quite well and met up with him in Leeds on several occasions. Nick's a genuine straight talking fellow, I dare say you couldn't be in his company if you had an attitude or one of life's piss-takers, because he would let you know within a matter of seconds. My wife describes Nick as a "real person". He's a guy who doesn't suffer fools gladly and from my own personal experience with him he's definitely better to know! On the boxing front Nick Manners is a solid part of Josh Warrington's team and you can see his rather imposing figure around Josh and his Dad on fight. Nick also runs his own gym Precise Accurate Training in Leeds so he still lives the sport today. As a fighter Nick was a winning fighter with a record of 11 wins, 5 losses and 1 draw, but out of his 11 wins he put 10 to sleep. It's fair to say Nick was a devastating puncher! I caught up with the colourful and proud Leeds man and I asked him where his boxing journey all begin. Nick said: I'm 51 years old now and I grew up in Gipton in Leeds.

My first boxing memory was as an 8 year old child and I used to watch all the great fights such as Muhammad Ali V George Foreman, Muhammad Ali Vs Joe Frazier. When Ali was on the telly my Mother would have us all sit down around the box glued. At the time in our street we were the only family who owned a black & white telly. I loved boxing as a boy, but I had no intentions of being a boxer at any point in my life. I would watch any kind of athletes doing their thing on the telly. I was in love with football and I even had trials with Leeds United with another friend of mine called Michael Smith, It was unofficial trials. What happened was I got suspended from school so me and Michael pretended he was poorly so he could come down with me. We went down to Elland Road to get some autographs. We were both 14 at the time and we just went to see if we could see our hero's around the ground. When we got there I seen all the Leeds team coming towards us, me being cheeky I was getting a bit lairy towards Frank Worthington, John Lukic and Kenny Burns. I was telling them I was a footballer and I remember one of them saying to me, "If you're that good how come you haven't got a team"? It wasn't I was brilliant, but I had a wand of a left foot and in the 70s left footed people were hard to find. I was also a hell of a runner so I could kick the ball and run like hell as well. I told them that because I was getting in trouble at school they wouldn't let me play football. I used to think of myself as a Tony Currie/Peter Beardsley type, that was in my head anyway but in reality id of been a donkey. I'm not if it was because I was so forward or not but me and Michael got invited to train with the under 16 youth squad. At the time the players used to train right out the back of Elland Road on Lowfield Lane. That day me and Michael scored 2 goals each and I even nut-megged a Leeds player. Afterwards me and Michael got in the bath with the Leeds team. I was that excited to be were all my hero's were that I actually went under the water to take a mouthful of water and swallowed it. I loved Leeds United that much that I wanted to savour the moment and get some of that water inside of me to remember the day. It was the greatest day of mine and Michael's life. My Mother had even wrote to Jim'll fix it for me to have a day like this but he never replied. I came out of that training session on cloud fucking 9… That was until me and Michael got around the corner and we heard "SIEG HEIL SIEG HEIL", of course that's a Nazi salute, I turn around and there was a load of National Front running towards us. Me and Michael had to seriously run for our life's. Remember we were just two 14 year old boys and these were grown men chasing us wanting to give us a kicking because of my skin colour. Eventually we seen a bus, the driver at first wouldn't open the doors because he was shitting himself but eventually he did. When I got home and told my Mother id been chased by the National Front she never let me go down there ever again. The worst thing about it is Leeds United were that impressed they invited me back as id impressed in the trial. Leeds even contacted my school to get in touch with me but I was never allowed to go near the place again. I was totally heartbroken and I never played football for a long time after that.

I was 19 years old when I first thought about doing boxing. When I was 19 years old I was in Everthorpe prison near Hull. When I was there a few people tried to pick on me because I was one of only a few black guys there. I was the only black guy on my wing. I quickly learned that the law of prison is, if you don't get caught you don't get done, so I'd bang them out with one shot! If you have a fight in prison, the chances are the authorities are gonna be aware because you're rolling around, but if you whack them out with one shot and put them to sleep, there's no argument and there's a lesser chance of you getting caught. I'm not boasting about it but it was something I had to do. I never lost a day in prison because nobody was awake to report me.

I learnt to punch properly in Armley jail. I would punch the walls with towels wrapped around my hands developing myself because I knew, only the strong survive in prison. I realised there was some serious hard guys in there and it was a dog eat dog society. I gathered that if a small man chins a big man, then chances are that small mans not gonna get touched again because he's already put that front on. If I was seen to be bullied and not stand up for myself in here, then it will open the floodgates, so I would bang them out. I would make sure if anyone tried it on with me I would let them know ASAP they didn't stand a chance with me and they'd think twice about coming at me again. I would get into a lot of fights in prisons, I was moved around to various prisons across the country. I don't say that as "I'm a hard man" but just because I got through it. I never really started proper boxing training until I was shipped to Durham prison in 1985. When I got there they put me on a three month lay down. It was quite a scary place was Durham at that time because Paul Sykes was in there at the time. He was manly It was spread around the prison grapevine that this guy was a monster. One rumour that went around the place was that he used to KO young offenders then bum them! I can speak for all my age group of lads that if you went inside one of the people you didn't want to meet was Paul Sykes! Tyneside's Viv Graham was also in there who I played basketball with. Big Alphonso Fredericks from Leeds and his partner Barbara Day the murderers were also in there. Barbara was on the woman's wing and I used to talk to her on the night shouting from her cell window. In Durham nick there was a mixed race fella from Newcastle called Manny Burgo who'd been an ex boxer, it was him who started giving me tips on how to punch properly in the prison gym on the bag. Around that time my brother Colin came to see me on a prison visit, he said Nick what's happening because every time you're getting locked up your getting bigger sentences, sooner or later your gonna get 'lifed' off and it'll be too late. He asked me what my problem was, so I told him when I'm out on the streets, it's between 6pm and 9pm I have nothing to do, so what I do is go looking for ways to make money. Colin told me he'd started going to a gym and he does that much work from 7pm to 9pm he's too knackered to do anything else. At the time I was doing a two and a half year sentence but managed to get early parole. In that time I'd been shipped to 13 different jails. The screws always told me it was for racial aggravation, I was like hang on a minute. How can it be for racial aggravation when its them calling me a nigger and a black bastard, and all I'm doing is turning around and responding by not allowing it.

From leaving prison I took up amateur boxing at St Patricks ABC in Leeds. The first night I would walk in that gym, Terry O'Neill the coach asked me if I wanted to spar! I found this a bit strange because I'd never even met him before. At the time there was two guys in the gym sparring with each other, one was Tony Massey, the other was York's Henry Wharton. I didn't even know who Henry was but watching him sparring I recognised that he had something about him. It just so happens that me and Henry were born on exactly the same day but one year apart it was so ironic. I would learn so much by watching Henry and how he held himself in the ring. Henry was a really humble guy but he'd beat you up in sparring. I never minded being number two in the gym to that man from the off. Henry had an extremely potent left hook and I was say he was the best fighter I'd ever been in the ring with, to never win a win title. Henry really put the work into boxing and in my view it was that little bit of inexperience that stopped him from becoming a world champion. The one fight Henry should of won which he didn't was Nigel Benn back in 1994. Henry in the fight started late and he had too much respect for Nigel's power and Nigel as a fighter. When Henry was training alongside me, he used to love Nigel Benn as a fighter. I said to Henry a couple of times in the years before he fought Nigel, you want to take a portion of respect away from Nigel Benn because your good enough to fight him one day Henry and you don't want to be thinking like that. Me growing up as a young fighter I used to love Chris Eubank. I got the opportunity to spar with Chris which I was really happy about. I always preferred Eubanks thinking boxing compared to Nigel's crash-bang-wallop style.

When I started amateur boxing I only really did it so I could beat people up. In them days I had to fight because of the racial tensions where I grew up. At times when I was growing up in Leeds, I had grown men trying it on with me just because I was black. At the time there was two things I could do when these incidents occurred, and that was bow my head pretend I didn't see and keep walking, or I could say "FUCK YOU, I've got as much right to be here as you and I'll tell you something I'm not going nowhere" then I'd stand and fight!

Regarding my amateur boxing career I had 17 bouts winning 12 of them. 11 of them I stopped as inside the distance.

I turned pro for one reason and one reason only... Money! To be honest as much confidence and positivity as I had, I was very insecure. I'd just come out of the nick and I didn't trust people easily. In boxing you just want someone to put your arm around you and tell you it's gonna be ok, but in boxing that's far from what happens. Regarding boxing promoters, I don't believe I got a fair shake. I don't say that with bitterness, maybe it was my character and these promoters felt like they couldn't deal with me. Of course I didn't get into when I was a young kid I was a young man, so I didn't feel like boxing owed me anything. I just thought I needed to learn to fight properly and I was gonna give it a go and of course it meant you could get loads of birds and loads of pats on the back. Me and our kid Colin had body's like adonis's, so if you go in there looking fit looking the part looking the business, well to a degree that fella's got to respect you before a punch has been thrown.

I wouldn't make my pro debut until October, 1990 aged 23 at Dewsbury Leisure Centre against Birmingham's Paul Murray. I beat Paul over 6 rounds. I'll never forget in the clinch Paul turned around to me and said "ere mate, we're both gonna get paid you don't need to hit us like that". I couldn't believe it I was in fucking shock for the rest of the fight.

Over the years a lot of really proper boxing people have told me they thought really highly of me as a fighter. I've always said why didn't you tell me then. I think I've always been a bit thick skinned and wouldn't of took any compliments like that anyway. I would go on to win my next 6 fights by KO, then I was matched against Hull's Tony Booth. Before the fight Tony Booth was shaken like a leaf at the thought of fighting me I know that, guy was really nervous. I was quite confident I was gonna deal with him pretty easy before the fight. I say that in all respect because I know Tony's a decent kid. On the night Leeds man Michael Gale was supposed to fight Tony that night, but Michael Gale pulled out. I was supposed to be boxing someone else but only over 6 rounds. When I heard Michael had pulled out of his fight with Tony, I went hang on a minute, I'll fight that Tony booth. I was told "NO NO Tony Booth's a bit too early for you Nick". I told my team I'm 6-0 and I'm at an age where I need to know if I can fight so I'll take the fight so they give me the fight over 8 rounds. As I was ready to walk out of my changing room my coach Terry O' Neill came in and said "You'll sort this fella out in 2 Nick". The second he said that I just went flat. I knew I was capable of doing it but I couldn't deal with the pressure when Terry said that to me. I knew Brendan Ingle would have had a real cagey plan for his fighter Tony Booth and it wasn't going to be a 2 round demolition job that Terry had told me it was gonna be. Tony Booth was a live opponent and it's no coincidence he went on to win 52 contests in a boxing ring. The fight itself well after 4 rounds I was gassing. Out of my full career the Tony Booth fight is my favourite fight because it taught me that I could fight. (The fights on Youtube if you wanna see it) I'm not saying I was world rated but that fight taught me I could get through a bit of adversity, I was knackered from that fourth round. I thought I won the fight, Tony booth thought he won the fight, I say that Mickey Vann gave it a draw because he was disappointed in me not performing a lot better. After the draw with Tony I would go on to gain my first defeat with the unbeaten Kevin Morton of Leicester with an 8 round points defeat 79-78.

From my first defeat led me to boxing on a big show at my beloved Leeds United football ground Elland Road in September 1992. Topping the bill was Henry Wharton defending his Super Middleweight Commonwealth title against Fidel Castro Smith. There were quite a few names on the bill like Herol Bomber Graham and Denzil Browne and I was facing Lee Crocker from Swansea. I remember it was a great privilege to fight at the home of Leeds United football club. I was a young hungry fighter trying to make my name in the 12 stone division so it was a massive opportunity for me on the big stage. I dare say it was one of the greatest nights of my life. So, I've started to started to warm up and focus on my fight with Lee Crocker and I've started shadowboxing and going through a boxers usual rigmarole. I also used to watch the fights before me and I was in the tunnel watching the fighting when suddenly I felt the atmosphere change immediately and I looked around and I saw all the security guards scattering and getting out of the way, then I saw this rather large figure coming towards me. I'm also with Jason Barker from Sheffield who was a former fighter, he was also known as Jason "pretty boy" Barker. Paul walks down and we're thinking he was coming down to give us some words of encouragement, I remember the BBC, Frank Bruno and all kinds of stars were there that night, well Paul walks up to us and says "are you both fighters?" which we tell him we are, he then goes right up to Jason barkers face, looks him right into the eyes and says "I'd rather fuck you then fight you". We looked at each other me and Jason and just moved away from him. They weren't the type of words you wanted to hear 30 minutes before a fight. I went back to my changing room thinking I don't want to be anywhere near that man, fuck that! I was alone in the room gathering my thoughts and getting into the zone mentally then suddenly "BOOM" the door flies open and in walks Paul Sykes, he shouts "here son I've seen you box before" to be honest I think he had me mixed up with Denzil Browne. So he starts saying he'd seen me box but I needed to do this better and that better and I needed to remember to do this etc. etc. etc. then he starts shadow boxing in my face and letting shots go, I've got a massage table in my changing room and I'm going backwards around it and he's still following me giving out all this advice but at the same time he is still throwing heavy shots. He wasn't being nasty then but I had to say "look Terry O'Neill is my coach and he'll here any minute Paul ready to pad me and get me ready" I don't think he liked me saying that and I could tell he had had a drink so he starts again but more of this shadow boxing. Well, I tell you the advice was still coming and I was starting to get a bit pissed off! To be honest he must have chased me around the table at least 3 times. Then something just crept into my head, I started asking myself "Are you bottling this Nick" I'm thinking I'm about to go out there and be warrior and this guy is chasing me around the table, it really wasn't ideal preparation to go and face a guy who had already beaten my older brother. I just refused to have this guy ruining my time to shine on the big stage. So, I've taken a step back and I've said to him "listen, I'm going to stand still now so you need to stop throwing punches Paul or you're going to connect and I'm not having it" with me saying that he kept throwing punches and shouting angry instructions and then I just totally snapped and banged him with a left hook and down he went, straight to sleep, he was out cold. Now panic sets in with me thinking I've killed him, then I start worrying I haven't killed him and he's going to wake up any second and kill me! This is Paul Sykes we're talking about here put yourself in my shoes. It's easy throwing a punch and banging someone out but it's the consequences afterwards that were starting to worry me. The first thing when I stopped panicking was I grabbed him by his Mac and put him under the shower on full blast, he started to slowly come around but he was very groggy, he made a loud groan and said "good shot that kid" then he got himself together and went back into the crowd. I never saw him again but I tell you what he shouted the loudest for me that night and I could hear his voice above all the others whilst I was fighting. A few people told me he was shouting some racist abuse but I never heard any of that. I won that night in 21 seconds of the first round by KO so that was my second KO of the night. I hit Lee Crocker so hard that he broke his leg in three places. Lee was in plaster to his knee for months after our fight. What I will say about Paul Sykes was fair play to the guy because there were never any comebacks after our altercation in the dressing room, he just let it go. I still have a scar on my left hand from that eventful evening. I went to get a tetanus after it too just in case. After my greatest night in Elland Road I was quickly brought down to earth in 3 rounds to Londoner Ali Forbes at Leeds Town Hall a month later. I gathered my stuff together by beating Jason Fores and Joe McKenzie both inside 2 rounds, only to lose on points over 6 rounds to Edinburgh's Sean Heron so I had almost a year off from boxing. I would come back to face some young kid from Wales called Joe Calzaghe who was 12-0, I'd like to say I trained to beat Joe but I had only 6 days notice for the fight. The reason id been away from boxing before that fight was the inconvenience of a few little prison sentences in between. When I fought Joe he was basically too fast and too fit for me. If I'd of beat him, I would of ruined his legacy because I'd of had a few more fights then just retired. I didn't train with the commitment and dedication Joe Calzaghe did or the history that he made. I know it sounds bizarre but I'm almost glad I didn't beat him so I never ruined that. I never came close to having a love or desire what real boxers like him had. I was very silly with my career because I then had another 6 months off from the Joe Calzaghe fight and fought Bruce Scott who was a fucking animal. It's funny but when I lost to Calzaghe I went up in the British rankings because of the performance I gave. At that time I'd asked for my contract back from Mickey Duff. I was chuffed I was able to say my manager was Mickey Duff when I finished boxing because he was a real somebody in the boxing world. In reality he was never going to let me leave him amicably. When I fought Joe Calzaghe he was managed by Mickey Duff also, I think Mickey was trying to get me a right good beating so I'd disappear out of boxing because that's what these promoters do if they don't like you. I got a lot of credit losing to Joe Calzaghe and I never got the beating Mickey Duff had hoped. So he put me in with Bruce Scott. When Duff told me I was fighting Bruce Scott at The York Hall in Bethnal Green I was like who the fucks he! Then I found out he was 16-1 and knocked most of his opponents out. I'd never seen or heard of Bruce Scott before until I boxed him. I remember seeing some bloke as I was going into the York Hall who looked like Mike Tyson but I never thought for one minute I'd be facing him. Then I seen him walking around with his top off in the York Hall but id still never clicked id be fighting him. I remember saying to my corner man Sharky Brown, I wanna see that bloke fight tonight because he looks fucking vicious! Next thing, I'm waiting in the ring waiting for my opponent and guess who walks through this fucking bull Bruce Scott into the ring staring at me and smiling. I never had any incline to who he was because I never really watched anybody outside my weight division back in them days and Bruce was from two weight divisions above me. When the bell went I quickly found out this fella could fucking punch rather sharpish! Even the punches that Bruce threw at me and missed, I could feel the wind as his punches whistled past my head. I'm telling you now Bruce Scott punched with bad intentions that night, I don't know what I'd done to him. He wanted to really hurt me that night before he stopped me in 5 rounds. I didn't really agree with the stoppage, I was more knackered than hurt but maybe the ref saved me for another day and he knew I was facing a much bigger guy.

After I lost to Bruce Scott I had back to back KO victories. I beat Sheffield's Paul Mason in 4 rounds to win the BBBofC Central Area Light Heavyweight Title in October 1997. Then I defended against Doncaster's Kevin Burton in 1 round before I walked away from professional boxing for good still a fairly young man at 30. The reason I packed in was at around 20 years of age I promised myself that if I wasn't ready to fight for a major title by the age of 30, then I might as well knock it on the head. Also at the time I'd been nominated by the BBBofC to fight Coventry's Neil

Simpson for a British Title Eliminator in Scotland, but the money they were offering wouldn't of even covered my training expenses. I even suggested I face Neil Simpson in his backyard of Coventry or my brother Colin could of put a show on in Leeds but it fell on deaf ears. From what they were offering I'd of been left with nothing so I told the BBBofC if that's how you want to treat me then I don't need the fight.

The only regret I ever had in boxing was not training properly. I should of really conditioned my body to be in top shape like my brother Colin did. For a while Henry Wharton told me Guinness was non-alcoholic and it's what us boxers should drink so I did. I would drink it and tell people I didn't drink but really I was because I didn't know. I wasn't really a drinker though but it doesn't go with the image does it. Boxers are demigod's and should stand up correct and look the part. Boxers are what everyone in the crowd wants to be, if you watch the crowds faces who are watching a boxing match, you can see they would love to be the guy in the ring. I didn't abuse myself with alcohol but I never trained to be the best Nick Manners I could be to be quite truthful. Boxing is the best leveller that I've ever come across, it just levels people and just humbles them. There's no lying in boxing you can't lie. You've got to expose yourself and you have to live with what you put out. I love the game of boxing still to this day in my gym like Neanderthals, they're shoulders are hunched and they can't look you in the eye or even shake your hand. Instead of walking they just shuffle along. I have to pull them aside and say, look calm down this is an opportunity to start again. Bit by bit I can see these kids changing as I'm moulding them into walking properly and even speaking right. I love it when I see these huge changes of these young folk who I have in my gym 3 times a week and it's not just me, this goes on in boxing gyms all over the country.

The two most talented fighters I've ever been in the ring with are Naseem Hamed and Joe Calzaghe. Originally and early on in my career I was in the Ingle camp and I would do body sparring with Naseem. I've always had fast hands myself and I don't say that in a bragging way but the only two people I've ever been in a boxing ring with and felt slow was Joe and Naz.

These days I have a gymnasium in Leeds I created myself I built the place from scratch. All I had at the start was a pair of pads, gloves and a body belt. In the early days I would charge maybe £15ph for a 1-2-1 session and with that id put £5 to my pocket, £5 for expenses and £5 to the sports centre I was using. Over time I started saving squirreling money away because it was all about getting my own place. An opportunity came for me to hire a small room and Thomas Danby college in Leeds and I had that place for 12 months. It was there I was finding my feet being a coach and making my living in becoming a boxing trainer. Also there I used to pad Leeds boxer China Clarke who was a really decent fighter, I told him not to waste the talent he had so what I did was get him in top shape then I sent him on to another gym because at the time I wasn't a professional boxing trainer. China Clarke went on to win the English Cruiserweight Title beating Wadi Camacho. I dragged China out of the boxing wilderness and sat down with him telling him he needs to go pro because when you get to a certain age you don't want to be thinking could I of done this that or the other in boxing. I knew China had that fight in him and I told him to get it out of him and he listened to me and went on to do alright in boxing. I would often get these kids coming to me and getting them into shape so I could myself get my padwork going and my hands going so they were using me and I was using them if you like. I was looking to find out myself if I could be positive and constructive to these young fighters and I believed I could. I discovered one of my best attributes was I was a good motivator and I was always honest with a fighter. Boxing's not a game where you can benefit a fighter by lying to him because he'll be found out then who's fault will that be.

I'm very lucky that I've persevered with boxing and I now have my own place called Precise Accurate Training on Macauley Street in Leeds. The place is my own business and its open Mon, Tues, Wed, Thur, Fri. Quite often I get kids through my door that think they've got to act a certain way in life to conform or fit in, to a degree I don't mind dealing with these kids who are unsure of what they want to do and where they want to go in life. Before they have the opportunity to make the wrong move, I'd rather have them in my gym and tell them to clear their head. I tell them to only be around people who don't want to do the wrong thing and you'll realise you can have a decent life by just being decent. I never judge any kid who comes into my gym. They're told that when they're training between 7pm and 9pm there do what I say and show people respect. I tell them that I may not be everyone's cup of tea but you're here to listen and learn. In my training sessions I don't mess about, you either do it or you don't and if you don't then there's no point in them even being in here. These days me and my brother Colin run the gym. Colin's recently come over to my gym as he was training at Burmantofts ABC in Leeds. My other brother Ricky Manners is an established boxing and promoter in Leeds. I will be forever thankful to Ricky for making sure I got the opportunity to win an established title and it was him that pushed me for that. The one thing I didn't want to do was be just a fella who people thought of as just a tough kid in boxing or just a banger. I wanted the words champion behind my name. No disrespect to anybody else but I didn't want a British Masters, at that time there was a traditional way of doing things like the Area, British, Commonwealth, European then the world which then you're the man. I always wanted to do it the right way and the Area Title I won meant I was the cock of my area. When I had that title I was asking lots of people if they wanted to fight me and it fell on deaf ears. Even a guy who went on to become a world champion I asked to fight him for it and his answer was "you don't bring the crowd". I told him bollocks I bring as much of a crowd as you do, I just wasn't interested in the risk of facing me.

When it came right down to it, I decided to stop boxing, boxing never stopped me and not many people can say that.

In 1998 I was used as a sparring partner by Chris Eubank for his first fight with Manchester's Carl Thompson. I was hired for 2 weeks but he paid me off after 3 days of sparring on full pay. One reason he paid me off and I quote Chris, "I asked for speed, but not that much speed". (You have to read that in Chris Eubank's voice).

These days I'm very much part of The Leeds Warrior Josh Warrington's team. After Josh won his commonwealth Title in Hull against Samir Mouneimne, Sean Josh's Dad approached me and asked me if I'd like to join his team at the back end of 2013. Our team are a winning team and were doing our best to represent Leeds itself and bring back the first world title to Leeds. Josh has been doing it since he was 9 years old and is fully dedicated to the sport. Josh has the same kind of focus, dedication, desire and drive as your Joe Calzaghe's and when you see a fighter like Josh you couldn't back against him. One thing that makes me so proud is finally we have an arena in Leeds that can support the fighters now, and I feel so proud walking out with Josh Warrington, that young kid who'd from a council estate. From a young age Josh has turned around and said I'm not gonna be a robber, thief or a dealer I'm gonna fight with these fists and you can try to take it out on my face. There's been loads of people in my life who've contributed in making me the person I am today. I'm thankful to my Mum and my whole family for supporting me and looking after me. I also met an old man by the name of Mike Cronack AKA Mighty Mike and he taught me so much in life. I lost him last year but I hope I continue to try to be a good person and help rather than hinder. I'm a Leeds man, a Leeds fan, I love where I'm from and I love the people I'm around. WE ARE LEEDS!

If anyone wants to contact Nick you can on 07943969643. You can also follow Nick on Twitter @mannersboxing also on Facebook MannersBoxing. 'Manners Maketh Men' also his other Facebook page MannersBoxing or by email preciseaccuratetraining@yahoo.co.uk

"I don't know if I wanted to top myself or if I just wanted someone to hug me".

Nigel Benn

Gary Sykes

It must have been around 2011 that I was sat watching Gary Sykes boxing on the telly with my brother in law. He turned to me and said, "Imagine if you met Gary Sykes and you found out he was an arsehole"! He went on to tell me he thought Gary Sykes was one of the nicest guys in British boxing who always came across very well on the telly. I had to agree, he was very much the opposite to your Chris Eubank Jnr, Luqmaan Patel, Wadi Camacho or Ohara Davies who people believe probably come in the brackets of being pure arseholes.

I went on to interview Gary Sykes for my first book 'Sykes – Unfinished Agony' about his namesake and fellow Yorkshire man Paul Sykes. From there on I've got to know Gary very well over the last couple of years. My brother in-laws initial first thoughts on Gary were very accurate indeed and I'm proud to call Gary a friend and we've had him over to our house several times over the last couple of years.

Gary's been retired almost two years now and it's fair to say from my own judgement of him he's found living life away from boxing a huge struggle. In fact he's been completely lost and if it wasn't for the fact he has such a wonderful partner in Natasha, I dread to think where Gary would be or what he would be doing now.

I don't want to sound like I'm now slating Gary because I've told him he has major issues in our many conversations regarding his silly shenanigans. None quite as stupid as when he phoned me one Sunday afternoon and told me he was travelling the 46 miles from his house to ours, only for him to turn up absolutely steaming drunk. I had no idea he was in the state he was when speaking to him on the phone not until he arrived. Me and my wife were horrified he'd driven all that way but even more astounded he'd got here in one piece and hadn't injured himself or someone else. I told Gary I was mortified by his actions and he even admitted the next day that when he woke up on my settee (I had to put him to bed) he had no recollection of how he'd even got there.

It's all very well me giving him advice on what to do and what not to do, but the fact is I was never a professional fighter who'd been used to the limelight at the very top of British boxing. For all the daft things Gary has done in the last two years since his departure from boxing and he's let me down on certain occasions but it's absolutely impossible to dislike him. He might be daft as shit but cards on the table there's no badness in him. I've never found him to be sneaky or pre-meditated, just a little boy who's now lost and struggling to replace something he's lost. He's looking for something that he'll never find or replace. For 17 years boxing was the only thing Gary Sykes knew or was good at.

I'd almost given up hope on adding my friend Gary to this book because he must have let me down about seven times when it came to interviewing him, but by some miraculous miracle he rang me one day when he finally had a stroke of "normalness" about him. I sat back and listened to how Gary came from just a council estate in Dewsbury to becoming a 2 x British champion.

Gary said:

I'm 34 years of age now and I grew up on Dewsbury Moor the place Shannon Matthews disappeared from in West Yorkshire. I actually grew up on the same road as Karen and Shannon Matthews.

These days I now reside in Heckmondwike. My first boxing memory was the fight on ITV between Nigel Benn and Gerard McClellan. How that never put me off boxing for life I'll never know. I was watching it not knowing anything about tactics or skill or anything like that, in my young mind of a 12-year-old, it was Britain against America and I was supporting the Brit jumping up and down at the telly.

I wouldn't start boxing myself until the age of 15, although I always wanted to box when I was really young, but my Mum wouldn't let me go. Mum thought it would make me have a violent nature. I used to play football and I played for two teams, I was quite a decent player, I also used to go running a lot before I started boxing. After a while I managed to somehow get permission off my Mum to allow me to go, just on a trial period to boxing. Near where I lived there was an amateur boxing club called Batley & Dewsbury ABC. This club was run by a gentleman called Keith Tate who'd been an old ex pro himself and he had even beaten the great Ken Buchanan as an amateur. I only really started going because I knew a few of the local lads near me who used to go, one of them lads were Jenson Garforth who was a national champion boxer. Jenson was one of the tough lads off my estate and I looked up to him if you like.

When I started boxing I completely sacked football off and boxing just took over my life from day one.

A big boost in 1999 to my love of boxing was when I was 15 when I came across a prime Oscar De La Hoya. I would watch videos of him fight after fight and I just wanted to be like him.

In my amateur club of Batley & Dewsbury I would go down and train with the juniors from 5.30pm until 7pm with Keith Tate. Then Keith would go home, he lived next door to the gym. I would stay and train with the seniors taken by Julian McGowan for another two hours because I was so keen. I've always said this contributed massively to my fantastic fitness and work rate when I became a pro. Truth be told I was only training to get fit, this was one of the promises I made to my Mum, I told her I would never box. It wasn't until Keith Tate came up to me one night and told me he'd booked me in for my medical in a couple of days because he had my first fight arranged in Redcar a week later. When he told me that I absolutely shit myself! I thought, what the fucks going on I was only coming to get fit. Then I thought I'm just gonna have to go through with it now. My coach Keith Tate was quite a strong-willed man and I didn't want to upset him. I felt like I'd been given my date for the electric chair.

So, the time came for me to box this little stocky guy from Redcar ABC, I can't recall his name but in the first minute of the fight I remember thinking in that first round was "this is it, I'll get this fight out of the way and I'm not coming back to boxing ever again it's too hard". In that first round the other guy hit me with absolute bombs! He was like a bull in that first round I wasn't used to it. I'd only light sparred previously to this and I didn't like it one bit. It did enter my head to take a knee and give up, but I have too much pride and I'd have never have lived it down from the other lads in the gym. I started coming back into it in the second round because he'd burnt himself out doing me so much damage in the first. In the third I gave him two standing counts and nearly stopped him, but I got a points decision.

I would go on to have 61 amateur bouts winning 51 of them. I won a NABC title, I also won a junior ABA title, beating Manchester's John Murray in the final of it. I beat Murray on a club show as well.

In only my 6th fight as an amateur Keith put me in the Boys Clubs championships with Gwyn Wale from Barnsley. I was very inexperienced, and Gwyn had won national titles for fun he was like a little man. Everybody was saying Keith was off his head for putting me in the ring with him because I was gonna get murdered. In the warm up to that fight I was in the same room as Gwyn, with only for a make shift screen separating us, the next thing I heard "BANG BOOM BANG", to me it sounded like a heavyweight hitting the pads. No kid my age could possibly wallop that hard. One of my mates looked at me while pulling a face with a look of sheer terror. "Gary that's the lad you're boxing making them thuds". I turned and had a sneaky peak to see Gwyn Wale full of tattoos murdering these pads, then there's me stood there like a right skinny little twerp. On the way to the ring I heard one of the arena bouncers laughing and saying to his fellow bouncer "huh, I know who my money's on". We got to the ring and when the fight started it was a piece of piss I danced around him in 2nd gear. After beating the tournament favourite, I lost to Paul Holburn in the next round from Sunderland.

I did go over to Germany and lost a points decision to former WBC World Champion Vitali Tajbert when we were both still amateurs. I didn't know who Tajbert was, so I didn't have any fear. After I boxed him and lost by four points the England coach said to me that they didn't want to tell me, but he was No. 2 in the world at the weight. Me and Amir Khan were over there representing our countries. I roomed with Amir all the way through our England training camps.

Amir was proper hyperactive as a kid and If Amir wasn't prancing around the room he'd be on his phone texting away, but it would be constantly beeping away and keeping all of us awake at night. It got so bad that when

Amir went to the venue to box, I nicked his phone charger and chucked it away. Sorry Amir if you're reading this but you would keep me up until the early hours when I would be boxing the next day.

In Germany after I boxed Vitali Tajbert I went to the saunas with Amir but before we went to step in some fella ordered me to take my shorts off. "FUCKING HELL" I thought, this is a bit seedy so we both thought fuck that got dressed and put our clothes back on and walked out.

Top American fighter Matt Remillard was another top amateur I faced and beat. In 2011 he fought Mikey Garcia but now I believe Remillard is doing a long strength for attempted murder.

I would go training down Crystal Palace in London with the elite of amateur boxing. One day in training I looked around the gym and everyone I was training with at the time were all signing forms to go pro. Don Broadhurst, David Dolan, Frankie Gavin, James Degale and Tony Bellew were all off to try and make their name in the pro ranks. I thought if I was gonna give it a go it may as well be now. Not being picked for the Commonwealth Games in 2006 kind of just gave me a nudge so I turned over and was trained by Rick Manners in Leeds 2006. I only had 2 fights with Rick in the first 14 months of being a pro, which of course just wasn't enough. After I left Rick I hooked up with Chris Aston and Frank Maloney and started boxing more regularly. When I started off boxing journeymen at the beginning of my pro career I found they didn't have any fear and I couldn't get motivated so it I made it a harder fight than was necessary. When I fought Ibrar Riyaz I even forgot my boots and I had to lend George Watson's boots straight after he had boxed, my trainer Julian had to run to the ring and take George's boots off him.

After every fight I would eat shit and go out on the piss for a few weeks. I'll never forget I was laid in the house on one of my sessions when Julian came to my front door saying that we'd been offered a British title in 3 weeks and did I want it! It was supposed to be against Ricky Burns but he'd sidestepped it to get a shot at the world title. The fight would now be against Manchester's Andy Morris on March 5th 2010. I took the fight and it was a 12-round brawl and was nominated for one of the fights of 2010, I was now the Super Featherweight British Champion.

When I first turned pro I never thought that I was good enough to win a British title. I still, to this day, watch that fight just for that moment when the ring announcer says, "and the winner from DEWSBURY", I've never had a moment in my life like that before it gives me goose bumps even now just talking about it all these years later.

After I won the British title I went on my usual sessions on the piss, to all the house parties being stupid. I know I could have done miles better for myself because before I won the British title I boxed Anthony Crolla in a 10 rounder and beat him easy, of course he went on to become a world champion.

One of the craziest things I've ever been asked to do in my boxing career was walk to the ring in a 'Find Shannon Matthews t-shirt', only a few days before she got found and it came out that her mam Karen was in on it, thank fuck for that, because I'd have looked a right dickhead as I'd already told her mam I was gonna wear one.

As a professional fighter I had 33 bouts winning 28 with 6 KO'S and losing 5. I was a 2 x British champion, English champion and I fought for the Commonwealth title, so I know I didn't have a bad career. I just wish I never did all the silly things regarding partying because when I didn't have a fight on I had no motivation I just didn't want to even be in the gym.

When I made my first defence of the British Title against Belfast's Kevin O'Hara I'd been on the piss for ages. I only trained for 3 weeks, so I feel it is very bad of me to say, but I beat him easily. When I beat Kevin, I went back on the piss for months on end. My trainer Julian McGowan was turning down fights for me because I wasn't even in the gym and I was the British champion. Julian said the reason he put me in the Prize Fighter was purely just to get me back in the gym away from the pubs and clubs. Normally people go in the Prize Fighter on the way up or on the way down. It's unheard of that a British champion would even go in them, well I did because I needed the rehab. I went from being in a pub to being in Prize Fighter in 3 weeks. Going in Prize Fighter was the biggest regret of my career because until then I hadn't lost a fight. I beat Stoke's Scott Lawton in the quarter finals by three scores of 30-27 and I looked really good. Until along came Gary Buckland who knocked me out in 45 seconds. When you watch that fight you can see me saying to the ref as he's waving it off "WHAT THE FUCK HAPPENED"! Up until then I felt I was invincible in a boxing ring.

After that bad KO I became more cautious which was a good thing for my next fight taking on the monster Carl Johanneson straight after it. I was still British champion even after my loss to Gary Buckland because you couldn't lose a title in the Prize Fighters three round format. I'd sparred Carl Johanneson a few months before I fought him and it's the only time I've ever been put down in sparring in my life. I went along because he was very to me being from Leeds, I was thinking it was gonna be just a steady spar then suddenly "BANG" and I was on the deck.

One of my biggest achievements in boxing was when I would go on to beat Carl in May 2011 over 12 rounds because I didn't think I would even go the distance with him never mind get the win.

After the Johanneson fight I got the chance of redemption taking on Gary Buckland again. I lost a 12-round decision but rather than win the fight I just wanted to prove to people that he couldn't knock me out again. I went to war with him rather than try to box and of course I wasn't a slugger I was a boxer, so I lost the fight trying to be macho.

When I lost my British title of course I went back to my party lifestyle. Around midnight one night I got a knock on my door and it was my trainer Julian. I was completely hammered but he told me we'd been offered a fight in Las Vegas against Adrian Broner for the WBO title and asked did I want it. Yeah of course I wanted to have it, then I closed the door and went to back drinking again. The next morning, I woke up and I was like "EH, WAS THAT A FUCKING DREAM?" I rang Julian up and he was like, "yeah we're boxing Adrian Broner in six weeks' time". For the first few weeks I was shitting myself training for Broner, then after I gained my fitness I started really believing in myself, I was training 4 times a day in beast mode. I even started training myself at stupid o clock to get my body ready but of course it fell through. Lamont Peterson failed a drugs test in his rematch with Amir Khan so the whole show was scrapped, and I was devastated because that was the best I'd ever sparred /trained in a build up to a fight. Their fight fell through and my 70K fight had also disappeared. When the fight with Adrian Broner didn't happen, I was that devastated I was thinking of calling it a day with boxing because I didn't have any titles and a career best purse had just gone down the swanny through no fault of my own.

An opportunity came for me to go back into Prize Fighter at the weight above me at lightweight. This one was being billed as the best one yet because it was full of champions like Derry Matthews, Anthony Crolla, Tommy Coyle, Terry Flanagan and Mongolian Warrior Choi. In the first fight I beat Hull's Tommy Coyle. Then I faced my old foe Anthony Crolla again to beat him for the second time. If that would have been a 12 round fight I'd have stopped him because I really beat him up. I would go on to lose a close points decision to Manchester's Terry Flanagan, who of course, went on to become a world champion a few years after. My fight in the final with Terry was that close that 76% of the Sky Sports viewers thought it was the wrong decision and that I should have won.

It wasn't all doom and gloom though because straight after the second Prize Fighter I won the English title beating Grimsby's Kevin Hooper on a unanimous decision in his backyard. After the fight I went back to the hotel with a few mates partying and tripped over a table and smashed my teeth out, I'm terrible when I'm pissed.

I made one defence of my English title beating Lancashire's Jon Kays at the Sheffield Arena on the undercard of Amir Khan V Julio Diaz in April 2013. After the fight I gave the English title up because I had my sights on regaining my old British crown. After back to back wins over Mark McKray and Femi Fehintola I was to get a shot at the British title which Liverpool's Stephen Smith had. Smith then vacated the title and promoter Steve Wood arranged for me to face Jon Kays yet again but this time for the British in my hometown of Dewsbury which I always wanted. I stopped Jon in our second fight in the 10th round but I felt like I'd aged overnight in that contest. If I'm being truthful I knew I'd seen better days from that point onwards. Jon even put me down in the 2nd round of the fight. When me and Jon weighed in we were

261

both slightly over, so me and Jon had to go over the road to the Dewsbury Sports centre and sit in their sauna together, bearing in mind the next day we had to go to war.

My first defence of my second stint of being British champion was Norfolk's Liam Walsh. He was one clever customer because when I was in my best days of boxing I was down to box him on two separate occasions and he pulled out. Then when I did box Liam he got me just at the right time and he had me down in the first minute of the fight. Liam was hitting me with such heavy body shots that if I never had such much pride I'd have called it a day and stayed down, my ribs were killing me the next day.

I did get another win against Ibrar Riyaz before I was to have my last fight against Olympic champion Luke Campbell up at lightweight for the vacant Commonwealth title in March 2016. I was done in two rounds by Luke and I knew that I was done in boxing.

After that fight I pulled a shocking stunt on my Mrs and went abroad for a piss up. Previously I'd been invited to Tenerife by the Walsh brothers for a training camp, but I'd declined. Well when I lost to Luke I told my girlfriend Natasha I was going to Tenerife training with Liam Walsh and co when really I went to Tenerife for 4 days on the piss. Those 4 days are still to this day a complete blur. Natasha doesn't know to this day I pulled that stunt and I'm hoping she won't even now. I think I should be safe because she doesn't read boxing books!

I did have a fight pencilled in to fight Sean Dodd but one morning I got up and thought "I can't be fucking arsed"! In the past when I've thought like that I've pushed myself and made myself go. Whereas that morning I didn't even go, and it was that day that I looked at myself in the mirror and I knew if I didn't have the desire to just even go jogging I was gonna end up getting badly hurt so I called it a day. I knew it was the right time to get out of boxing that morning. I'd done nothing but boxed from 15 to 32 and now it was gone. What else was I gonna do!

Boxing gave me a lot of good times and none more so than when I went to 10 Downing Street to see the Prime Minister. I'd been sent down by the folks of Dewsbury because of all the bad press Dewsbury had received over the Shannon Matthews fiasco. I have a picture of the then Prime Minister David Cameron holding my British belt over his shoulders.

At first when I retired I was so happy because I could eat what I wanted to. When I was going jogging and it got hard I could stop instead of having to keep going to push myself.
Now, I miss it so much that I even have thoughts to make a comeback but it's never really a serious thought, I know I'm done. I know there wouldn't be any titles if I did come back, basically I'd be just a name for some up and coming kid to have on their record and I've never wanted to be just a name. I was a 2 x British champion.

Since I've retired I've been a bit lost I don't mind saying. I've crashed my car because I was drunk, I'm just so glad nobody got hurt and I've well and truly learnt my lesson. I've been an idiot and I've been lost as a person. Before I was Gary Sykes the champion around town, now these days I'm just Gary Sykes so I feel like I've got an identity issue. Any boxer that's reading this please take note from me, because I had the party lifestyle and although I had good times and I didn't want to miss out, it cut short my career and I know I could have done so much better. I burnt the candle at both ends.

Now I've finished boxing I have no trade, so I've got to start all over again. When I was a boxing champion I had so many hangers on, people I didn't even know would be ringing me attaching themselves to me. I'll tell you something right, this year when it was New Year's Day I received three texts of best wishes. Back say 6-7 years ago I wouldn't even read them they would be that many. If that doesn't put things into perspective I don't know what will.

I wish Josh Warrington had come along when I was on the scene, so I could have hung around with him. When you look at the boxers from say Liverpool and Manchester their all close together. The only friends I had were pissheads and I got drawn in.

When I was boxing it kept me in order I had real discipline when I wasn't being stupid.

Boxing's still a big part of my life now but I only watch it from my armchair. Funnily enough I watch more boxing now than I did do when I was fighting.

I had some right laughs in boxing, one time I was with Amir Khan in Croatia at the Olympic qualifiers in 2004 and I nearly had a fight with Eric Donovan from Ireland who's just gone pro now. We all got put out of the qualifiers in the first round apart from Liverpool's David Price so we all went to a nightclub. When we were in the nightclub Amir wasn't even drinking and he had his top off swinging it around like a complete nutter. I was getting with this bird, but I had no idea Eric Donovan had been cracking on with her and when he came back from the toilet he lunged at me and it had to be broken up by about 12 people, it was absolutely crazy! Amir was always doing funny shit and I still haven't forgotten the prank he played on Luke Campbell when he was asleep and took a picture. Another funny story was the time I got trapped in a lift for over half an hour with James Degale and Tony Bellew, James started crying I kid you not.

I just wish I'd have got with Natasha earlier on in my career rather than at the end of it, Tash is very sensible with money and she'd have stopped me blowing huge amounts of it on shite. God I was so shit with money and at times I craved a real job like a bin man or working in Lidl, so I could allocate it weekly. Instead I got it thrown at me all at once when I was just a young and immature kid. It was like letting a dog loose on his food then wondering why it ate till it was sick.

I wish I could go back and do it all again differently but of course I can't.

"The run home was my school bus, the long runs in the cold nights were my parties, the gym was my playground".

Josh Warrington

John Pearce

I first heard John Pearce's name when I was about the age of 12 years old from around the Middlesbrough boxing scene. He was a bit like the Loch Ness Monster to me as a kid. I had never seen him in the flesh, but you knew this myth existed because everybody spoke of this guy in Middlesbrough's gyms.

The first time I met him I must have been around 14-15 years of age and I went to a sauna with my gym friend Carl Vallily (Commonwealth Gold 2010 winner Simon's brother). Me and Carl were sat talking away when we noticed this fat bloke coming in, he must have heard us talking about boxing because he told us he was a boxer. "What's your name mate"? I said, being my usual cheeky nosey self, I've never been backwards in coming forwards in anyone's company that I've been in. "John Pearce" was his reply. I remember swearing at him "NO FUCKING WAY YOU'RE THIS JOHN PEARCE EVERYBODY TALKS ABOUT"! I remember it clearly to this day, John, at the time, was probably around the 15stone mark and didn't look like this model Middlesbrough legend that I'd heard so much about for the last few years. I liked John immensely from our very first meeting though. I wonder if my friend Carl Vallily remembers that day also.

John Pearce comes from a really strong boxing background. His great uncle Jimmy Pearce fought in the 1940/50s. His Father John Pearce was also a really good solid pro with a hell of a left hook, this must have been where John Jnr got his legendary left hook from. His younger brothers Mark and Paul were also decent fighters who both won national titles between them.

For me personally as I was growing up, John was a bit of a role model but not just to me, but to many of my friends around the boxing scene also. When John won the ABA'S for the first time in 1996 he was asked to hand trophies out at my club show, the Old Vic ABC, it was a loser's trophy as was the norm for me, but he always had time to talk, was very well mannered and he comes from really good stock.

I can only speak well of the full Pearce family in Middlesbrough and I'm sure anybody who knows them will be nodding their head in agreement reading this. Some of the most knowledgeable boxing conversations I've ever had were with John Pearce Snr in his old haunt the Brambles Farm pub.

For as good as I knew John Pearce was as an amateur, I'd always wondered why he never turned pro! After winning two ABA titles and a Commonwealth Gold in Kuala Lumper in 1998, 27-year-old John must have had the world at his feet and for all the times that I'd seen John over the last nearly 20 years, it was a question I'd never really got around to asking him until now.

Anyone who has seen the Wellington Middleweight box could tell a mile off he fought like a pro even in the amateurs and would have been greatly better off by turning over into the paid ranks.

One thing I remember looking back at John from around 1995-99 was the amount of times I'd seen him looking out of shape! I know the pro fighters can do it, you've only got to look back at Ricky Hatton's career or more recently Tyson Fury's but John, for most of the 90s was on the England squads (Now GB Team) and when he let himself blown up like he did, it must have left a mountain to climb before he joined up with England's elite at the Crystal

Palace boxing camps. One memory I have regarding John Pearce was an old girlfriend of mine in 1997, told me that when she was working in the Porthole Café opposite Albert Park in Middlesbrough, she said "That boxer friend of yours come in our café this morning and bought two dinners, people were looking at him in disbelief of how much he was eating". John by his own admission didn't drink, smoke or take drugs, but food was his vice. I suppose the people who don't live or have never been to Middlesbrough wouldn't understand the addiction of a "Parmo" once you tried them. Crystal Meth users will never understand the withdrawals you get from not having the famous "Boro dish" once you've tried it.

I must say from my own personal experience of writing this book, out of the 20 people I've chosen, John Pearce was the one I was looking forward to the most! Many of the boxers I've met in life can be a bit of a let-down, there's an old saying, never meet your hero's because you'll only be left disappointed, well John may have only been an amateur, but in my eyes he's as big a star as anybody in this book. The talent he had was frightening, his style was unique in a boxing ring and he must have been fucking awful to fight. John Pearce was from the same mould as a Gennady Golovkin but with more of a noticeable left hook to the body. When I would watch him when I was a schoolboy I would watch him cut top amateurs in half with that deadly left hook to the body of his.

Many years ago, John sent me a few clips of his ABA quarter final bout with Carl Froch in 1999. When you watch that bout you can see Froch almost running for his life and he was in a sheer panic anytime that Pearce was in reach of hitting him with that rib crunching shot of his. Not only was John Pearce a terrific pugilist but he's a wonderful fella. One thing I found very tragic back in 1998 was when John won the Commonwealth Gold, the town of

Middlesbrough never really did anything for him, I'm not saying he should have had an open top bus parade but for a genuine salt of the earth lad from just a council estate to go and do what he achieved it should have been recognised more. He's without doubt written his name in Middlesbrough folklore for good reasons.

Often when people think of Middlesbrough they think of Bernie Slaven, Chubby Brown, Chris Rea, Brian Clough or the Parmo. Well if you think of Middlesbrough and boxing in the same sentence he's without doubt one of the names people will think about. It was an absolute privilege and honour to add John Pearce Jnr to this book. It may of taken me longer than all the rest of the book to pin John down due to his hectic schedule, and also the threat of a possible injunction should I not leave him alone (Joking) but I finally sat down with him and asked him where it all begin for him in boxing, and how he became Britain's number one middleweight of the 1990s.

John said:

I grew up on the Brambles Farm estate of Middlesbrough and I'm 46 years of age now and I live in Acklam in Middlesbrough now.

My first ever memory of boxing is of my Dad taking me to some gym. It's one of my earliest memories that I can even think of, at this time my Dad had stopped boxing, but he was going training. I never went to do any boxing I was only maybe 3-4 and was just toddling around the gym whilst my old man trained just to keep in shape. I was stood behind the bag and my Dad was tippy tapping the bag until his natural desire must have taken over, then he really hit this big old leather bag hard, and it hit me straight on the chops and my head also banged off this big old-fashioned radiator. My Dad stopped and picked me up immediately, I was bawling my eyes out hysterical. I guess you could say my first ever memory was a painful one in a boxing gym because I can't remember anything earlier than that day.

As small as my Dad was and I mean he was only a featherweight in his prime, he could really work a bag. My Dad had great feet with a terrific left hook so that's maybe were I got it from. The funny thing is my Dad never wanted me to ever become a boxer, he always encouraged me to play football.

From as far back as I can remember when he came in from work, because he had his own building company did my dad, I would run and get his gloves out from underneath the stairs and wanted to box him. I used to spar my old man, he'd be on his knees and I'd go hell for leather on his head with these giant gloves because I was only little. More often than not he'd say, "no son, come on let's play football over the Brambles Farm school fields" and most of the time, as soon as I'd get there I'd be whinging to go back home to spar. Football was never enough for me so I'd pester him to take me home so we could spar. He always gave in if I let him have his tea first. Even as I got older sparring with my Dad I still couldn't hit him with a handful of rice. My Dad taught me that Mayweather like defence before I'd even heard of Floyd Mayweather. It was my Dad teaching me these little things that turned me into what I was as a boxer.

For many years I badgered my Dad to take me to a gym, instead of him taking me to boxing he took me to an old friend of his called Fred Kidd. Fred was a diamond of a man and he taught a self-defence class in an old church just near North Ormesby market in Middlesbrough. It was a bit of karate, judo, wrestling etc... A bit of everything apart from boxing. My Dad thought taking me there was going to pacify me and that I'd forget about going to boxing. Looking back, I knew my Dad had been a professional fighter in youth and I couldn't quite understand why he wouldn't let me become a boxer, I thought he was just being cruel towards me stopping me doing what I wanted to do. He didn't really want me to box because he'd been shafted so many times himself. I must admit I've been the same with my daughter Jade who now boxes, so I understand now but I didn't back then. I've gone on to do the same thing as what my Dad did to me if you like.

I went on at my old fella for what must have been years, until one day he came in from work and told me he'd spoken with John Dryden who runs a boxing club in the next area from me North Ormesby, and that I could go to his gym that night. I was so excited to have finally been allowed to go aged 11.

When I started boxing, what my Dad had been teaching me for many years was how to box the way they did in the pro game, this didn't go well with the amateur game truth be told. I'd start dropping my left hand in the gym and I was always told to get my hands back up, lots of little things that I was picked up on. I was told to forget everything my Dad had taught me and was told to start again with the basics by the coach John Dryden in his North Ormesby ABC.

Looking back, it was one of the most intimidating things I'd ever had to do because I'd walked into a place where there were some absolutely fantastic boxers there such as Frankie and Paulie Cunningham, Lee Richardson, Peter Cronin, Neil Johnson, Jimmy Fewster, Peter Connors, Brian Graham, Lee Harrison, Ste Davies and the ex pro Graham O'Malley. Sparring with Graham was an eye-opening experience in itself, he knew all the old tricks like standing on my feet or pulling my head guard down on purpose. They were all a real top bunch of kids and many of them had won national titles by then. When the gym was based in North Ormesby and ran by John Dryden and Richie Cosgrove I would only go when my Dad took me, I never really got into it until the gym moved to above the Wellington pub in the town and became Wellington ABC in 1983. Before then the gym had been owned by John Spensley and John had all his pro's in there.

I had my first bout for the "Welly" as it was known, when I was 14. I boxed at my home show at the Priory Social Club on Marton Road in Middlesbrough. I fought a kid called Tommy Oliver and he was from United Services in Hartlepool and he bashed the life out of me. I would also lose my next one because as a kid I was too weak. I could box but when somebody got close and put it on me I would struggle. If I was allowed to be kept long I wasn't bad but I struggled with anything else boxing wise until I was around 15.

In My first 13 fights I'd won 6 and lost 7 and going into my 14th bout in the schoolboys I was gonna face a lad called Gary Robson from Whitburn ABC who was the schoolboy champion. He was a really good kid. At the time there were five in my weight group in the schoolboys. Myself and my clubmate Carl Blenkinsop and a lad Michael Plews from Joe Walton's ABC who I later fought, and a lad called Mark Halliman who'd had 21 bouts and won 19, the 2 losses he did have were against Joe Calzaghe in the schoolboys the year before.

Me and Blenky were sat talking and Blenky said that if he drew Mark Halliman he'd be pulled out, I said the same I said if I draw Robson my Dad will pull me out because he was too experienced and too good for me at the time. Well around ten minutes later my Dad came back and told me I was boxing not once but twice and that I was on first. I thought great I'm boxing someone else who "is it Dad I asked"? I was sure he was gonna tell me I was boxing Michael Plews who was my schoolfriend at the time, so it wasn't as scary, but with that my Dad said, "you're boxing Gary Robson"! I remember my stomach turned and I was thinking, Dad you must hate me you horrible old bastard. That was all that was going through my mind in the warm up to the bout was that my Dad must hate me! I later found out that Gary Robson had had 52 bouts and won 49 of them, he was a really good lad. At the time I had only had 13 bouts and lost more than half of them, so I hadn't fought anybody yet. My pain and anguish sort of went away for only a moment when my Dad turned to Blenky and said, "And you're on second, you've got Mark Halliman"! So, my old fella had not pulled either of us out and stuck us in with the two stand out kids in the whole competition. I would get beat but that was the first time I realised that if I had a bit of self-belief I go could on and do well in the boxing game. Gary's experience took over in our fight and he was a worthy winner. Against him that day it was the closest I'd ever come, junior or senior to taking a knee and going down. I'd rather somebody shot me from behind than take a knee I would always say when I was boxing. My friend Blenky lost that day too but he gave a fantastic account of himself. Halliman from Shildon ABC was another stand out kid who I would look at thinking I'd love to box like him, so Blenky did himself proud that day. After the fight I was sitting in the corner all depressed and fed up having a major sulk to myself. I'll never forget Jimmy Somerville's Bronski Beat song 'Small Town Boy' was on and I was listening to the lyrics which said, "RUN AWAY RUN AWAY RUN AWAY" and I was really contemplating running away from home for good.

I had 30 junior bouts in total and I won the NABC'S which was my highlight. That was the first national title that I picked up. In the semi-finals of the NABC'S I beat a good lad called Anthony Maynard from Birmingham, he went on to become a decent pro himself in later years.

I would also face Middlesbrough's John Mett three times who was from our main rival club in the town the Phil Thomas School of Boxing. John Mett himself was a 2 x schoolboy champion and a bit of a knockout merchant. Even as a kid John didn't put his opponents down he liked to knock them clean out he was a man in a boy's body he was a right little monster. John was a bit of a boy as a kid, in his school he was the hardest in the place. Quite often I would get messages from other kids at his school saying, "John Mett said he's gonna knock you and Blenky out in the same day". When I won my NABC'S title I asked my Dad if we could get a fight on with that John Mett from Phil Thomas? My Dads reply was "we'll leave it for another couple of months". I asked my Dad for that fight and my Dad wouldn't put me in with him, and to be fair as a junior he was a walking nightmare for anyone because he was as strong as a bull and had a punch as hard as a mule's kick! Before I had the three fights with John Mett, if anyone ever asked me if I'd win I would always say we'll see how it goes, he's only got two arms and two legs like me, so we'll see what happens. The only time I've ever said anything different was when I said I was gonna do this, that and the other to John Mett. It was big news around Middlesbrough that me and John Mett were fighting and when I was asked how it would play out, and because I'd knocked my last 4 opponents out my confidence was sky high, I told everybody who'd listen that I guarantee the first shot I landed on him he'll go over. In the fight itself it worked out just as I'd said and I caught John and he went down in the first. He got up tough as teak and came at me again only for me to catch him with another headshot and as he was going down I caught him with a body shot as hard as I could and he was down again. He was utterly

275

slumped in the corner, but he gets up like something out of a horror film, I'm convinced he's gone and it's only a matter of seconds before the ref jumps in to call it all off. For some miraculous reason he let Metty go on and as I walk forward and dropped my hands to throw my speciality left hook to the body the next thing I knew was that I woke up in my own corner. My Dad later told me he hit me in the middle of the ring and I slid across the ring on my back into my own corner. I'll never forget it I remember looking up and I could see the referee looking over me and I was thinking what's he doing up there? My Dad also told me that when my head hit the floor it knocked me out with my eyes shut, then my head bounced again to wake me up. I somehow managed to get up but of course I was in no fit state and the referee stopped it. At the time I was going mad saying he's worse than me I wanna carry on, my Dad later on said my eyes were well gone. After the fight I had concussion badly and I was being sick on the way home. Getting hit by John Mett was like getting hit by a sledgehammer and even in our other two fights where I beat John I could bloody feel him. It doesn't matter how good your chin is, when somebody like John Mett hits you, you feel it.

Boxing's a dangerous sport and you can be badly hurt even when you win in one round. I'll never forget I fought a lad from Hardwick Lads, the club that Kelvin Travis runs in Manchester, called Craig Walker and Craig was like John Mett in that he could really punch. It was the Everton Triangle show in Liverpool and we had about 6 of the Welly lads on. When I got in the ring with Craig I'd expected a big monster from what I'd heard about him, but in reality, there was this slim lad in front of me the same build as me who was just a little beanpole. I looked at him thinking he can't be a knockout artist because my Dad had been telling me for the last two weeks he was really tasty. I just thought it was my old fella being evil trying to scare me. I went on to knock Craig Walker out in the first round, but we exchanged left hooks and he caught me right behind the ear, so when I went back to the corner I seen my Dad smiling and I thought FUCK! Have I been knocked out???? I honestly didn't know I'd just won. My Dad then slapped me twice on the face and I was watching him, and his lips were moving, but I couldn't hear him. Then the ref grabs my hand and walks me to the centre of the ring with the other guy I'd just fought, and I was convinced I'd been knocked out. Even when the master of ceremonies announced and the "winner by knockout", and as soon as he said that I thought, aah fucking hell nor I've been sparked! It wasn't until I heard "Pearce in the blue corner" did I realise I'd won the fight by KO. My mind had just drawn a blank for the last five minutes.

In the juniors I could box if I was allowed to box, and I could make people look silly, but what let me down was my lack of strength really until I became a senior boxer. It was around changing from the juniors to the seniors that I had around 15 months away from competing with a bad back. I had also torn a ligament in my right shoulder. What I used to do was that I used to have my right arm bandaged up to my neck, and train with just my left hand. I think that was primarily where I became extremely good and powerful with my left hook as that was all I had for so long in the gym. I'd often train just walloping away at the bag throwing a left hook to body. Hours and hours, I would practice this shot until it was perfect and very potent. I was never ever out of the gym and lived the life, but I was also a greedy fat pig!

I first went in the ABA'S in 1991 as a welterweight. Before that I'd been on the young England team, but I never really got going until I'd say around 1994. Over the years I had always had little niggling injuries but what I decided in 1995 was that at the start of 1996, whether I'm injured or not I was gonna go in the ABA'S because I'd missed the last few years going in them through silly injuries. In 1996 I was 25, my first daughter Jade was born, and I'd decided that this was gonna be my last year in boxing. In 1995 I'd had one contest because I'd been out with a bad back. I was in my Nana's house and I got a phone call off my other coach John Dryden. John told me he had a fight for me in 7 days' time at Spennymoor's show but it's at 12st 10lbs. At the time I was 14st 3lbs and I'd only just got back into training, so I wasn't really that bothered about taking it. At the time me and my partner Nik didn't have any money and John Dryden told me they'd offered me £50. I'll take it was my response I didn't even ask who it was against. £50 was a lot of money when we had no money in our bank. "Who's it against John anyway"? I asked. Some fella called Micky Thompson and he's ranked number 4 light-heavyweight in Britain and he's 6ft 4 tall. Now bearing in mind I was only 5ft 9 that was gonna be quite a bit of difference one might say! The fight itself happened and me and Micky nearly killed each other until the final bell. Micky won on points but to this day he's more than a friend to me and I'm very close to him, he's like family.

So, the 12th of January 1996 came and injured or not I didn't care, I was going in them ABA'S and I was out of boxing for good. My journey that year in the ABA'S was Granger Park's Alan Exley who I stopped with a body shot in the North East round in the 1st round. Alan was 35 at the time and was giving it one last go. He told me he was pissed off when he drew me. Next up was the Yorkshire round and I was to face Hunslet's Darren Rhodes who was a very good fighter. Darren won everything as a junior himself and had also beaten my younger brother Mark in the schoolboys a few years back. I would gain revenge for my brother Mark with a points win over Darren. Darren went on to be a decent professional for many years after. In the pre-quarters I was matched against Craig Harvey and I knocked him out with a body shot. In the quarters I took on Yinka Bello from Parade. He was one of the favourites to win the ABA'S that year, but I got the victory on points. In the semi's I was to face Shildon's Glenn Wharton who was another standout junior. I caught Glenn very early on in the fight and ended up knocking Glenn out. In my first ABA final I was to take on Birmingham's Wayne Elcock of Erdington ABC and I beat him in 56 seconds of the first round. I was told Wayne was a good stylish boxer, so I jumped on him as soon as it started. I gave him a count believe it or not with my backhand and I couldn't punch for toffee with it. The referee let it go on and I finished him with a few body shots to become Britain's number one middleweight.

The year after it would be my first of my trilogy with Hartlepool's Ian Cooper. I faced him in the January of 1997 and I just didn't turn up, Ian well and truly beat me a million percent that night. That was my ABA journey over until the year after when I would face Ian again in the North East round in January 1998. Ian had not only beaten me in 97 but he went on to win the full tournament by beating Triumph ABC'S Jim Twite in the final. In my return with "Super Cooper" as his fans were shouting, I was much more switched on than in our first battle and I stopped Ian in the fourth round to go through to the Yorkshires where I met Bradford's Donovan Smillie. Before our fight Donovan was giving it the big un with his crowd and making cut throat signs to me. I picked my bag up and got out of the way as if I was scared whilst he was shouting the odds. Blenky asked me what I was doing but I never got involved with that shit. Of course, when we fought it was a different story and I knocked him cold. After the fight Donovan was in a bad way and needed hospital treatment.

In the quarters I faced a guy from the Royal Marines called Robert Fordster and I knocked him out also in the 2nd round. In the semi's I faced Mark Redhead from New Astley ABC. The year after he'd go on to get to the final only to lose to Carl Froch. Mark was a good opponent, but I was too strong for him and I knocked him out in 3rd rounds. For the final I faced Triumph's Jim Twite. Jim's a top guy and when we were on the England team I had so much time for him he was a lovely guy. Jim was a southpaw which wasn't my favourite type of fighter to come up against, but I beat him on points to gain my second ABA title. Funnily enough the year after Jim would face a young David Haye and Jim knocked David out sparko.

In 1998 the ABA'S wasn't the only thing I'd win as I went over to Kuala Lumpur to claim the gold medal in the Commonwealth games also, but before I went over to the Commonwealth games I would have to go into a "box off" at the Liverpool multi-Nations in the June of that year because of Repton's Andy Lowe. The same thing happened at light-heavyweight with Courtney Fry and David Haye also, of course Fry was picked ahead of Haye for that competition.

I would box in total three times to claim the gold with a victory over a Ghanaian, my opponent for the quarters pulled out with a damaged hand so I faced the competition favourite Belfast's Brian Magee in the semi's. Brian was an extremely clever fighter to box. His timing, distance and the way he pulled away was the best I'd ever been in a round ring with he was exceptional. I would beat Brian on a comfortable points victory so that got me in the final to face India's Jitender Kumar who I also beat on points.

In 1998 I was now a double ABA champion and Commonwealth gold medallist so if ever there was a perfect time for me to go pro it was then. At the time I was 27 and I did seriously consider it. Hartlepool promoter Dave Garside took me to Liverpool to meet manager John Ireland. In hindsight I really really wished I'd have turned pro then. I'd had a couple of offers when I was younger from the late Gus Robinson, but I didn't have any bargaining power as I hadn't achieved anything back then. Truth be told my old man was very anti-pro boxing because he'd been shit on himself as a fighter. My old fella used to tell me that all you are is a promoter's meat and they're the butcher. They decide how to slice and dice you in whatever way their please. Scotland's Alex Morrison had sent me a letter around the time when I came back from Kuala Lumpur but regrettably I just left it. My mind was purely on the 2000 Olympics in Sydney but of course I didn't end up going.

In 1999 I went looking for my third ABA title. In the North East rounds I would box twice facing Guisborough's Stephen Swales, who'd go on to win it the year after. If I hadn't have pressured Stephen like I did in that fight I would have had a really nasty night against him. What a beautiful boxer Swalesy was and he was the last Englishman to beat Ricky Hatton in the schoolboys of 1994. After our fight I said to Stephen he needed to stick with it as I wasn't going to be around in that game that much longer and he was the future of the middleweight division. He was the man to fill my shoes in my eyes.

In the Yorkshires that were straight after, I received a walk over and it was just as well because I damaged my hand on Swalesy's head.

In the North East final, I would face my old foe Ian Cooper again in the final for the third and final time of our trilogy. I liked Ian an awful lot but at the time we had a major rivalry because of the people he knew and the people I knew. Of course, Hartlepool and Middlesbrough were only 12 miles apart. Things had been said in the build-up and I felt I had a big point to prove because we were both one each in fights. I went out and caught Ian with a left hook and I instantly felt my hand go. Instinctively in a fight the adrenalin takes over, but I knew something wasn't right with the inside of my hand. I would stop Ian again to claim a 2-1 victory in our fights but afterwards, when I went to the physio he told me I would have been better breaking my hand as it would have healed quicker. Luckily, I received a walkover in the Yorkshires into the next round so I had a bit of time to heal. In that time, I trained as a southpaw because I only had the one hand in the gym. There was no compromise with my fitness as I was still going out doing my endurance running and things like that. It was in the quarter finals I was to take on a fella from Phoenix ABC, a guy named Carl Froch. I had watched him in the final the year before against 6-time ABA champion and my England teammate Chris Bessey at the weight below me. Bessey beat Froch that day but Froch caught Chris at the end of the round, Chris got his silly legs on, but the fight finished and Bessey got the victory. If the fight had been longer than I think Froch would of went on to KO him possibly like he did in the dying stages of his fight with Jermain Taylor in 2009.

My Dad and Blenky told me before the fight that I had nothing to prove, but as I only had one hand I needed to pull out. I said, "Absolutely not"! He's only a young lad. If I can use my left hand for half of the fight, I'll be alright. I didn't listen, and I went into the fight with the future British boxing legend. Just before I walked out I had my hand freezed up. I've watched that fight repeatedly and I know I didn't win. The last time I spoke to Carl he thought I'd just nicked it, but I knew in my heart the right man got the decision on a split decision. It was a lovely gesture by Carl many years later when he did an interview with Boxing

News that he rated me as the best and the hardest fight he's ever had. Many years later I got to spend a bit of time with Carl and he told me he was really bricking it before he fought me. Carl has openly spoken in books about his issues that he had in his amateur days with his lack of confidence. I could never understand how he had them issues because the heart that man had was something else. It's beyond me to think that he thought at times he wasn't good enough it's frightening, and it was just down to his age and sheer lack of experience at the time I would say. When I boxed I always had this thing where I wouldn't look at anybody before I boxed. I would just stand and face my Dad in the corner because it was just something I didn't want to do. I know all these fun and games go on in boxing but that was never me. I can't get into all that staring people down shit because if I did I'd start laughing.

Many years later Carl was also interviewed for a boxing magazine and he said that he found it really intimidating that I wouldn't face him. In his second fight with George Groves at Wembley in front of 80,000 people he said he did it to George Groves and he said it worked a treat for him.

Looking back on my life in boxing at 46 years old now I have massive regrets. I know I underachieved and I didn't do the things I should have done in boxing. I should have turned pro after the 1998 Commonwealth games when I was 27. When I had the chance of going pro with Dave Garside I was scared, and I now know that was silly but Dave's a big intimidating man. Dave did so well for Hartlepool's Micky Hunter in his career and Ian Cooper and so many other fighters he had. I should have turned pro with Dave Garside and I now look back and regret it so much. At the time I felt I didn't need to go pro though because I had a good job, so I was never chasing the money. Also, at the back end of my England career me and Audley Harrison were funded athletes which always helped financially. I know I've said it before, but it really wished I would have at least went pro so I could have said I'd given it a go. I also wish I'd never gone to the world games in Tallahassee 1999 for 19 days when I didn't want to go. I would end up going and I wasn't in the slightest bit interested in even being there. When I got there my mobile phone had ran out, so I was in a training camp with no way of contacting my Wife and little 3-year-old girl Jade. In truth I wasn't even going to get on the train to go because I found it so hard to leave them. My last sight leaving for that trip was my baby Jade crying screaming "DON'T GO DADDY" being hysterical. I know she didn't understand but it didn't make any difference to me, I was totally broken. Even when I got to the next stop at Darlington and Nigel Wright got on the train I was still inconsolable. During that trip to the world games it was just constantly on my mind I couldn't switch off. Ian Irwin and the other coaches agreed that they wouldn't send me away for more than 10 days at a time which was very good of them. At times I was allowed to stay at home and train instead of meeting up on certain camps because I struggled missing Jade and my Wife. For instance, when we were expected to do the warm weather training for Kuala Lumpur I wasn't expected to do it, I'd told them I didn't need to do it.

When I lost in the world games in 1999 in Tallahassee, the next morning I wanted to go home but head coach Ian Irwin wouldn't let me. He told me that we had gone out there as a team and we were going home as a team. I actually took enough money out there to fly back on my own. I begged Ian to be allowed to go home so I could see my family. Ian reminded me that the Olympics in Sydney were just around the corner. He told me if I stayed he wouldn't send me to Ukraine qualifiers, but I'd have to go to Greece and Liverpool for the other Olympic qualifiers. I just wasn't cut out to be away from my family for that length of time.

Back home in 1999 I boxed the top American Rodney Griffin at The Hilton Hotel in London. It was a U.S.A V England international boxing evening and I received a thumb in the eye. I lost by a count-back. My eye got trapped in my eye socket which it still is to this day. The eye socket is versatile apparently and it can fracture, and slam shut on the eye which is what happened to me. To this day I have double vision from that day. From that fight I was expected to travel to Greece to go to the other Olympic qualifiers and if I didn't get in there I could go to the Multi-Nations at Liverpool. Of course, with this new eye injury it just wasn't possible. The England team then sent Carl Froch in my place to the Liverpool qualifiers and he got beat by a Polish kid.

My Olympic dream was over. I think hand on my heart, even if I'd have qualified for the Olympics I wouldn't have gone anyway because my second daughter Kelsey was born just before I'd have been due to fly out.

I never retired from boxing and haven't to this day. I kind of just slipped away quietly. I was actually going to make a comeback for the Manchester 2002 Commonwealths when I was 31.

Looking back over my time in boxing I'll be honest I've had many sleepless nights. It eats me up because of my own mistakes. I should have done so much differently and because of that I did things wrong and I stayed away from the sport. I'm bitter only to myself for the things I should have done. I even got offered a job on the England squad but didn't take it. I'm involved with boxing now but it's only because my daughter Jade is boxing now.

The best I ever fought has to be Brian Magee and also the French lad Jean Paul Mendy has to be up there who was number 3 in the world when I fought him. He was an awful southpaw and he just tied me in knots. He wasn't brilliant on the eye but no matter how much I pressured him he just seemed to slip out of the back door. He went on to fight for the IBF world title against Lucian Bute in 2011.

In my gym, the Wellington, I used to spar and let the kids hit me to bring them on but there was a couple of them that I couldn't have done that within a month of Sundays, one being Tony Robbo. He was a little walking monster and the other was Michael "Tatty" Hollinsworth.

One of the most talented people I've ever been in any gym with by far was Blenky (Carl Blenkinsop) what a complete waste he was, his talent deserved far more respect for the dedication he had to the sport. The amount of people you see doing that when they get to 16-17 when they realise they like a drink is tragic. Another guy from the Welly who was a magnificent fighter was Frankie Cunningham, I would stay there watching him for hours and hours on end. His diligence and the way that he trained, I would sit and stare how he threw his left jab and try copy it. Another top guy in my gym was little Neil Johnson who went on to become a pro at flyweight under Barry Hearn. My Dad used to make me watch Johno's feet and the way that he moved. When I was a kid I would watch and admire Brian Graham. The way Brian whipped that left hook in was mesmerising and how he would walk people on to his left hook it was if he asked them to move into the correct position, so he could wallop them it was magic how he did it. A guy who used to come in with Brian Graham was the infamous Lee Duffy from South Bank. I was only a kid when the Duff used to come to our gym and train. I used to go watch the lads on a morning and Lee would be in there with Brian and John Black.

I always wanted to be in the gym and I would make any excuse to be in the place. John Dryden wouldn't let me train on a morning because he used to tell me I was doing too much but I would be in and hanging around. Lee Duffy was a big heavyweight and I can't really say because I never saw him spar, but when you watched him on the bag, he did look classy. Lee really could throw the combinations and boy could he punch. Considering Lee had never competed as a boxer he did look like a million dollars, not only that but he was awfully fast for a heavyweight. Another lad who was a big part of my early learning was Paul Forrest and I sparred hundreds of rounds with him. Paul was like a little pro even as a kid with his good head movement and he was very tough and strong. I got so much from Paul sparring with him because he had a real good pro style even at like 14-15. Paul would be obsessed with Barry McGuigan and Julio Cesar Chavez. Me and Paul would sit watching stacks and stacks of boxing videos together as a kid watching all the great fighters and trying to study them. Of course, Paul turned out to go pro and be a decent one at that. Jason Duffy, Vernon Ferguson, Robbie Aldridge, big Dean Wilson, Anthony and Tommy Crutchley, Nathan Thompson, Neil Fairclough, Andy Illingworth, who we called Superman because he looked like Clark Kent who was a very funny lad, and Mark Teasdale were all fabulous lads to be round in the gym. Mark and I did loads of sparring as I got older and he would come forward all night. Not only did Mark look Mexican he fought like one also and he's a really nice fella is Mark. Speaking of Mexican looking guys, I couldn't forget to mention little mad Michael Debnath. Michael got quite far one year in the schoolboys and he drew Birmingham's Matthew Macklin. Many years later Matthew became one of my England teammates and he always used to ask how Michael was and tell me about the fight they had. I think the difference between Michael and Matthew was Matthew

287

was too experienced in the ring and in general and he went on to take a points decision but that was before getting put on his arse by Michael in the first round. Debnath was a classic case of a good kid in the gym getting to maybe 16-17 and then throwing it all away because he found out his love for girls, drinking and nightclubs etc... Another Welly ABC lad I won't fail to mention is a guy called Imran Hussain. Now Imran went to our gym from 1989 until 1999. He never competed because he suffered from epilepsy. When Hussain came in the gym for the first time he was a little bit overweight, but he learned all the basics, still didn't lose any weight but was keen as mustard and trained hard. When Hussain moved up to the seniors from the juniors, he was there as regular as clockwork. Every time you saw him in the gym he would always be talking boxing and he was a lovely kid as well. He wasn't one of these kids who had an attitude. Well one day I'd noticed Hussain had been losing weight, but I didn't think anything of it. Until one day I drove past him out jogging and beeped my horn and waved, then 2 hours later I seen him again still jogging a few miles away from the first time I'd seen him I couldn't believe it. Hussain as well as boxing training had taken up running and he lost all his weight. When I was in the gym nobody could keep up with me, I was the type that if somebody did a tuck jump I had to do two. Well Hussain got that fit he was almost up there with me. Even to this day everything revolves around his love for boxing, he is seriously boxing's super fan. If I've ever been unsure about anything on boxing, the one thing I do is go straight on the phone to Hussain and he knows the answer and he's one of the nicest guys you could meet. If you cut Imran Hussain in half all you'd find is one massive boxing glove and he's a bit of a Welly legend for sure.

The hardest I'd ever been hit must be by a young David Haye without any shadow of a doubt. I'll never forget one

Sunday morning he was brought into the England squad to train with us seniors. I was actually brought into the office by the coaches to be told this skinny kid from South London who'd just been to the European juniors was coming to train with us for the day. I was asked by Kelvin Travis to move him around and basically don't bash him up too much. At the time I was at the top of my game. I never ever tried to bash anybody especially some young skinny gangly kid. I was told to just move him around with my feet and put a little bit of pressure on now and again to let him know I'm there. We set away sparring and David's that relaxed he's almost vertical. Well I can honestly say I've never felt power like I did when he hit me that morning. I was numb, my whole body buzzed from head to toe. What happened was that I just threw a lazy jab at him, with that he dropped that shoulder and threw a right hand which caught me right on the forehead, if somebody had hit me with a sledgehammer at the same time then David's punch would have hurt more. I got proper "zapped" like a flash of lightening. From that moment on in our sparring I had to majorly bash him. I don't mean that in a nasty way, but I had to bash him to keep him off me just to keep him under control. I sparred so much after that and he may have been a little wary to be as full on with me again but saying that he was only a baby starting out in the game. As soon as David was in our camp he was like you see on the telly, just a cool confident little character even as a boy as he was then at 17. David went to the Multi-Nations in 1999 and when he was picked Ian Irwin and the other England coaches took me in the office to ask my thoughts of David from our sparring together. I said "What do I think! I said Jesus Christ you couldn't leave him behind in the under 19s, get him put in the full England team. He punches like nothing I've ever felt in my life and he's skilful".

I also did many rounds of sparring with Audley Harrison at Crystal Palace. When I used to go down fat I'd get put in with big Audley to teach me a lesson. I would normally be too quick for Audley and my work rate was too much for him. I didn't think Audley enjoyed it because with me being only 5ft 9 and him 6ft 5 I was like a little Willow the Wisp. The only way I could get any real success in there with him was sinking my body shots into him. I couldn't get anywhere near his face, so I just used to wallop body shots into him. Audley actually asked me to go easy on the body shots because he'd just had a hernia operation. I said, "well where am I going to hit you Audley I can't reach your chin you're too big"!

Many times, I would watch big Audley Harrison against David Haye and let me tell you something, boy could that get heated. Audley would be very wary of David in the spars. The thing with Audley was that when he fancied the job, Audley was unstoppable! From watching their old spars over the years, I thought Audley would have beat David when they fought in 2010 as pro's. Many times, in our training camps Audley would turn up and he either couldn't be arsed, or he'd turn up like a man possessed. Audley was never in the middle it was either one or the other. In our training camps for the 1998 Commonwealth Games Audley was absolutely on fire. I was only just beating him on the 3 x 800 metres in the mornings and all the way through that competition Audley stood out, because he had a different demeanour. In the camp beforehand Audley was like a roaring lion he was the alpha male, he was pissing up trees and all sorts and of course he went on to take the gold like I did. People seem to forget Audley had only gotten out of jail a couple of years earlier as well. I'll always remember our team and a few other boxers from fellow countries were all on a bus and it wasn't moving. This day it was red hot and there wasn't any air conditioning on the bus and we were all sweating and getting irritable in Kuala Lumpur. The Canadian Super-Heavyweight who was also in Audley's group was also on the bus, but he was down at the front. I could see Audley was getting seriously agitated. As he was getting more and more agitated I was having a bit of a giggle at him. Also a few of the others on the England team like Stephen Bell and little Gary Jones started taking the piss out of Audley. So, with us lot winding Audley up, he then stands up saying "I'm gonna say something to this fucking driver". With that Audley grabbed hold of a metal pole on the bus above his head and ripped it clean out of the ceiling. Then he went down the front of the bus screaming all sorts and being so irate. Well the big Canadian Super-Heavyweight who was massive by the way completely shit himself when he seen big Audley turning into the Incredible Hulk. Now if I remember rightly I think Audley beat him in the quarter finals. It's funny because the big Canadian was a huge menacing thing, but that little incident totally deflated him and Audley steam rollered him, completely butchered him cold in the first round.

The whole 1998 tournament in Kuala Lumpur was one huge laugh after another. Little Gary Jones the light-flyweight from Tower Hill ABC, myself and featherweight Stephen Bell of Louverlite ABC we acclimatised really badly, so we couldn't go to sleep. Belly had brought a Gameboy and me and him would take turns on this Gameboy. Me, Gary, Belly and even Levi Patterson were all very close. Levi was my sanity because he had a kid as well, so he knew what I was going through. Me and Belly would take turns on the Gameboy, but many time we would get bored and want to cause mischief. When we were away we were placed in two rooms. In one room there was Folo Okesola, Audley Harrison, Courtney Fry and Andy McClean, and the rest of us were in the other although Chris Bessey was in a room on his own. Well one-night Belly's Gameboy had gone missing and I wanted it. After a good while of me and Belly arguing we both realised some fucker had stolen it. So, a penny must have dropped because whilst I was calling Belly all the dickheads under the sun, I paused for a minute and said hang on a minute, its them bastards next door they've nicked it. Belly said "ya right we need to do a dorm raid". So, me and Belly stripped off, and Belly used to wear Y-fronts, so me and Belly put a pair of Y-fronts on our heads and went creeping bollock naked just with these undies on our heads. We then ran in the room and the first bed we came to was Folo's, so we both jumped on his bed shouting "WHERE'S THE FUCKING GAMEBOY WHERE'S THE FUCKING GAMEBOY"! Poor Folo was laid in his bed screaming absolutely screaming. It turns out poor Folo never had it we'd just woke him up in the middle of the night for nothing. It turned out Birtley's Andy McClean had had it. A couple of nights later I couldn't get to sleep again. I looked over at Belly and he's reading lads magazines and I'm bored shitless. So, I said to Belly get the camera and follow me. So, went into little Gary Jones' room, and I got my balls and put a ball each in little Gary's eye sockets when he was asleep While Belly snapped away. Then I put my cock along the bridge of his nose and Belly snapped that, anyway when I dropped my cock on Gary's nose it woke him up and little Gary's jumped up all fiery to fuck, he was going to knock me out he was threatening to knock Belly out and then smash Kuala Lumpur up. Me and Belly couldn't move through laughing so much we were crying. It was imperative to never leave your camera about because what me and Belly would also do, and remember this was 20 years ago before digital cameras, we used to get somebody's camera and say somebody had taken 12 pictures, we'd take the other 23 of each other's arses so when our teammates got them developed they'd had a few good ones and the rest were either arse or cock and balls. I suppose doing shit to each other kept us sane.

Whilst I was in Kuala Lumpur I missed Jades second birthday and that broke me. At times before the tournament I had made up my mind I wasn't even going to go, it was my family who forced me on the train at Middlesbrough, Nik my Dad and Blenk forced me otherwise I would never have gone.

Just before my 40th birthday in December 2010 I got diagnosed with cancer I went and got myself Non-Hodgkin's Lymphoma which was a nice surprise. I've been on my treatment since then and I've had two lots of chemotherapy. I'm on maintenance treatment at the minute. All they do is every two months there give me an injection in my stomach. The cancer itself is not something that can be removed and its' something that I'll always have, and I've learnt to live with it. It's been shrunk a hell of a lot since it was first diagnosed. I still train, and I still spar, and I still do the things that I've always done in life. I have good days and bad days at times.

My eldest daughter Jade is now boxing herself so I'm down the Wellington ABC as much as I can go down there with her and watch over her. Me and Jade, who's 21 and a lightweight now spar regularly down the gym where I learnt my trade. Jade is doing really well and I didn't even want her boxing like my old man didn't want me boxing. I also do a few rounds with the lads in the gym, but I haven't done for a bit since I had my last chemotherapy which wasn't too long ago.

Boxing has given me a really respectful outlook on life. Boxing has also given me discipline and made me humble. I'll never think I'm better than anybody else because it's made me grounded.

I have to thank my old man without any shadow of a doubt. Also, John Dryden, Blenky and a million percent my wife Nik and my girls Jade and Kelsey. Nik's been around me when I had made a pig of myself then had to lose all the weight. I never drank but like I said before I was a pig and I would be horrible to be around. I loved my "Parmo's" and chocolates I was terrible for. Them times when I was making weight and Nikki was eating Chinese in front of me I wanted to stab her eyes out (laughs).

I don't follow boxing on the telly anymore. Obviously with me being a coach with the Wellington ABC I follow the amateurs. Sometimes if there is a big fight on a Saturday night my phone is like a disco. People phoning me up for tips or Blenky phoning me up to tell me how much money he lost.

Like I've already said my little girl Jade boxes now. She started late which was totally down to me. I've done what my Dad did telling her "you can't" and I shouldn't have done. Jade, to be fair, she's as passionate about boxing as I was in my prime. Jade's style, well she's a body puncher like her old Dad.

I've made some wonderful friends for life from my life in boxing. Spennymoor's Mickey Thompson, my close friend Carl Blenkinsop (Blenky), Stephen Bell I speak to all the time. I speak with Kelvin Travis quite a lot and in my opinion, he was the best coach not to be on the England team. Kelvin is so knowledgeable on the fight game. Little Gary Jones I speak to him weekly as well as Crook's Nigel Wright regularly. When I first got my cancer, Chris Bessey was straight on the phone full of concerns for me because somebody had told him. Audley Harrison's sent me things from California sending me therapy stuff and a 'How to beat cancer' book which is so touching.

Only a few years ago my friend Tony Robbo put on An Evening with Carl Froch in Middlesbrough. To be honest I was dreading meeting him. When I packed up Carl kind of took over from me. I'd always looked at him in a different view because Carl was a young lad and full of himself but when I sat down with him I got a shock at how much of a nice bloke he was. I was taken back and caught off guard if you like. We still text each other from time to time, because we fought each other in a boxing ring the respect will stay there to our graves.

For all you guys reading this thinking how bad my cancer is I'll say this, it's not going to beat me, not a cat in hells chance I have my kids and my wife to look after. I haven't got time to be ill. The days I am bad, I have Nikki, Jade and Kelsey to run around after me. Also, Nik's Mam Kath and her Dad Ray have been worth their weight worth in gold helping us all. I also have a business partner and good friend Ped AKA Peter Barnes that money couldn't buy. When I have my bad days, Ped looks after me with work. He also looks after Nik and the kids. Mickey Thompson, Blenk and his Mrs Andrea are always there for me which I can't thank them enough for.

My amateur club the Wellington ABC was and is still to this day run by a funny old character by the name of John Dryden. John's had everyone through his hands, all the rough lads, but he commands respect. John doesn't give a fuck who you are, he's the boss and he takes no crap. John was never bothered about anyone and he would always get a grip of them. John's still in the gym now even in his 80s. Even now at his age he's in the gym every single night it's on which is at least three times a week. John still takes the kids on the pads and now he takes my daughter Jade on the pads. He's still exactly like the way he was when he used to take me on the pads as an 11-year-old boy. John reminds me of another old school coach who's also had champion after champion through his hands for donkey's years and that's Frank O'Sullivan from Birmingham City ABC. Frank is still to this day coaching the kids, he was the guy behind the Yafai brothers.

Basically, John Dryden has been a massive part of my career just as much as my Dad. When my Dad and John got too old to take me on the body bag which I loved, then Blenk came into it. Carl Blenkinsop is now a tremendous coach at Phil Thomas School of Boxing in Middlesbrough. He's got some cracking Juniors at that club. He's teaches them the basics but then they put their own twists on it which is boxing in a nutshell. I think if it wasn't for boxing then your John Dryden's and Frank O'Sullivan's wouldn't be still here boxing is what keeps them going I don't care what anyone says.

I would never have been involved in boxing if it wasn't for my Dad John Pearce Senior. From day one I've always looked up to him and I always will. I used to call my Dad my left arm, as if you take him away out of my corner I'll have nothing, I couldn't have boxed with one arm. What my Dad did for me was insurmountable. Me and my brothers will always have a healthy respect for him. No matter how little he was, he was always the boss in our house. The most wonderful thing I have ever seen in my Dad in the gym over the years was that he loves the underdog. Even if a kid came in the gym and he wasn't gonna make it as a boxer, he would always spend his time showing them things over and over. My old fella is never one for ignoring anyone like that.

Afterword

So, you've read 20 different folks' tales of pugilism. Not pretty reading a lot of it was it?

As much as us the armchair avid followers bang on about just how great boxing is there's a different side that only the fighter really knows. A side that isn't as glamorous or appealing as the big promoters on telly let you believe it all is.

When you look back on the 20 interviews, the words that jump out at me are "regret and if only" but of course hindsight's a wonderful thing when you can look back with a mature head and a knackered body.

Not every young fighter coming through the ranks can be as sensible and as level headed as Joe Maphosa and Josh Warrington. Oscar Wilde's famous quote of "Youth is wasted on the young" is very fitting when you take in the accounts of Kevin Mitchell, Gary Sykes, Andrew Buchanan and Matthew Burke's chapters. Even my friend Esham Pickering, whose interview I didn't include because he asked me to pull at the last minute, had tragedy and bitterness towards boxing written all over it.

As much as we, the boxing public love the game it's certainly not a game is it and Gary Sykes was spot on when he said boxing's a ruthless business and an unforgiving sport. Also, Nick Manners' expression when he said "there's no lying in boxing because you get found out sooner or later" is very true. If you lie in boxing sooner or later, it will be a very painful experience getting exposed like a rabbit caught in the headlights on a dual carriageway.

Only a few years ago I'd become sick of being laid off from work or being passed around from agency to agency doing labouring or FLT driving jobs because I had no real trade, so I enrolled in college. I'd always thought about learning to become a barber many years ago, but I thought I was too old at 36. I'd started a men's barbering course to be fully qualified in 8 months. Brilliant, I thought, I'll set up my own boxing/Celtic barbers in a couple of years and be my own boss. Why didn't I think of doing this sooner as I was flying through my course? 3 months into it I would hit a snag, a big one. To learn men's cuts it must be learnt from making lines in the hair at different parts of the head. The devastating problem for me was I was seeing double lines or double scissors as they were hovering over the scalp. The reason for this being is whilst I was an amateur boxer myself I sustained an eye injury. Back on November the 16th 1995, as a 15-year-old I boxed at The Coatham Hotel on Redcar seafront at Lingdale ABC'S show. I boxed a lad called Paul Durose from Tom Hill ABC in Doncaster at flyweight and lost on points. It's funny because I'd never seen Paul from the day we boxed until one morning late in 2011 in Wakefield. Both of us were there that day because we helped out coaching at different gyms, as it was in the Boys Clubs quarter finals. It's bizarre because we were no longer flyweights, I can't speak for Paul, but I was more like a cruiserweight. "Do they call you Boyle, I think I boxed you 15 years ago?" he asked. It was lovely catching up with Paul after all those years since our bout in Redcar. We chatted for a good hour and he even apologised for being the reason that I wear glasses. I don't think there's another sport out there that leaves you with the respect you gain for your opponent for life, after trying to bash each other's brains out and you can only find that in boxing.

Around an hour after the fight I started to see double. I didn't tell anyone I just went to bed and had hoped it would be gone by the morning. All weekend my double vision stayed it was that bad that I had to close one eye even walking about and doing my glass collecting job over that weekend. Of course, when I went to school they were rather alarmed and one of the teachers drove me to the hospital where I had to go every week for three months. What had happened, the doctors said, was very common in whiplash victims and I was left with a lazy eye. The correct term is a Monocular Diplopia and I needed glasses, still do even to this day.

It's all rather bizarre because it was only amateur boxing with head guards and I mean how bloody hard does somebody 8st punch for god's sake he wasn't exactly Gerald McClellan! But it was classed as a freak incident and my eyes evened up, to an extent, after months, so I went on to box again several times after that. To this day if I look at something long distance and put my hand in front of my face I'll see two hands, and vice versa. It's the reason why I'll never be able to drive a car also. So, something came back to haunt me as a 36-year-old man that was just something I did as a 15-year-old boy. Not to mention getting my nose rebuilt at 33 years of age because I boxed with my face.

As I'm writing this now I think boxing still is the most exciting sport in the world. Whether you're doing it yourself in small hall shows for a poxy trophy, or you're sat in your front room having the lads round for a big PPV fight and you've had a bet and a few beers. I will always be in love with boxing and I take my hat off to any young kid sacrificing the best years of their life to try and make a better life for them and their families. Fighters like Joe Maphosa and Josh Warrington who can't go out to their mates 21st birthday parties or aren't allowed out on New Years Eve when the wives and girlfriends are giving them earache telling them how boring they are.

I was in young Joe Maphosa's company not too long ago when he was sat there eating dried nuts on a weekend when it was supposed to be his time off. That's real dedication, what these young soldiers put themselves through many of us will never have any idea of. The 12-week camps and training 3 times a day! It may all look unbelievably glamorous under Eddie Hearn's bright lights of Sky Sports, but it takes a special kind of person to go running in the bitterly cold rainy mornings. "Marvellous" Marvin Hagler once went on record to say, "It's hard to get out of bed at 4am to do your roadwork wearing silk pyjamas".

One of my close friends growing up was Middlesbrough's Stephen Truscott. He would have 36 amateur bouts as a school boy winning 28 of them. Stephen was then kicked out of the gym for a season for misbehaving outside of boxing. Only to come back as a junior aged 15 and have a further 28 contests winning every one of the 28 on his second stint in boxing. In one season he won the Boys Clubs, Schoolboys and junior ABA title, he did the clean sweep and that will never be done again. He also won another Boys Clubs title the season after beating Nottingham's Nicky Cook before walking away from boxing for good at 17 years old and he never boxed again. Stephen's former trainer had all kinds of messages from Frank Maloney and Frank Warren offering him all sorts to come back because obviously they realised his huge potential, but it fell on deaf ears. In all my years watching boxing I've never seen anyone as invincible as Stephen Truscott and if you go on YouTube and type him in then I'm sure you'll understand my point when you've watched a few of his fights. It was an absolute honour to receive a black eye so bad that he closed my eye up completely in sparring I could never lay a glove on him. I know Stephen doesn't really like talking about his boxing days these days from speaking to him over the years, but he can be so proud of what he achieved. The three national titles he won in the season 96/97 were all against top London club Newham ABC lads. After Stephen's third win that season I was told the Newham ABC coach said, "Well he's beat all my lads now I've got nothing left". Stephen was a complete one off and an exceptional talent.

In all my years of following boxing and getting to know certain fighters close up. None and I mean absolutely none can compare to the gentleman that John Pearce mentions in his chapter called Imran Hussain. I was made aware of Imran by so many people before I met him because he would always be around the Middlesbrough boxing scene. To say this guy loves boxing more than the entire people in this book wouldn't be far wrong because this fella is a walking, talking boxing encyclopaedia. Imran never boxed on a competitive level because he had epilepsy, but he was a member of the Wellington ABC in Middlesbrough for over 10 years. When I watch a lot of boxing on a weekend I can become "all boxinged out" and will forget about it for 3-4 days. Anybody will see, if you have Imran on social media, that when he's at work on his 15-hour security shifts, he's posting videos at all hours about boxers nobody but him has even heard of. I went to Glasgow with him last year to the Josh Taylor Vs Ohara Davies fight and it was a great day out. We watched all the fights and met many ex boxers as they always attend these big boxing events. Even before we went to the boxing I took him to my good friend Alex Morrison's home in the East End of Glasgow to talk more "shop". Anyway, after the boxing had finished when we were heading back home and travelling the 200 miles I asked Imran if he was ok to drive home and did he want a Red Bull to waken himself up for the long journey. He turned to me, smiled and said, "I'll be ok as long as you talk boxing to me". I was fucking sick of boxing by that point! He's one of the nicest guys you could wish to meet and there's not a bad bone in that fella's body. If any of you guys have Facebook, you MUST add Imran Hussain if you like boxing!

Marvellous Marvin Hagler once said, "if you cut the top of my head off and look inside you will find one big boxing glove" and I imagine Imran's head would be full of the same.

Dominic Negus certainly had a point when he said, "Us boxers aren't the most academic of people". I've been in gyms and had some right laughs at other people's expenses. I've took senior boxers on the pads and they've completely missed the pads and punched themselves in the face almost to the point of knocking themselves out.

Another funny memory I have in a gym was while I was timing the lads sparring I was also giving orders out outside the ring. This particular time I shouted 10 press ups, only for the two fella's in the ring to stop sparring and get on the floor, I was lost for words. Also, another time some young boxer was telling me about the time he watched a film and it was based on a true story... The film was Back to The Future! You don't half get some funny fuckers in boxing gyms I tell you and guys completely not a full shilling but we all love a laugh in life don't we.

In May 2014 I did a charity night in Saltburn which raised £600 for a guy's cancer charity. The night was called an Evening with Wayne Alexander because the clues in the name and I sold 130 tickets. This night was the same night as Floyd Mayweather's first fight with Marcos Maidana. In the early hours Wayne had had one too many rum and cokes and he fell asleep missing the fight, and I took loads of pictures of him and I in all sorts of poses. The next morning Wayne kind of laughed it off but asked me to delete the pictures. I figured it would be slightly beneficial to do as he asked considering just how hard he punched.

I'd like to thank every single gentleman for giving up their time and speaking to me and making this book possible.

The one thing I didn't want to do was put people in just because they were a good boxer but have to ignore the fact that they might be a complete prat outside of the ring. I've carefully and personally not picked the 20 whose stories you've heard in this book, and I respect them all a great deal.

I'm also very proud to announce that this book is supporting a registered charity which is the Middlesbrough Cancer Ward at James Cook hospital. This has been chosen by the one and only John Pearce. I'm sure I speak for everyone reading this when I say we are all 100% behind him in his biggest fight of all, and it isn't Carl Froch this time, if only it was.

Thank you so much for your interest and support on the Tales of Pugilism Facebook page and long may it continue.

Many thanks, always a pleasure Jamie B xx

Coming soon from Warcry Press

Lee Duffy
'The Whole of The Moon'

by Jamie Boyle

A book which has taken over 25 years to arrive. The definitive story of the man who held an eight year reign of terror over the town of Middlesbrough.

Containing many first hand and previously unheard accounts from some of Duffy's closest friends and associates, this book will finally confirm who the man was and what he was really all about.

No stone will be left unturned and this book will not shy away from controversy, but will aim to provide an unbiased and balanced view on the 'Borough icon .

Make no mistake, this will be the definitive book on Lee Duffy, there will be no more 'ifs' and 'buts after its release.

From the author of the best selling Paul Sykes books 'Unfinished Agony' and 'Further Agony' Jamie Boyle.

Also available from Warcry Press

Sweet Agony

by Paul Sykes

Not heard of Paul Sykes? Mentioned in the book, "Legends" by Charles Bronson, an A to Z guide of the men Bronson had regarded to be the toughest in Britain. Referring to 'Sykesy', Bronson describes him as "a Legend, Born and Bred" and writing: "I first met Sykes in Liverpool in the early 70's and at that time he was probably the fittest Con in Britain. A notorious hard man from Yorkshire, a fighting man in every sense. A lot of people never liked him, perhaps they even feared him but I respected the man for what he stood for". Bronson goes on to relate an incident said to have taken place in HMP Liverpool, where Sykes 'allegedly' killed the prison's cat and fashioned it into a "Davey Crocket" style hat, I think you get the jist!

Sykes had also been billed to fight Lenny Mclean at London's Rainbow Theatre on 20 November 1979, but this fight never materialized. Lenny Mclean, in his autobiography 'The Guv'nor', later explained: "A week before the off, Sykes went into a club in Wakefield where he lives, got well p*ssed and had a ruck with four doormen. He did them all but one of them got lucky and put a cut above his eye that took eight stitches to pull together". and the fight was off.

Sweet Agony is his own story of Prison, Life and his rise to the Heavyweight Title Fight against John L Gardner.

Also available from Warcry Press

'30 Years a Fighter'

The Fighting Memoirs of
Kevin 'Bulldog' Bennett

with Richy Horsley

30 Years A Fighter is the story of a unique fighter, Kevin 'Bulldog' Bennett, written with Richy Horsley.

Benny as he is known, was an amateur boxing champion. A professional boxing champion and a world bare knuckle boxing champion. How many people do you know have achieved that accolade? Nobody, only Kevin Bennett he is the first one.

He had his first fight at age 11 and his last fight at age 41, hence the title '30 Years a Fighter.'

The Forgotten Champ

with Nick Towle

He was the Hackney Rock, the 'Mini Marciano', king of the British and European heavyweights, yet somewhere down the line John L Gardner became the 'Forgotten Champ'.

Terrorised by a brutal father, shunned by his peers, his was a torrid childhood in the deprived East End where his only friends were his doting mother and an Alsatian called Vic.

But a chance encounter with Dr Who and the wiles of his gangster brother led Gardner to the attention of unscrupulous boxing moguls who turned him into an irresistible force but took his spoils in the process.

At his peak, Gardner was nigh-on unbeatable. He faced down the gruesome Paul Sykes, went toe-to-toe with Ali and had a strange encounter with Freddie Starr and a UFO.

He fought the law, battled a rampant gambling habit and ultimately stared down his most resilient foe - the 'Big C'.

In this absorbing and unflinching account of his stellar career, Gardner lifts the lid on how he was betrayed by some of the biggest names in boxing. How he conquered half the world but preferred to shun the limelight.

Moving, funny and at times tragic, his remarkable story is a must-read for all fans of the noble art.